global masculi.

SERIES EDITOR *Michael . Kimmel*

Men face common issues – the balance between work and family, fatherhood, defining masculinity in a globalising economy, health and reproduction, sexuality and violence. They are confronting these issues all over the world in very different contexts and are coming up with different priorities and strategies to address them. This new international series provides a vehicle for understanding this diversity, and reflects the growing awareness that analysis of masculinity will be greatly impoverished if it remains dominated by a European/North American/Australian matrix. A number of regional and thematic cross-cultural volumes are planned.

Michael S. Kimmel is a well-known educator on gender issues. His work has appeared in numerous magazines, newspapers and scholarly journals, including the *New York Times Book Review*, *Harvard Business Review*, *The Nation* and *Psychology Today*, where he was a contributing editor and columnist on male–female relationships. His teaching examines men's lives from a pro-feminist perspective. He is national spokesperson for the National Organization for Men Against Sexism (NOMAS) in the United States.

ALREADY PUBLISHED

Robert Morrell (ed.), *Changing Men in Southern Africa*

Bob Pease and Keith Pringle (eds.), *A Man's World? Changing Men's Practices in a Globalized World*

Frances Cleaver (ed.), *Masculinities Matter! Men, Gender and Development*

Lahoucine Ouzgane (ed.), *Islamic Masculinities*

IN PREPARATION

Adam Jones (ed.), *Men of the Global South: A Reader*

about the author

Victor Jeleniewski Seidler is Professor of Social Theory in the Department of Sociology, Goldsmiths College, University of London. He has written widely in the field of gender, particularly in relation to men and masculinities, as well as in social theory, critical theory, philosophy and ethics. His most recent book is *Transforming Masculinities: Men, Cultures, Bodies, Power, Sex and Love* (Routledge, 2005).

young men and masculinities

global cultures and intimate lives

VICTOR J. SEIDLER

ZED BOOKS
London & New York

In memory of my brother Michael,
2 October 1950–2 April 2005
and remembering my older brother Johnny,
28 July 1944–27 May 1982

Young Men and Masculinities was published in 2006 by
Zed Books Ltd, 7 Cynthia Street, London N1 9JF, UK,
and Room 400, 175 Fifth Avenue, New York, NY 10010, USA
www.zedbooks.co.uk

Copyright © Victor J. Seidler 2006

The right of Victor J. Seidler to be identified as the author of this work
has been asserted by him in accordance with the Copyright, Designs and
Patents Act, 1988

Designed and typeset in Monotype Van Dijck and Gill Sans
by illuminati, Grosmont, www.illuminatibooks.co.uk
Cover designed by Andrew Corbett
Printed in the EU by Biddles Ltd, King's Lynn

Distributed in the USA exclusively by Palgrave Macmillan, a division of
St Martin's Press, LLC, 175 Fifth Avenue, New York, NY 10010

A catalogue record for this book is available from the British Library
Library of Congress Cataloging-in-Publication Data available
Library and Archives Canada Cataloguing in Publication Data available

ISBN 1 84277 806 4 Hb (Zed)
ISBN 1 84277 807 2 Pb
ISBN 978 1 84277 806 7 Hb
ISBN 978 1 84277 807 4 Pb

contents

'Nothing is ever the same as they said it was.
It's what I've never seen before that I recognize.'

Diane Arbus, *Revelations*

'Focusing on the person, the self, and the emotions
– all topics difficult to probe in traditional ethnographic
frameworks – is a way of getting to the level at which cultural
differences are most deeply rooted: in feelings and in complex
indigenous reflections about the nature of persons and social
relationships.'

George E. Marcus and Michael J. Fischer,
Anthropology as Cultural Critique

preface

young men, global cultures and intimate lives

families

Intimate relations and family life have undergone enormous changes in the West since the 1970s, to the degree that in the new millennium we remain unsure about how to think about them. With globalisation and new technologies of mass communication these uncertainties have been reflected in urban and, increasingly, in rural settings globally. The issue is not simply to decide who is to be included within the sphere of family and intimate relations, but to account for the increased rate of separation and divorce, and to register the fact that families across heterosexual and gay relationships have become so much more complex.

We can no longer assume, as we still did in Europe and the United States in the 1960s, that there is a norm of the 'nuclear family' against which other family forms are to be judged and evaluated. This assumption was part of a pervasive ethic of normalisation within the positivist traditions that prevailed in the social sciences whereby if, for example, you grew up in a family with a single mother or where a father had died, you learnt to keep quiet about it at school, wanting at some level to feel that your family could somehow be 'normal'. This vision of 'normal' heterosexual 'socialisation' has haunted studies of the family within sociology since the 1950s and can still shape the ways we think about relationships between young men and masculinities in diverse societies and cultures.[1]

Parents often seek to protect their children when they are in fact protecting themselves against knowledge they cannot face. This tendency has begun to change, at least in urban middle-class cultures in the West, as there is an aspiration towards more open emotional communication between parents and children. It has indeed been a striking change, across diverse cultures and classes, as men as new fathers have wanted a closer relationship with their children than they had with their own fathers. Yet it has sometimes created uncertainties, since fathers can feel uneasy about the exercise of their own authority because they do not want to threaten their close relationships with their children. Sometimes this can lead to mothers exercising the traditional role of authority that fathers have abandoned, along with the feeling that their partners present themselves as 'friends' to their own children. This can make it difficult for fathers to set boundaries and limits for their children.

In the context of high divorce rates, with relationships deemed much less likely to last, one consequence is that parents can focus more on their relationships with their children, which will continue in some form regardless of separation or divorce. Parents can, paradoxically, invest more in their relationship with their children than in their adult relations. It is important not to generalise, but to be aware of diverse patterns of intimate relationships that also affect the shaping of the gender and sexual identities of young women and men.

In urban settings in diverse cultures we need to be aware of the complex intimate relations people have shaped for themselves. It can no longer be assumed that 'families' live together in the same space. Sometimes adults choose to live in their own spaces; it can no longer be assumed that people live together, even if they have children together. Sometimes women choose to have children on their own, or with men whom they do not have an intimate relationship. In lesbian families there might be close relationships with men as friends who can be actively involved in the bringing up of children. Increasingly people negotiate intimate relationships that seem to work for them, without assuming that there is a pattern to which they should conform. Often there is little surviving sense of a single pattern to which everyone should somehow adapt, whether in straight or gay relationships.

Some people have experienced their parents staying together in a relationship where there was little love, and they are less prepared to do this themselves. Parents want relationships that work for themselves as well as for their children, though this can be difficult to negotiate. But these issues around family and intimate relations, and what works to provide a stable and loving environment within which young people can thrive, have become central moral and political concerns, especially with the emergence of the religious right within the United States and the spread of evangelical Protestantisms globally. Often these concerns have centred on attacks on gay and lesbian families, even though the research has shown positive results of growing up in loving relationships in which young people are listened to and cherished for themselves. Yet there has also been widespread concern about the violent behaviour of young men and interest in how they should be brought up and educated.

For the postmodern family there is no longer a single pattern that is regarded as 'normal' and against which other forms of intimate relations are to be evaluated. There is a wider recognition that individuals have to discern honestly what works for them through negotiating with their partners about their individuals needs, wants and desires. This involves individuals being 'present' in their emotional relationships in a way that their parents might not have known. For an earlier generation there were clearly defined gender roles and expectations, and people did what was generally expected of them. For instance, men presumed they would get married and that children would follow. There was a strong moralisation of family relations within modernity that was still very much alive in the 1950s. There was a normalisation of the heterosexual family in which both men and women felt they had to fulfil prescribed roles, at least in public. If their emotions and feelings did not accord, they would often learn to keep them to themselves. There was still a stigma attached to divorce and often women were blamed for the breakdown of relationships.

It is in the context of particular intimate relations that gender education takes place within the home and boys learn how to behave as boys, and girls learn how they are expected to behave as girls. But these definitions have changed, and in diverse cultural settings such gendered expectations have to be renegotiated as parents deal with the tension between the expectations they might continue to have at home and the visions of greater gender equality children might learn about at school. There is a complex interplay between home and school. It can be difficult to negotiate across these differences, for example when young girls from traditional Asian backgrounds in Britain learn to challenge their own mothers, wanting them to stand up for them in arguments with their fathers. Young girls might feel obliged to live a 'double life', registering disappointment when even their brothers do not speak up on their behalf. They do not want to dishonour their families, but at the same time feel it is unfair that they cannot enjoy the same freedoms as their friends at school. They might refuse to help at home unless similar demands are made of their brothers. They might feel that it is also unfair when they are punished for things their brothers are allowed to do.[2]

Young people grow up in very different kinds of families. Within some families there is still a clear demarcation of gender roles and a gendered division of labour that goes largely unquestioned. This often goes along with clear expectations of what boys and girls are expected to do. It might be that girls are expected to help their mothers in the kitchen but that this is an area from which men are largely excluded. Changes can be brought about by the experience of, say, Asian families living in the West. Different families make different accommodations; feelings about a daughter's future will vary. Some fathers might be more encouraging, especially if their own mother was more independent. Again we have to be wary of making generalisations. At the same time we have to be open to the influences that cross cultural boundaries. Changes often characterise particular generations, especially when there is a desire to assimilate into the dominant culture.

A questioning of gender roles has characterised Western societies for more than a generation. This process has now become global, taking different forms in diverse cultural settings. Sometimes parents will express their uncertainties to their children, but often they will feel a need to be clearer in such discussion than they might feel within themselves. Often there are issues about the kind of conversations that can take place between the generations. If parents have listened and legitimated their children's emotions since they were very young, it can be easier to maintain some form of contact through the teenage years of withdrawal. But these are difficult years, when young people are exploring their own identities, confronting the existential issues of life and death that their parents often refuse to acknowledge themselves. Often young people want their parents to 'be there' while being allowed the freedom to explore their own realities.

authorities

Traditionally fathers were expected to discipline their children, and in different cultures we find echoes of the threat 'wait till your father comes home'. But to exercise authority fathers had to maintain a distance from their children, since closeness was assumed to threaten their position. This distance often prevented them relating emotionally to their children. This created its own form of melancholia, as fathers felt trapped in a distant relationship they could not change. They wanted to feel closer to their children but felt trapped in their position of authority. They could feel obliged by their wives to exercise discipline; it was thus a test of their being 'man enough'.

Sometimes fathers were taught by the larger culture that they could take up their relationship with their children at any time, so that it did not matter if they were heavily involved with work in the early years. Yet they could come to feel betrayed as they recognised, too late, that this was untrue and that the distance that had been created through the early years could not be undone. As fathers they could often feel isolated and alone, wanting to reach out to their children, but knowing that the time had passed. If a younger generation of men influenced by feminisms and ideas of gender equality have sought more equal relationships with their children, they have nevertheless often felt unable to create clear boundaries out of a fear that these might threaten the closeness they seek.

When we think about how young people relate to paternal or maternal discipline we also have to understand how they think about themselves as 'adolescents' and whether this is simply a designation others assign to them? When and how do young people question parental forms of authority within different cultures and traditions? Does this reflect a lack of respect, and how are relations of respect renegotiated within families where young people feel that respect has to be earned? Do we need to gender and sex the term 'adolescent' and question the implications of a fixed stage, which has the same features across diverse cultures and societies, of physical and emotional growth marking a transition between childhood and adulthood?

Is adolescence thus a transitional stage, a liminal phase in which young people are somehow caught on their way to adulthood? Is this what allows adults to say, often too easily, to their teenage children that what they are going through is 'only a phase' and that they will get 'through it' before they know. This registers a difficult and challenging time, especially for the adults, who can find it very hard to relate to their 'adolescent' children. Adults often consider young people to be 'out of control' and feel they have lost connection with the person they used to know, who might have become overassertive, demanding and uncommunicative.

Young people go through physical and emotional changes in their early teenage years that can be difficult to come to terms with. A moment comes when they no longer experience themselves in relation to their parents but as 'individuals' in their own right. They are no longer a son or daughter who is happy to define him- or herself in relation to the family. They resent being treated as children, because as teenagers they know that they are no longer children. They want to be given responsibilities, but at the same time can be so absorbed in their own inner processes that they withdraw from the social world of the family against which they are defining themselves. They want to know 'who' they are for themselves, which often means rejecting how they are defined by others and involves a period of intense experimentation through which they explore what they want and need for themselves. At some level they know they are not adults and do not really want to be part of the adult world. Rather, they are concerned with defining their own values and beliefs for themselves.

With hormonal and bodily changes this can be a period of intense emotions and desires. Sometimes it can be difficult to live with these mood swings. I can recall how deeply I felt within relationships and how crushing it was when they broke up. It seemed the world had ended and that I would never love again. I was probably only 14 at the time, but the future did not count since I lived so much in the intensities of the present. Attachments and emotional relationships were absorbing, though they were rarely shared with my parents. I never thought that it was possible to share emotions with them, and was shocked to discover later that some parents actually talked to their teenage children. My parents, who had been refugees to Britain from Nazi-controlled Europe, had grown up in a very different world. Though my mother could be understanding and was open to friends coming over, I did not imagine that I could share what was going on within me.[3] There was an uneasy balance at school between sporting masculinities that were more easily affirmed and the uneasy masculinity of those who performed well academically. Some boys could prove themselves in both spheres and they were often given seniority. But there was no singular dominant or 'hegemonic' masculinity, since these were cut across through relations of class, 'race' and ethnicity. Some differences were stigmatised more than others. If there were different spaces in which you could affirm your masculinity, there was tension between an inner experience as young men and the cultural masculinities through which we felt we had to prove ourselves.

In the 1950s, with the images of Charles Atlas the bodybuilder in the newspapers, there was a sense that 'real men' do not have 'puny' bodies; nor are they 'softies' or 'wimps' who show their vulnerability and emotions to others. As boys we did our best to build our bodies as we read about heroic masculinities in adventure stories, like the Famous Five, which still carried the promise of empire and images of heroic masculinities. These were fantasies we learnt to identify with, even if they had little connection to the realities of everyday life. In some ways they provided standards against which we judged ourselves and found ourselves wanting. They provided images of young masculinities not widely questioned until the advent of the women's movement and gay liberation in the West in the early 1970s.[4]

identities

Since the 1970s young people have learnt to thinking differently about issues of gender, sexuality and power. The questioning of the women's movement in the early 1970s was related to broader patterns of change within the labour market. Young women were no longer ready to subordinate themselves to men and they no longer accepted that they had a biologically determined responsibility for the children and for housework. Learning from feminisms, even if not identified with the movements, young women across different classes, 'races' and ethnicities felt that if they worked and brought money into the home men should share responsibility for childcare and domestic work. But they were also clear that if their partner was not prepared to enter a different, more equal form of gender contract, they were ready to leave the relationship and live on their own. The renegotiation of gender relations spread across global cultures as visions of greater gender equality and sexual justice were transforming expectations of intimate relations in urban areas, and also increasingly in rural areas. However, they were also meeting resistance with the revival of religious fundamentalisms that worked to sustain and reinvigorate patriarchal relationships.

Interviewing men who grew up in the 1950s in Britain makes clear that they often felt that a future was mapped out for them. If they had a greater sense of themselves as teenagers than did their parents, with more spending money and more time for themselves, they expected nevertheless to get married if they were heterosexual and soon after probably have children. As male identities were tied to waged work, the bringing home of the first wage packet being ritually marked within working-class families as a sign of manhood, they were also connected to fatherhood. As a father, a man had affirmed his masculinity. Often this came after a period of national service or military involvement – the other way young men affirmed their male identities. These cultural norms provided a level of security in relation to male identities that a generation growing up after the war were not to experience in the same way. Never having fought for their country, they could feel they still had to prove their male identity, which had never been properly tested through war.

So when we think about young men in specific histories, cultures and traditions we are thinking about the particular conditions through which they engage with the social world and affirm their male identities, sometimes through questioning and refusing prevailing cultural masculinities. They can carry different expectations from their fathers and different ambitions for themselves depending upon their histories, cultures and societies. For example, a man who had lived in Pinochet's Chile in the years after the bloody coup against Salvador Allende's Popular Unity government on 11 September 1972 told me on a trip to Santiago how he often felt the shadows of the past fall across his life. As a young man growing up, there were questions you learnt not to raise and silences you felt obliged to respect. Young men I have talked to described how the closing of the public world had produced an intensification of their inner emotional lives and spoke of the significance of pornography as a way of exploring their sexual identities. Watching videos with your friends created a private space of exploration that taught about desires that could not be talked about in public. Looking back, the men insisted on the significance and value of pornography, notwithstanding what they recognised as degrading images of women.

listening

It is difficult for parents to listen to their teenage children when they have no interest in sharing their ideas and beliefs and when a perceptible gap divides the generations, at least for a while, during which time there exists no common language that allows the bridging of differences. If young people encounter the adult world within particular historical and cultural contexts, we also have to acknowledge that, for a while at least, they may not be interested in communicating with an adult world they largely reject. Unlike the experience of earlier generations of young men and women, the uncertainties of a newly globalised world leave young people unsure of what the future holds for them. Young men might have the vague idea that they want a relationship, but a future of marriage and fatherhood might no longer seem so certain. They recognise that the future is open in ways an older generation often cannot grasp because in a globalised economy, with the decline of traditional industries, there is no longer the assured work their fathers might have taken for granted. The future often presents itself as full of risk and uncertainty.

Young people growing up with global images of gender and sexed relationships are often taken up with an exploration of their own desires and identities. They search for an intimacy that allows them to be vulnerable and close. But, in contrast to the sexual politics of the 1970s in the West, young people do not want to be defined or categorised in relation to their genders or sexualities as straight or gay or bisexual. Attracted by postmodern visions of open and fluid identities, they often reject the idea of fitting experience into pre-existing categories. Similarly, young people, especially in urban areas, no longer have a confident belief in pre-existing family forms and seek to define their intimate lives within the possibilities opened up by global cultures. Within postmodern urban cultures, individuals often feel they have to explore their own bodies, desires and sexualities. It is through this self-exploration that they seek to negotiate a relationship that meets their changing needs and desires. They appreciate that negotiations also involve compromises and a respect for the needs of others as they define them.

Within newly globalised cultures and changed worlds there has been a breakdown of communication between the generations. Too often adults still think of 'adolescence' from the point of view of an adult experience. Young people are defined through what they lack, namely adult responsibilities. At the same time there is a widespread awareness that new technologies and the Internet mean that young people are communicating with each other through diverse virtual realities. They are speaking and listening to each other across the traditional boundaries of the nation-state. They can share their own sources of information and are often sceptical about what adults have to say. They know they are growing up in a radically different world in which the experience of the past seems to carry less weight.

Faced with the uncertainties of a globalised world, young people can feel that their parents have little to teach them. They can feel more open about homosexualities and racial and ethnic differences, though they can also reproduce the intolerances of earlier generations – this is especially true of those young men who still define their male identities through a rejection of vulnerability and emotions still regarded as 'feminine', and so connected to an unspoken fear of gayness. Homophobic speech is often a form of self-protection since heterosexual identities are often established through an inner rejection of homosexual desire. It is through a rejection of 'softness' that young men still affirm their heterosexual male identities.

Yet within diverse urban settings there seems to be a greater willingness to listen across genders and sexualities. But in some cultures this cannot be said so confidently in relation to 'race' and ethnic differences. Rather, a focus upon issues of gender difference can work to silence an awareness of diverse 'race' and ethnicities. In Chile, for instance, this is evident in the dominant indigenous group of the Mapuche. While there is a recognition of a Chilean identity and a wide mestizo culture, there is a disavowal of indigenous inheritances within the present. This is very different from Mexico, where people more generally claim that everyone is mestizo. If there is a glorification of the Aztec cultures in the past, there is also a disavowal of racial and ethnic differences in the present. People do not like, for example, to be reminded that most of the people serving in a restaurant have darker skins.

Often young people in Mexico grow up to take these differences for granted since they reflect relations within middle-class families where maids from indigenous backgrounds cook, clean and look after the children. Often there are ambivalent emotional relationships, since young people tend to disavow their relationship with women who have cared for them. So we need to be careful to specify who is listened to, and in what cultural circumstances, and who is silenced. Sometimes young people feel they 'know best' and do not have to listen to anyone. Often they inherit complex cultural inheritances and traumatic histories that shape their experiences in the present and also their capacities to connect openly with others in their intimate relations. Recognising ways that intimate lives are tied up with national and global cultures allows us to explore what young men are learning to become.

power/authority

A postmodern culture recognises a crisis in traditional forms of hierarchical respect. Young people are no longer prepared to accept the cultures of deference that their parents took for granted. An egalitarian ethic has spread across global spaces within a widespread consumer culture that encourages young people to recognise themselves as equal citizens, as bearers of rights and responsibilities. It is not that they do not believe in authorities, but they have questioned traditional authorities that expect to be obeyed without question. They want to know who is speaking and with what authority, and what they have done to be owed respect within a democratic culture. How have they earned their position of authority? With what authority in relation to their own experience do they speak?

Within many cultures in the South young people suspect an authority consolidated through a historical relationship between a dominant white European masculinity and the project of colonial modernity that saw the subordination of indigenous cultures as a marker of progress. This allowed a dominant colonial masculinity to speak with the impartial voice of reason. This impersonal voice that often spoke with the authority of scientific objectivity assumed enormous authority in relation to the colonised other, deemed to be uncivilised.

A discourse of hegemonic masculinities has often not questioned this impersonal and impartial voice but has made it its own within a structural theory of masculinity as one social practice among others. Discussion that unwittingly makes an implicit identification between men and masculinities renders it difficult to explore how men have grown in relation to particular masculinities, and also the tension and unease which men often feel in relation to prevailing models. As long as we think of masculinities as locked into relations of power with each other, it is difficult to understand how men can change through processes of transforming masculinities in specific cultures, histories and traditions. We have to learn to speak always from a particular position so as to question the impersonal voice of an objective rationalism. If there is space for bodies and emotional life within Bob Connell's understanding, in *Masculinities*, of the theoretical framework of hegemonic masculinities, it is as the subjective consequences of objective structures. This makes it particularly difficult to explore the contradictions in young men's experience and the transitions they make during their teenage years. Rather, Connell is locked into thinking about the diverse confrontations young men have in relation to the adult world.[5]

Connell's structural theory has been vital in analysing how patriarchal relations embody relations of structural violence, but it remains
largely within the terms of a modernity framed by a dominant white
European masculinity. Employing a theoretical framework that is
established through reason alone allows little space for the diverse
voices of young men themselves. The distinction Connell draws between, on the one hand, emotional life as 'therapeutic' and, on the
other, 'politics' conceived exclusively in structural terms works readily to disdain the voices of men he would otherwise want to listen
to. There is little space for dialogue theoretically, even if there is in
the empirical studies, in which young men can explore their diverse
relations with their inherited masculinities. Nor is there a space for
them to explore how they have become the young men they are, or
to challenge traditional relationships of authority within the family,
where they are expected to listen and obey rather than be heard and
respected themselves.

Within a hierarchical vision of respect, obedience was owed to
those in positions of power. Within more democratic family relationships, respect is earned though experience and behaviour. Young
people are concerned to question hierarchies, including hierarchies
of masculinities, that close off dialogue and communication. They
do not want to be told what to believe, but insist on the freedom to
work out their own beliefs and values. They want space for their own
relationships and often want their parents to support them without
expecting too much in return. This can be difficult for adults to
accept. But if we are to question the grand narratives of modernity,
including those framed in terms of masculinities, we have to be open
to listening to what young people have to say.

We have to recognise that young people are not necessarily challenging all forms of authority or setting authority in opposition to
freedom. Rather, they want 'good' authorities that are not based upon
the obedience of those who have been silenced. Similarly they can recognise the need for discipline in their own lives, but are questioning
of forms of obedience that are expected to be automatic. They want
to be part of shaping new forms of familial and intimate relationships.
They recognise that the models we have inherited from the past no
longer speak to the present in which we live. They want the respect

and trust of their families, knowing that they need the time and space to explore their own beliefs and values. If this is a time when young people take risks, it is also a time when they demand honesty and straightforwardness from those people who would work with them.

Young people in democratic societies often want to be able to exercise more power over their own lives. If they have grown up with more equal gender relations both at home and at school they can be less concerned with the issues of gender equality that concerned an earlier generation. As younger women in the North seem sceptical about identifying themselves with feminism, partly because they do not want to limit the opportunities open to them, so young men are less concerned with the relation between men and feminism than they are about how to live meaningful and open lives as men. They want to explore 'where they are at' without the moralism that still haunts traditions of sexual politics. At the same time, moralism can have a particular appeal in Latin America, for instance, where there is often social distance between the radical intellectuals and the social movements to which they connect. In this context it is easier to disdain men's groups as concerned exclusively with improving the personal lives of men, while feminism alone is somehow concerned with 'changing the world'. We find here echoes of an unreconstructed Marxism that has yet to rethink deeply enough its relationship to a masculinist project of modernity.

Young men often do not want to be identified with or defined by the power they have in relation to women because they know that in many areas of their lives they experience themselves as far from powerful. They do not want to live the masculinities of an earlier generation but wish to explore 'what it means to be a man' in their own worlds. They do not want to have to deny their love, warmth and tenderness to live out a vision of masculinity that no longer seems true to their own experience and possibilities. They want to engage with the structural violence of a globalised world and the different messages they receive within that world while being able to transform their intimate relations as they shape different masculinities that allow for more equal gender and sexed relationships. Struggling for institutions to be transformed within democratic cultures, they seek a more equal distribution of global resources between North and South.

They recognise that transforming masculinities is part of a process of review for young men as they create more open, equal and loving relationships both with themselves and with others.

acknowledgements

Many people have supported me through this project that brings together work that I have done over many years in Britain, the United States, Europe and Latin America. As I have listened to many men engaged in a struggle to create more equal and loving relationships, I have learnt to appreciate the vital significance of history, culture and traditions. Within diverse cultures that define themselves as largely secular I have learnt that modernities have been shaped through the secularisation of dominant Christianities. In Europe I was forced to engage the differences in the struggles that men had, in both hetero-sexual and gay movements, with inherited religious traditions that they generally disavowed, in order to make sense of the differences between the men's movements in Scandinavia shaped through diverse Protestant traditions and the very different experiences in Italy, Spain and Greece.

This involves the insight, partly shared by Foucault, that in order to grasp different levels at work within contemporary subjectivities, we need to explore the resonances with disavowed Christian tradi-tions. To investigate the different ways in which boys grow into young men, it means also recognising how dominant Western tradi-tions have been shaped through traditions of patriarchal masculinities that have worked to silence alternative voices, histories and experi-ences. It is partly through learning to disentangle our own complex inheritances to establish a deeper connection with ourselves that we can learn to listen differently to others. The women's movement challenged men to rethink their inherited masculinities and create more equal relationships with partners and children. For those grow-ing up in Britain, this has involved learning to name the ways our intimate relations were tied up with global cultures of empire within late capitalism.

At school we learnt to feel proud that the world was largely col-oured in pink, which indicated the breadth of the British Empire that was to be decolonised through the late 1950s and 1960s. This shaped its own inheritance of unspoken superiority that reinforced the white male supremacy we did our best to identify with. But the narrative did not fit easily for me, since I was marked as different through the traumatic history of the Shoah – the Holocaust – which had had such a devastating effect on my family. As boys growing up to be young men, I and my peers very much wanted to belong within a culture that demanded that you paid a price if you were to assimilate. We were ready to pay the price whatever the disorganisations it brought in its wake.

We were ready to watch other boys to learn the masculinities that were expected of us, even if they were in tension with what we might be learning at home. It was probably through a sense of difference that I learnt to question an identification of men with prevailing masculinities. It was through a sense of liberation brought about through rock-and-roll and dancing as a teenager that I learnt that the body had an emotional history of its own, offering a different reality from what is often lived in everyday life. These were contradictions in lived experience that I learnt to listen to and respect. In time they taught me to how to discern tensions between the inner voices of young men and what they might feel obliged to say in order to conform with what was expected through prevailing masculinities.

Through the years I have received the consistent support of my men's group, and have benefited greatly from the discussions, both personal and intellectual, I have had at different times and places with many people, including David Boadella, Bob Moore and Terry Cooper, to whom I am grateful for their particular insights into the emotional lives of men. For discussions over the years focused around issues of men and masculinities, I would like to thank Paul Alsop, Tony Dowmunt, Anna Ickowitz, Tony Seidler, Paul Morrison, Terry Cooper, Richard Morrison, Martin Hargreaves, Michael Wibberley, Patrick Nash, Anthony Stone, Joanna Ryan, Ulla-Britt Lilleaas, Sheila Ernst, Jeff Hearn, Michael Kimmel, Bob Connell, Sheila Rowbotham, Caroline Ramazanoglu, Dean Whittington, Danny Kelly and Fran Tonkiss. For discussions on broader European masculinities I thank Jorgen Lorentzen, Claes Ekenstam, Luis Jimenez and Michael Kaufman. For discussions in relation to Latin America, I have benefited greatly from conversations with Juan Carlos Ramirez, Ana Amuchastegui Herrera, Benno de Keijzer, Gloria Carriega, Juan Figueroa Guillermo, Patrick Welsh, Jose Olavarria, Teresa Valdes, Matthew Gutmann, Mara Viveros Vigoya, Norma Fuller, Luis Jimenez, Daniel Caziz and Teresa Ordorika.

Nearer to home, the sociology department at Goldsmiths, University of London, has long provided a space of intellectual support. This book marks a celebration of the thirty years that I have been teaching there and allows me to acknowledge my appreciation of the many generations of students from such diverse backgrounds that have been so lively, encouraging and supportive. So many have responded positively to the ideas as they were first forming, and their excitement and enthusiasm have kept me going, even when the times were tough. They have recognised the importance of work on men and masculinities, which has always been an integral part of the MA in Gender, Culture and Modernity, a course initially framed with Caroline Ramazanoglu and Ross Gill. The department has been a very lively and stimulating intellectual home, and through its different incarnations has been very supportive. Karen Catlin, Doreen Norman and Sheila Robinson have provided the love and administrative support that have enabled us to thrive as a department. Around the work I do in relation to gender there has been much support from many colleagues over the years, including Brian Alleyne, Les Back, Vikki Bell, Kirsten Campbell, Marian Frazer, Ben Gidley, Paul Gilroy, Monica Greco, Michael Keith, Celia Lury, Kate Nash, Pam Odih, Nirmal Puwar, Nik Rose, Marsha Rosengarten, Brett St-Louis and Fran Tonkiss. Recently the interdisciplinary project set up with Joanna Ryan on Embodied Psyches/Life Politics has proved a lively and stimulating space to explore interrelations between the psyche and the social.

I would like to thank Michael Kimmel for his warm welcome of this project for the series and the enthusiasm of Anna Hardman and her colleagues at Zed, who have been helpful at every stage of production.

My partner Anna Ickowitz has watched this project grow over the years, and her Brazilian friendships have given me an inner relationship with Latin America that made this work possible. Dealing with

transcultural issues within our relationship has prepared me to recognise cultural differences that so often go unnoticed as they are
silenced within the power of rationalist discourses. In the work that
we have done together and in sharing the bringing up of our children
Daniel and Lily, who are now adults, we have learnt from our own
experiences what is involved in bringing up a new generation with
respect, love and emotional honesty. Daniel and Lily will have their
own stories to tell, as they will have their own emotional work to
do, as they find their own ways in the world. Hopefully they will
continue in their commitments to make this world a better place in
their own unique ways.

I

introduction: young men and masculinities

teenagers

Young men today are growing up in an increasingly globalised world, one far removed from that of their parents. This has to an extent been true for each generation: young men need to define themselves in opposition to their parents. Yet, with the advent of global media, generational expectations have transformed not only in the relatively prosperous North but also in the South. Reaching an age where they no longer want to define themselves as children, they are nevertheless unsure of their status as adults. As teenagers growing up in a world shaped by new technologies, young men can feel caught between different realities, wanting to define their teenage existence but often uneasy about the adult designation 'adolescent'.

Teenagers might be adolescents for others, but they themselves often reject this medicalised definition that frames them as objects of an adult gaze. Adults have long tended to view these years as an unsettling and disturbing 'phase' that young people have somehow to 'get through'. Though aware that a globalised world offers a different future for their children, parents are often constrained by their own expectations about work and life. They have often lost touch with their own teenage years. Having forgotten what they lived through, they tend to relate to 'adolescence' as a foreign territory that needs to be disciplined, controlled and regulated through expert scientific observation. Unable to communicate with their children, parents often fall back on authoritarian traditions, which further alienate young women and men.

It is difficult to connect with teenagers, in diverse cultural settings, unless as adults we can recall what we ourselves lived through during these years. We have to remember the intensity and passion of our own teenage years if we are to appreciate what young people live through. As we recall our own refusal to tell our parents what was going on in our lives, so we can appreciate that teenage children will often refuse to speak to their parents. Keeping secrets is a mark of independence. They will talk to their friends in a way they will not with their parents. They do not expect their parents to understand, and, though at particular stages of development they may want their parents to 'be there' for them, they often refuse to account for themselves.

I remember growing up in London as a teenager in 1950s' Britain as part of the first post-war generation that had money of its own to spend. It was a new world of rock and roll; there was a sense of excitement that a new category of 'teenager' was being born with us. Accompanying the conflicts between groups of 'mods' and 'rockers' on the beaches of the south coast in Britain there was a developing awareness that 'adolescence' was not just a period that young people 'go through', but that teenagers were creating a new world for themselves, shaping a post-war identity not really known before.[1]

Yet within the new globalised economy and the global transformation of work relations there has been a radical shift in teenage experience across different classes, cultures and traditions. With the widespread use of computer technologies young people have access through the Internet to a diversity of aspirations and definitions of teenage experience. Many young people have access to music and cultures from across the globe and can draw upon sources of information and imagery unknown to previous generations. This has helped transform the relationship between education and civil society, particularly within the West, where the school was traditionally conceived as the institution responsible for 'socialising' individuals into the norms and values of the dominant culture.[2] Knowledge was gained at school, and young people were often dependent on their teachers for knowledge of the world beyond their family and local culture. But in the new millennium children who have access to these new communications technologies can cross boundaries of class, culture and ethnicities to control their own sources of information. This can encourage them to question traditional forms of authority as they recognise the possibilities of living differently.

Young people are also growing up in a world of greater gender equality than that of their parents. This can create its own confusions for young men, unsure about what it means to be 'a man' alongside women who take for granted the claim to equal rights, even if they do not call themselves feminists. Young women across the globe growing up with the benefits struggled for by the feminists of the 1970s and 1980s have a new sense of direction and entitlement to gender equality. But they can also refuse to identify themselves with feminism.

There is a widespread perception, encouraged by global and local media, that feminism is 'man hating', and in an oppositional relation to men. Even if these women know that feminism does not have to go hand in hand with a disdain for men, they sometimes perceive older generations of feminists in terms of getting together in consciousness-raising groups. Sometimes seeking to define themselves against their mothers' feminist generation, and – in the West at least – having had more equal relations with young men in their education, they can conceive gender equality in different terms.

As differences have opened up between different generations of women within diverse cultures and traditions, so too there are differences between an older generation of men, who responded to the challenges of an earlier feminism centred upon their relationships with women, and a younger generation of men, who tend to focus on the contradictions and tensions in their experience as men. Within very different cultural and social settings they can be keen to discuss relationships between men and diverse masculinities while refusing to engage so exclusively with the relationship between men and feminism that was the central concern of an older generation of men. They are also more likely to refuse to identify 'men' as exemplars of particular 'masculinities', as Bob Connell seems to do in *Masculinities*, and will often refuse a discourse of 'hegemonic masculinities' that cannot illuminate men's embodied and emotional lives.[3]

histories

Young men and women often unknowingly inherit the painful and traumatic histories of their communities and countries that their parents have refused to share with them. This is often a feature of migrant communities. For example, Muslim and Hindu communities in Britain carry the history of the partition of the Indian subcontinent in 1947, which is rarely shared with the second generation. Communication can break down between parents and children when the latter are being educated into a world that is obviously very different to that their parents knew. Fathers often feel respect is due to them because of their position within the family, maintaining family honour and tradition. Young people, for their part, can feel a sense of betrayal as they are educated into British ways. They may feel torn between different worlds, obliged to live different identities at home and with their friends at school. It is difficult to reconcile these conflicting pressures, and they may find it impossible to share their concerns at home.

More generally, as traditional forms of authority became widely challenged in the late 1960s in the West, individuals within both mainstream and migrant communities began to question the authoritarian relationships they had with their fathers. Many who became new parents in the 1980s and 1990s wanted a closer and more intimate relationship with their own children.[4] This involved a transformation of intimate relations that seemed to spread around the globe with new technologies and forms of communication often beyond the concerns of traditional feminisms. This was often double-edged. Women wanted greater gender equality, but this was often made possible through the employment of poorer women. In Latin America, for example, women from shanty towns would live as domestic workers in middle-class families, taking responsibility for both children and domestic labour so that both parents could go out to work. Children left in the care of these women would sometimes develop close and loving relationships with them that mothers could find threatening and difficult to negotiate. Often there would be a tension between the love the children felt and the hierarchy and disdain they experienced, especially from their fathers in relation to these women.

This was not so different from what was happening in the West, where greater gender equality was often achieved among the middle classes through the labour of poor migrant women, who would be employed to care for young children. Often children would bear resentments at their parent's absence that they might find it difficult to express, as middle-class parents would often compensate by buying their children gifts as a substitute for their own presence. Parents might return home exhausted after long hours of work, within a neoliberal economy that had seen an extension of the working day. If they earned good salaries there was often a prevailing anxiety about the security of work, and an awareness that there were many other people waiting to take their job if they put a foot wrong.

Since the 1960s there has been a generation of more liberal forms of childrearing, especially among the middle classes. Often parents have found it difficult to set limits and boundaries for their children, thinking that these are a sign of the authoritarian relationship they have rejected. Parents did not want to hurt the relationship they had with their children and were fearful of damaging the intimacy they had established. But they were also uneasy about the long hours of work, experiencing guilt in relation to their children because of their absence. There is often a tension between the importance they accord to their relationship with their children and the time they put into it.

Research in Latin America has indicated that there has been a very significant shift in attitudes to fathering, which has shown how important is the relationship with their children for a new generation of fathers (Fuller 2000; Valdes and Olavarria 1998). The research shows how they think about their futures through their relationship with their children. Unsure of their intimate relations, amid high levels of divorce, parents will invest a sense of their future in their children, knowing that these relations will persist even if their marriage breaks up. But there is also a desire, framed differently from earlier generations, to protect their children from the 'painful histories' of dictatorship that have marked so many Latin American nations.

Often it has been important for parents to feel – possibly because of their own absence at work – that their children are happy and contented in their lives. But this can encourage parents to discount and invalidate their children's experiences as they do not want to acknowledge their unhappiness or depression. Parents often assure their children that these feelings are groundless, and children can be left feeling they are somehow obliged to their parents to convey an image of continuous happiness. Often this means that young people learn to conceal their emotions, and a split can open up between their inner experience and what they learn to show to their parents. They can learn to hide their emotions because they do not want to add further to their burden, nor to be told that they are ungrateful for the gifts that middle-class parents are able to give to their children. These are emotional patterns that can help shape intimate relations across cultures. Though framed differently within specific cultures, there are often transcultural lessons to be learnt.

The need felt by a generation of parents in Argentina, Brazil and Chile in the 1980s and 1990s to protect their children from their painful experiences of military rule can create an unreality in the relationships between parents and children. Children often know unconsciously about these painful emotional histories that have been 'passed on' by their parents, even if they have never been spoken about openly. These displaced emotions can encourage a variety of forms of acting out by a younger generation who have not lived through these events. Sometimes the consequent political differences have led to splits in families.

A young woman shared her experience with me when I attended a conference in Santiago, Chile. Her father, who had been in the military, and her mother had taken different sides during Salvador Allende's government of Popular Unity. Her parents had separated and she had gone into exile with her mother to Sweden. Eventually she was to return to Chile. She has never really spoken to her mother about her experience of imprisonment and exile. Somehow a silence had been maintained in their relationship, and even now she feels that her mother might not be ready to talk. Within the terms of Chilean culture she had learnt to behave appropriately – that is, not to hurt others. Often this means, especially for young women, being more attuned to the feelings of others than to your own needs. Not wanting to upset others, this woman has learnt to accept silence from her mother, and a different silence from her father, whom she has also not questioned about these years. She has learnt to keep her feelings to herself, not recognising the possibility that they *could* be talked about and that she might be able to move towards some form of resolution with her parents.

Chile lived through a terrible period after the coup that overthrew Allende's government on 11 September 1972, when so many people were beaten, tortured, forced into exile, or even killed. Parents were concerned to protect their children from the effects of this traumatic history and did not want to open up these wounds for themselves. They learnt to leave the past behind, fearing that it would merely bring unresolved pain to the surface. Chilean culture can encourage people to think that, since you cannot change the past, it is better to forget it. There is a particular movement of the arms through which people express the notion that it is best not to make a fuss, at least publicly. As with many Catholic societies, there tends to be a sharp distinction drawn between inner emotional life and the proper behaviour that people learn to assume in public. They do not expect to be questioned in public about their private feelings. Boundaries are created between public and private lives in different ways within different cultures that help shape gender relations and forms of communication.

Often parents will not share their painful histories with their children, not wishing their shadows to fall on future generations. They do not want to see the signs of these unspoken painful histories in the sadness and depression that the younger generation carry. They prefer to tell their children that there is nothing to feel depressed about, even though they themselves might know otherwise. Since the young did not live through these difficult times, parents prefer to think they remain unaffected by them. They do not connect the high rates of tranquillizer and other drug use among both older and younger generations in Santiago with the silences that exist between the generations. Possibly in the name of protecting their parents, children learn to keep their own counsel as they internalise what it is best not to ask about. But this can leave young people with their own uncertainties and haunted feelings, experiencing horrors that they cannot define.

male superiority

Young men often grow up taking their superiority for granted. Seeing that their sisters are treated differently, they take for granted their advantages as men. This can help to sustain rigid forms of masculinity in which young men can feel they continually have to defend, to be on guard to prove their male identities. Sometimes trapped into feeling they are not 'man enough', they will feel that it is through risky behaviour that they can affirm their masculinity. Traditionally a sense of male superiority has worked to legitimate male violence against women. For example, research suggests that in a quarter of Chilean families women and children have experienced male violence.

As we reflect upon the sources of male violence within different cultures we need to think about the transition that boys make to become men. If young men, for instance, see their fathers taking out their anger on their mothers, they can grow up feeling that this violence is deserved and legitimate. Young men in Latin cultures might learn to think that it is particularly justified if a woman has been unfaithful in some way, if she has insulted or sworn at her husband, or even if she is simply determined to get her own way. It is a sign of male dominance within patriarchal cultures that women can sometimes blame themselves for this, thinking that if they had somehow behaved differently they would not have caused their husbands' violence. This shows how vital it is to intervene in the process of young men's learning in their transition to manhood within many patriarchal cultures. If women still think they deserve to be beaten, then this reflects a failure of educational systems and the nature of gender injustices within patriarchal societies. It also marks a failure in that young boys often become men precisely through their acceptance of male violence. They learn to identify with their fathers and to reproduce violent behaviour in their own relationships, so affirming their superiority in relation to women.

Yet, increasingly, young women in both the North and the South are learning to refuse these relationships. Rather than feeling they should blame themselves, young women tend to be horrified at the violence their mothers have had to endure. Brought up to think they have equal rights as women, they question the terms of male superiority and insist upon more equitable gender relations. They want relationships that are different to their parents'. In the urban middle class, but also increasingly in rural areas, where the mass media have shown alternative gender roles, young women are increasingly refusing to cook and clean for their partners. If they are working and bringing in money to the household, they expect domestic tasks to be more equally shared. They prefer to be on their own, especially if they can afford their own accommodation, than to be with a partner who expects them to be subordinate.

This marks a significant shift within a single generation across diverse global cultures and traditions, and involves a reordering of gender relations among young people across social classes. For instance, in Spain – linked through Catholic tradition to Central and Latin America – there has been a decline in the birth rate. Women wishing to defend their rights are refusing to enter relationships with men who still uphold traditional masculinities. This is in contrast with Protestant cultures of northern Europe, especially Scandinavia, where the promise of greater involvement on the part of men has encouraged women to risk having children with them. Often they are disappointed when men return to work soon after the birth, sometimes refusing the paid leave that the state offers to them, but there is at least the expectation of greater cooperation and gender equality.

In Latin America there is a growing discussion about young people as the bearers of rights – not simply rights granted by the state but also rights that allow them to make demands upon the state. But if it is accepted that young people have bodies, within states still dominated by the Catholic Church, they are often not recognised as having sexualities. Rather, their identities as rational selves or as spiritual beings are defined in part through the rejection of a sexuality identified with the 'sins of the flesh'. This is particularly true of young male sexuality, regarded as 'animal' and somehow beyond the control of reason if it is released. These cultural traditions shape male superiority in particular ways, making it difficult for young men to acknowledge themselves as sexual beings without a sense of shame. This is sometimes echoed in Eastern traditions, where, for instance in Thai Buddhist culture, there is a reluctance to talk openly about sexuality. Young people learn to speak appropriately in ways that often refuse to acknowledge sexual desire in language. This can be an issue for young gay men in Thailand, who can often feel constrained to act out heterosexual masculinities in public.

Traditionally in Latin cultures shaped through Catholic traditions, a young man who had made a woman pregnant would have been forced by both families to marry her. Their relationship would have both compromised them as individuals and, moreover, reflected upon the honour of the families. Since sexuality is a mark of impurity and since women are brought up within a Catholic culture that defines celibacy as a moral ideal, sexual relations are still often marked by a sense of shame. Young people who are better informed and live within more secular urban cultures can still be unconsciously influenced by negative attitudes towards sexuality. These ambivalent feelings can still be difficult to name within more secularised societies. Young people might find it difficult to own up to these feelings or negotiate them honestly within relationships. This can make it particularly difficult to negotiate around issues of contraception. Young men often feel uneasy talking about sexual feelings and desires.[5]

sexualities

Within Catholic cultures in both North and South there has been a long historical identification of sex and reproduction. People supposedly have sex in order to conceive and have children. Reproduction is defined as the 'proper' use of sexuality that is otherwise being misused if it is 'simply' sex as pleasure. This reproduces a moralistic tradition in relation to sexuality. Young people who want to think of themselves as having broken intellectually with these traditions can find themselves caught emotionally. This can make it difficult for people to speak about sex openly and honestly in both heterosexual and homosexual relationships. Rather it produces its own silences, where people feel 'taken over' by desires that are beyond their rational control. They might feel bereft of an emotional language in which to share their experience of sexuality. This can also 'speed up' sexual contact, making it difficult for young people to take time over their sexual relationships. This can foster a focus upon genital sexualities within Latin cultures, as well as a tendency to move with great speed towards coital relationships.

The forbidden nature of sex takes a particular shape within Catholic cultures, even where they have become secularised; this can add to its excitement. This vision of sexuality as being overtaken by something they cannot expect to control makes it difficult for young men and women, in different ways, to reflect upon themselves as sexual beings who know themselves sexually. It can also limit the possibility of taking time to reflect upon their sexual desires and so negotiate their individual needs within relationships.

In the dominant secularised Protestant culture of Britain it was well into the 1960s before the women's movement encouraged women to explore their own sexual desires. Feminism encouraged women to explore their sexuality and so question a traditional notion of sex as a duty owed to men by women – and not only within working-class communities. Women were not expected to enjoy their sexual experiences, and if they did they would rarely talk about it. Rather there was still the notion that men could not 'really help themselves' when it came to their sexual desires, and that sex was a right that was owed to men within marriage. Women and children had long existed as male property, and a husband had sexual rights over the body of his wife. Women would talk about tolerating the experience but often not really knowing how to enjoy it for themselves. Reclaiming the sexuality of women was a vital contribution that feminism made to women's lives, and potentially it transformed relationships between young people. It was through the recognition of embodied identities that feminism questioned the terms of an Enlightenment rationalism that had been made in the image of a dominant white European masculinity.

In the Catholic cultures of Latin America, negative attitudes towards sexuality take on a different shape as sex is shamed. Traditionally it has been important for men to conceive of themselves as 'protectors' of their female partners. If she worked and earned money, he would still insist upon paying for them when they go out, even if it is with her money. He might not worry about her working so long as she still did the domestic work and cared for the children. Although she had to do a double shift, he could not be expected to help, since traditionally you could not expect a man to be in the kitchen. Within a culture of male superiority there was a sharp distinction between men and women, masculine and feminine.

Men often learnt to fear the feminine within Catholic traditions, which identified Eve as the first women who brought evil into the world. So men had to protect themselves against women, whom they learnt to distrust, and so also against their own femininity. Heterosexual masculinities were partly shaped through a fear of emotions that came to be identified as 'feminine' and so shaped homophobic fears that emotional vulnerability indicated homosexual inclinations. Traditionally, if a man started helping with the house and children this would be deemed a threat to his masculinity. He had instead unconsciously to protect himself against the influence of women, even if he could not frame it in this way. On a video shown at the Santiago conference in 1992, in a session on adolescent masculinities, a young man explains that he always walks in front of his wife so that he can protect her if a car comes towards them unexpectedly. As he says, 'I think this is the man's role.'

In a context of traditional gender roles it can be difficult to negotiate more equal sexual relations, as young men remain focused upon the satisfaction of their own desires. Sexuality is not framed as a matter of mutual pleasure and desire. In Catholic cultures, as the connection between sexuality and reproduction is increasingly questioned, men can still feel uneasy about the pleasures of sexual desire. In different ways for men and women, excitement can be tied to questions of risk, especially for young people. Women can feel that part of the excitement of arousal lies in the possibility of conception, so that with the risk of pregnancy taken away (for example by a vasectomy) the intensity of desire also diminishes. A young woman from a rural area might say that it is because she loves a young man and is ready to have a child with him that she is ready to have sexual relations. She might be ready to take the risk of unprotected sex as the risk adds to the intensity and somehow serves as proof of her love. Young men in heterosexual relationships might want to resist the use of condoms because of the widespread perception that it somehow 'takes away' from the pleasure. But they might also fear the interruption in a sexual experience that is framed as a passion beyond the control of reason. They might also fear a loss of erection when they put on the condom, or just feel embarrassed about doing this with a woman they do not know well. Often intimacy develops with these potential mishaps, but if there is a lack of intimacy young men will not want to risk the embarrassment. They will not want to compromise their 'reputation' with other men. They might be so concerned with affirming their masculinity that they readily risk the possibility of conception or of contracting HIV or STDs. This has its own rationality within a strong patriarchal culture.

In urban centres in Latin America we might discover more equal gender relations, in which traditional expectations have been questioned. Young women and men might think about sexuality as a matter of pleasure, but there will often be tensions between what they might say in public and what they feel in more private and intimate spaces. They might be uneasy with their bodies and feel they can only be sexually active in darkness. At some level they might want to speak about their desires but lack confidence and be embarrassed when it is a matter of communicating openly with sexual partners. They might have inherited cultural notions which suggest that speech serves to interrupt desire and so diminish passion, making it hard for them to learn that speech can also intensify desire and bring closeness as individuals risk expressing how they feel as sexual beings and how they like being touched and how they can be aroused.[6] In Catholic cultures people can feel that pleasure is interrupted if they express their desires in language. It is as if speech can bring forward a hidden awareness of sin, since bodies have for so long been identified with the 'sins of the flesh'. This can mean that sexual passion becomes an affair of silence in which few words are spoken.

It is only when prevailing negative attitudes towards sexuality are questioned openly, and young people develop an emotional literacy that allows them to speak about their desires, that they will be able to feel more relaxed with their embodied sexual identities. This will involve a rethinking of sex education and its significance in the shaping of gender and sexual identities. As young people learn to recognise how exploring their sexuality in safety with appropriate contraception can be a part of exploring their identity, so they will be able to be more open and honest in their sexual relationships. As people reach towards greater gender equality, they will recognise how respecting people's feelings and emotions can be as significant as respecting their ideas, beliefs and values. But this involves revisioning cultures that have long disdained the body. As we learn to take pleasure in what was for so long devalued and rejected we learn to recognise ourselves as embodied beings who no longer have to 'take flight' from our bodies and sexualities.

Our rights as sexual beings become integral to a renewed vision of sexual citizenship and democracy. But this involves learning how different cultural and religious traditions in the North and South shape the ways young women and men learn to feel about their bodies, sexualities and emotional lives, within an increasingly globalised world. It involves learning to name the continuing influence of these traditions, which have often been disavowed within secular cultures that often like to think they have broken with them in their move towards modernity. It also shapes the ways many young men feel about their inherited masculinities and the learning about themselves they need to do as part of a process of transformation.

2

masculinities, histories, cultures and religions

modernities

Within the discourses of modernity that have shaped the disciplines of the social sciences and humanities it has often been difficult to identify the different currents that developed during the process of secularisation of religious traditions. The ways that modernity has been framed by a secularised Protestant culture within Northern Europe and the United States has tended to shape the universal terms through which other cultures have learnt to understand themselves. Through being presented in universal terms as 'scientific', these modernities have often worked to undermine the significance of religion and traditional culture. In the terms of a secular modernity religious traditions have been conceived as a form of 'backwardness' that inevitably gives way to the advances of reason. The implicit vision of history as progress means that 'religion' becomes an object of cultural research. This has tended to blind people to the ways in which, for instance, Catholicism has remained a formative influence within Latin America that needs to be studied in its diverse forms within different countries.

Such a study might usefully examine the various histories of conquest, as they were shaped by different alliances between the cross and the sword. We have to trace the histories of genocide, and the various equilibria reached between colonisers and the colonised that still echo in the present. Rather than assume a vision of historical progress that insists upon the present and the future, we must be prepared to reflect upon historical memories that carry the wounds of conquest. The survival in Mexico of indigenous cultures and their refusal to wither and die, a fate that had been anticipated in the nineteenth-century evolutionary visions that informed the philosophical basis of the social sciences, means that we have to allow for competing histories, cultures and memories. We have to question the singular vision of the nation-state that would argue that 'we are all Mexicans' because within a vision of mestizo 'we are all mixed'. This reflects the singular vision of Catholicism that was alone a path to truth and salvation. It was only through the Church that souls could be 'saved'.

Modernity presented itself as a secular vision that replaced faith with reason. With time, faith would give way to reason; it was the task of reason to investigate the sources of religious belief. Within a vision of history as progress there was a particular Protestant shaping of modernity that presented itself as universal. This made it difficult to recognise how Catholic traditions have remained formative in the constructions of gender identities in Latin America, partly because people did not want to acknowledge the continuing influence of Catholicism. This threatened claims to modernity and made it difficult also to appreciate that there were different modernities that possibly needed to be understood in different terms. The ways in which Catholicism has shaped men and women's relationships to their bodies, sexualities and emotional lives needed to be explored in their own terms, rather than in the secularised Protestant terms of modernity according to which 'others' had to evaluate their experiences and discover themselves 'lacking'.[1]

As Gramsci recognised, the vision of time and temporality within the social sciences is shaped by an implicit evolutionism.[2] Modernities define their own visions of 'backwardness' and imagine their own evolutions through different stages of development. This view was vital for the European coloniser's vision of the indigenous as belonging to an 'earlier stage of development', and thereby as having somehow outlived their historical usefulness. This view informed discourses of the 'primitive', interpreted to mean that there was nothing to be learnt from indigenous cultures, which would inevitably die out of their own accord. This worked to relieve the moral responsibility for the destructions of conquest and served as moral legitimation for the European colonisers' barbarism and cruelty. Christian legitimations that spoke about the saving of souls, on the assumption that whatever suffering was wrought hardly mattered when set against salvation, transmuted into evolutionary justifications that spoke of 'different stages of human development'.[3]

Modernity offered a vision of the future and allowed a break with a 'primitive' past. Since the Europeans had everything to teach and little to learn, they were relieved of the moral burden of colonialism. Trapped within the terms of 'nature', the colonised could not hope to survive, let alone develop on their own terms. Only through accepting a subordination to 'culture' could the indigenous hope to make the transition from nature to culture. In this way they were demeaned in their own eyes. They were to be blamed for their own poverty as their cultures were appropriated.

[handwritten margin note: Nature ↓ evil. inferior. ↓ Subordinated 2 culture.]

ethics and progress

Simone Weil was an early critic of the brutalities of colonialism. In her later writings she questioned an ideology of progress that continued to inform and shape the social sciences. She recognised how Roman visions of power and greatness had shaped Western culture to such a degree that young people still learnt to identify with the victors, as if conquest somehow proved the moral validity of their ideas. Often this helped shape particular forms of forgetting, as people learnt to focus on the present and the future, since the past had little to teach them. Not only did the powerful inherit the means to write histories in their own image; their victories were morally legitimated through the equation of virtue with power.[4] This was a vision that Marx failed to question, in his assumption that new modes of production signified a path of development. The influence of evolutionary ideas in some of his later formulations obscured the destruction and cultural catastrophe that was wrought through conquest. For Marx, whatever brought capitalism was somehow to be welcomed, because it was a 'necessary stage' in the development towards socialism.

Standing on the edges of European fascism, both Gramsci and Benjamin in different ways questioned the temporalities that informed evolutionary assumptions within orthodox Marxism and the social sciences more generally.[5] They were no longer prepared to sacrifice present pleasures and joys for visions of future salvation. They named the Christian visions of self-denial and self-sacrifice that informed these evolutionary conceptions as if sacrifices in the present would win 'salvation' in the future. Even though Marx was drawing on Jewish sources to establish a 'this-worldly' ethic in which people could value fulfilment and self-realisation, notions of revolutionary self-sacrifice shaped later Marxist traditions. Often it was easy to devalue the present in the face of promised redemption in the future. The present was imagined as a preparation for a 'better' future and the past was understood as an earlier stage of development that has been transcended. It was partly through a Hegelian vision that the past was to be 'superseded', as if everything of value in the past had been absorbed into the shaping of the present. This was to give secular expression to the Christian idea that the Old Testament had somehow outlived its historical usefulness and been replaced by the New Testament and so was 'silent' in the present.

Benjamin has helped to question notions of evolutionary progress that have been taken for granted in temporalities within the human sciences. Sacrifices and cruelties in the past have been legitimated in the name of a brighter future, echoing Christian visions of redemption, in which present sacrifice brings salvation in a world to come. This orders a relationship between present time and future time that shapes individual lived experience. If, in Catholic traditions, people feel that they have been 'born into sin' and that they carry a sense of guilt since learning that Christ died 'for their sins', it can be difficult to break with these feelings, even if they have been questioned intellectually. People might feel a sense of guilt that they no longer relate to their Catholic formation. This forms an unease and intensity in bodies which shape sexual relationships.

Relations to time and temporality are formed differently within the Catholic tradition, which allows for confession and so for a new beginning. But it can still be difficult in Mexico for men to admit that they have made mistakes and caused suffering to others if they fear losing face within the social hierarchy. Even if they acknowledge wrongdoing in private, they may do everything they can to maintain face within the public sphere. This relates to the different ways public and private spheres are shaped within Catholic and Protestant cultures and so to the different relations between public and private ethics. In Latin cultures there is more emphasis upon public behaviour and on the importance of being seen to have behaved correctly towards others. This might make it easier, for instance, for men to have affairs as long as they do not draw it to the attention of their partners. Even though others might know, they learn not to talk about it, at least publicly.

Within a Protestant modernity there is more emphasis upon consistency between public and private spheres, and on taking responsibility for your actions. With no ritual of confession, people can find it hard to allow for pleasure, which can be regarded as self-indulgent, if not sinful. People have learnt to discipline themselves individually, and to practise self-regulation. People might be equally concerned with being shamed in public, but find it harder to escape their own feelings of personal betrayal of the ethical ideals they have internalised. With no escape, people have to live with their sins for eternity, so shaping a different relation between ethics and time.

histories

In the historical centre of the Mexican city of Puebla, where the first international conference on masculinities was held, one experiences the physical dominance of the cathedral within a strongly traditional city. On entering the cathedral one is confronted with a representation, in a glass box, of the suffering body of Christ. His suffering is made visible through his bleeding body, and Catholics are immediately reminded of the guilt they carry because he died for our sins. People who have grown up Catholics, even if they have subsequently broken intellectually with their faith, say how immediately this embodied guilt can still emerge for them. They have grown up with these images as children. They function like Catholic doctrines embodied in somatic actions, such as making the sign of the cross, which can be so automatic that people are hardly aware of their movements. Such images of suffering can have a traumatic effect on children, reverberating long after they have separated consciously from the Church.

The suffering body of Christ works as a constant reminder of the presence of death. It helps to shape a particular relation to time, as death enters awareness as an eternal presence in life. Within a Catholic tradition people are constantly reminded of a death that cannot be escaped or placed at the outer limits of life, as so often happens within Protestant modernity. One learns that time is eternal and that the time in which one lives is of little consequence. As one is reminded of death so one is also reminded of suffering, which in relation to the suffering body of Christ comes to signify love. It helps to sustain a vision of life as sacrifice, and an awareness that however much one might be called upon to sacrifice in one's life, it counts as nothing when compared with the sacrifice to death that Christ made in order to redeem the world.

How does this help to shape a particular sense of the meaning of life as sacrifice? Whose life has value? Do different temporalities interrelate with each other in Mexico? Though the Church insists on imposing its own calendar, there are different temporalities formed through their relations to the cycle of nature. As Catholicism shapes a linear vision of time that traces back to an origin marked by the birth of Christ, so it has had the power through conquest to impose its temporalities upon indigenous peoples who inherit a seasonal and cyclical vision of time. Within the social hierarchies created around the notion of 'Spanish blood' as a marker of civilisation, blood remains a crucial signifier. Contemporary Mexico is still haunted by the idea that it is only through your Spanish blood that you can 'count for something'. People have learnt to be shamed by their indigenous origins, and, even though they might constantly say 'we are all mestizo – mixed', people are very aware of differences of colour.[6]

Though the presence of Guadalupe as a black saint is absolutely vital within contemporary Mexico, this is partly to be set against the 'whiteness' of Jesus and a more general identification between 'whiteness' and 'goodness'. As in other societies colonised by Europeans, there was often, especially in the early twentieth century, a strong sense that people could evolve towards 'whiteness', and that through different generations moral progress could be identified through the whitening of skin over generations.[7] In Mexico, where there is an abiding sense of social hierarchy, the way one looks determines the way one is treated. Middle-class children in Mexico City often unconsciously learn to distrust indigenous peoples, identifying them with crime and violence. Often restricted to their own neighbourhoods, they grow up in different worlds, with relatively little contact. It is as maids and gardeners that they see the indigenous.

One is expected to dress and carry one's body in ways that reflect one's class position. In a town like Puebla one soon learns that one is not to wear shorts unless one is *gringo*, and that sandals are only worn by the poor and the indigenous. There is a strong sense of appropriate behaviour through which one's position in the social hierarchy is reflected. Within a dualistic moral culture there is a sharp division between good and evil, and people often feel uneasy with ambivalence and uncertainty. People feel they need clear guidelines to be able to make judgements and position themselves clearly in relation to others. It is very important to maintain appearances, so that one often finds a public adherence to the rules, even if there is private transgression.

hierarchies

Catholic cultures often sustain social hierarchies that can be in constant tension with their democratic visions. It is difficult to sustain ambivalence within a dualistic moral culture that draws categorical distinctions between 'good' and 'evil', 'angel' and 'devil', 'virgin' and 'whore'. In Puebla, known as City of the Angels, there is a social order that is presented as if it were divinely ordained, with different orders of being. People have a strong sense of position, and this is both gendered and racialised. Even though the middle class now dress informally, they learn from an early age how to give orders as they speak to their 'inferiors'. There might be a personal concern that crosses lines of class, but social distances are maintained. In Britain or the United States there is more fluidity: young people might work as waiters to earn money in the summer without feeling that serving others is somehow beneath them.

The Conquest continues to echo in the disavowed racialised relationships that exist in the present. In a restaurant there might be a clear racial hierarchy reflected in the different positions of service, despite the claim that 'we are all mixed'. Since the Revolution young Mexicans have learned at school that the Conquest was a cruel and monstrous attack on 'our' Mexican culture. Indigenous culture was claimed and appropriated as 'Mexican', while historically marginalising and silencing indigenous peoples as uncivilised and lacking education. Somehow education came to be the marker of civilisation and allowed hierarchies of wealth, power and position to be taken for granted. It was only the 'higher classes' who, through their education, could promise the nation a future, since the indigenous supposedly remained trapped within the confines of nature.

Even though the revolution in Mexico transformed political ideologies and produced land reforms, its sense of history remained ambivalent. It fostered a vision of progress tied to science and technology that brought different elements of the nation together in a unified vision. But it sustained its own myths of mestizo and a shared identity as *mexicanos* that made it difficult to come to terms with traumatic memories of conquest. It went some way to question social hierarchies, but it also wanted to heal social divisions and bring the nation together. Though the power and authority of the Church was questioned, it was somehow able to sustain its control over morality, which was shaped in its vision.

Since ethics is so easily identified with the morality of the Church, it can be difficult to recognise alternative ethical traditions and the different visions they carry. Through its long history the Church has worked to naturalise a distinction between 'human equality', which supposedly exists in the eyes of God, and notions of 'social inequality', which are supposedly 'political' and so have little to do with equality. In schools middle-class children learn to accept inequalities as part of 'their reality' as if they cannot be changed. Though the state insists that citizenship is taught in every school, it often finds it difficult to engage with the moral concerns of young people as they question the unequal world and relationships they discover. Unable to give answers, teachers often learn to deflect the questions, and children can be left in a state of unease, unsure of what to believe and often feeling a level of guilt for the inequalities they cannot explain.

Rather than question social hierarchies, ethical concerns are shaped towards acts of charity and goodness that affirm the moral worth of individuals within a social world that cannot be transformed. Middle-class children learn that others are poor because they are 'bad', or else 'lazy' and 'uneducated'. The poor come to be blamed for their poverty and the rich learn that they have no responsibility towards the poor other than charity. This is the way that God made the world; if he had wanted to make it more equal, he would have done. Everyone faces their own challenges and fate: who are we to question the wisdom of God? In this way the Church remains crucial, as Gramsci recognised, in getting people to accept their fate without question: this world has to be tolerated as a 'short time' in which people prove themselves worthy of an eternal justice in a 'world to come'.

cultures

Rather than assume that issues of male violence are universal in Latin America, and that within patriarchal cultures we can translate methods that have worked in North America and Europe, we need to understand the specificity of masculine cultures within Mexico and the part that Catholic traditions have played in legitimating male power and authority. The power that men are able to assume very much depends upon the cultural legitimation of their authority. If a man feels that it is his duty to discipline his partner, and that women cannot be trusted to speak the truth and have to learn obedience for their own good, then violence will flow more readily.

If masculinity is defined exclusively in terms of individual power relations, as it tends to be within Connell's work in *Masculinities* (1995), for example, then we do not have to investigate cultural sources of power and the ways male power is legitimated within particular cultural and religious settings. This argument is echoed within those feminist traditions that maintain that because women confront male power right across Latin America, so cultural, historical and religious differences are irrelevant. This makes it easier to accept universalist theories of 'hegemonic masculinities', which disavow the cultural and religious forces that Gramsci reflects upon in his notions of hegemony and counter-hegemony in the *Prison Notebooks*.[8]

It is telling that Coriac, a project on male violence in Mexico City, works with issues of both violence and parenting, but has tended to avoid consideration of sexuality. There has been a tendency to examine issues of violence in relation to male power only within an individualistic psychological framework that is blind to issues of sexuality, culture and religion. Within the secular and individualistic assumptions of psychotherapy it is hard to appreciate the restlessness that is produced through the shaming of bodies and sexualities within a Catholic culture. Unless the shared historical, cultural and religious assumptions of the 'therapist' and 'client' are explored, rather than disavowed, it is difficult to explore their formative power and the ways in which a particular culture continues to shape ways men feel about their bodies, sexuality and emotional lives. Where there are strong cultural distinctions between public and private lives, as in Mexico, this will produce particular difficulties in relation to intimacy, especially where men have grown up to identify emotions as 'feminine' and where there are strong homophobic fears within the diverse cultures.

memories

The conservative government of Vicente Fox in Mexico has recently been supporting a proposal to limit the teaching of history in school and to exclude the teaching of pre-Hispanic cultures. They want to focus upon science and technologies in the present, and to forget the past, which can be divisive to visions of a unified Mexico. Yet the past refuses to die, and questions remain. On a trip to Cholula – a heavily indigenous town that was dominated by the Catholic presence in Puebla, which for a period vied with Mexico City to be the capital of Mexico – one encounters a Catholic church built on the top of a hill that was once an ancient temple. Walking through the pyramid a visitor is aware of the power of pre-Hispanic civilisations. The Spanish marked the Conquest by building their church right on top of the pyramid, to mark their victory and register their superiority. They built a number of other churches in the area to reinforce their spiritual domination.

A visitor walking around the remains cannot but ask whether the indigenous feel a particular relationship to these monuments, which Mexicans might claim to be their own. One wonders about the ways different memories are brought together, and whether in the unified vision of the nation other memories are being silenced. Resistant to the notion of collective rights of indigenous peoples, the project of nation-state building set out to create the vision of a unified history and culture upon a discrete territory. This was a project that did not ignore differences of history, culture and religion, but was anxious to subsume them within a national narrative of the Mexican state that would take priority. People would be allowed their own memories as long as they did not threaten the priority of the nation-state and the narratives it imagined and produced for itself. So middle-class Mexicans learn to be wary of the idea that the remains at Cholula carry a different significance in collective memories. They want to appropriate these sights as part of a unified 'Mexican' memory, while at once they might regret the construction of the church as a marker of domination.

Rather than acknowledging that different peoples might have different memories, and so read the remains at Cholula in different ways, the construction of a revolutionary history in Mexico seeks to provide a unified vision of historical imagination. But against this is the fact that in Mexican families the presence of Indian blood can still be a source of shame, and a woman who claims 'Spanish blood' can still shame her husband. This indicates the continuing presence of a discourse of 'blood', which travelled with the Inquisition from Spain, even if it was already present within indigenous cultures.

It was partly through the imagination of the Reconquista and the Inquisition in Spain that people in 'New Spain' were encouraged to re-enact conflicts through a dominant Spanish heroic masculinity.[9] Rather than re-enact the visions of the Spanish Conquest, there are every year re-enactments throughout Mexico of struggles between the 'Christians' and the 'Moors' in which the victory of the Christians is celebrated. Spanish hegemony is represented through Spain's power to impose its own early victories in the Reconquista in this newly conquered land. People dress up, make up their faces and create elaborate costumes for these ritual confrontations. The Christian victory evokes the dominance of a militaristic Spanish masculinity allied to the Church, even though it is ritually performed by those whose ancestors were often on the losing side. The ritual re-enactments confirm where the sources of power remain, even though people in different periods might have preferred their own meanings.

In these ritual reminders of struggles that were originally fought in another place and time, there is an implicit consolidation of the power of whiteness. The Christians are often imagined as 'white' in their struggle against the dark-skinned Moors, reminding people of an unconscious identification between whiteness and goodness in a Mexican culture where issues of race are still difficult to address directly. People have to deal with their own skin colour knowing that this indicates an indigenous connection that is largely disavowed within the ideology of mestizo. Though privilege is not directly related to whiteness, since it is also a matter of wealth and social position, social hierarchy is still reflected in skin colour. It is still something that people feel they might have to compensate for, since they cannot wipe it away. It is the sense that 'darkness' needs to be compensated for that can threaten a sense of male identity. It can help produce another level of unease and tension within relationships, as people do their best to behave correctly in public and dress according to their social position. But skin colour remains potentially threatening because it is visible.

visibilities

In Catholic cultures, where there tends to be a sharp division between public and private spheres, it often matters a great deal how people present themselves in public. Research shows that men may behave well towards their partners in public, since they are concerned not to be shamed or lose face, but act violently towards them as soon as the front door is closed. In Mexico, some of the tensions that men take out on their wives emerge from the silence that exists around issues of race and masculinity. There is a tension around whether men can sustain their honour and self-respect in public if they feel that their colour can be used against them. These differences are disavowed within the notion that 'we are all mixed', but this does not mean that some people are not darker than others, and that skin colour cannot be invoked as a source of shame.

This can create an anxiety about being publicly exposed. For example, men can find it difficult even to concede a lack of knowledge when asked for traffic directions, and will often answer in an assured manner so as to sustain a certain public image of themselves. There is a constant struggle to maintain one's position and not lose face in front of other men. Masculinities remain competitive relations, and if people have to strain to sustain their image in public, they have the power to humiliate and abuse their wives and children in private. This radical disjunction between public and private spheres and the need for men to act appropriately in public can make it difficult to research into men's beliefs and relationships. There will be a tendency to give the acceptable response and conceal private ambivalence and unease. For if masculinities demand that men affirm their control over their emotional lives, then they may fear that the interview process will leave them exposed and vulnerable. They will not want to admit violence towards their partner, especially if they feel that this might shame them in the eyes of the researcher. We need to develop culturally appropriate ways of researching men and methodologies that recognise cultural and historical differences.

As men learn to protect their image in public, it can often be difficult to know what they really think and feel. Often people become identified with the image of themselves they want to portray; they are so used to sustaining a distinction between inner experience and what is considered acceptable behaviour that it can be difficult to read what is behind the front they present. This can produce its own forms of paranoia, as people are unsure of what others, especially men, might think of them. The Catholic emphasis on honour can make it more important to conceal vulnerability, at least in public, since people do not want to be shamed in the eyes of others. Given complex racialised histories, people often have to deal with tensions in the public presentation of self of which they are barely aware.

The Hollywood film *Frida* draws on the life of Frida Kahlo, and her marriage with muralist Diego Rivera, in post-revolutionary Mexico. Kahlo's paintings are notable for portraying externally her inner wounds. Her husband wants her to believe that his sexual relationships with other women are of little consequence, because 'having sex is like shaking hands'. She feels shamed by his affairs but does her best to sustain her image in public. However, her paintings together form an exploration of both this mental pain and the bodily pain she carries as a result of a bus accident when she was young, which crucially shaped her identity as a woman. She makes visible in her paintings hurts that would usually be hidden and covered over in public.

Whereas Kahlo has the courage to recognise how her husband's affairs added to her inner pain, and to acknowledge the difficulties she has dealing with his lies and deceits, Rivera is more concerned with sustaining an image of himself in public. He is concerned with imagining an inclusive vision for the present and the future through the large public murals he creates. He wants to give dignity to the different indigenous, peasant and labour traditions within Mexico in ways that can bring them together around a belief in the future that science and technology seem to offer. He is a public artist whose work is acclaimed both in Mexico and in different art centres around the world.

Kahlo was not publicly recognised, though many people knew about her paintings. She had an unusual kind of imagination that was prepared to question the masculine public visions of the nation-state and focus attention on a more private and intimate imagination. She was prepared to reveal the pain and humiliations that a public masculinity often wanted to disavow even in its revolutionary manifestations. She too expressed hopes for a better future, but she refused to forget both the pains that she carried in her body and the collective traumas and sufferings that created different memories and histories in Mexico. She suggested the presence of memories that were often disavowed, and made visible in her body the pains that would otherwise be silenced.[10]

Many Mexicans felt uneasy that the film was made in English, and it took time for them to accept its images, but they nevertheless appreciated what it was trying to do. It reminded them of an important post-revolutionary period in their history, and through Kahlo's pictures it made visible a different imagination that was more fluid and suggestive than many of the murals they had grown up with and learnt to admire. Kahlo's work was not widely exhibited in her lifetime; only at the end of her life was there a major exhibition, which she was obliged to visit in her own bed, so sick was she by that stage. Through her private pain she made visible in her paintings an intimate imagination that refused to ignore the suffering that women so often carry on their own. She implicitly questioned a Catholic tradition bringing the private and public into a different relationship with each other. She refused to sacrifice her bodily pleasure, but in her work imagined a new ethical vision in which women and men could come together in more equal and loving relationships. She refused the idea that sexual desire was shameful and insisted on greater openness and honesty in intimate relationships; she was unwilling to tolerate her partner's affairs or maintain a public image that was untruthful to what she knew herself.

Cultural theorists have learnt to draw distinctions between urban, rural and indigenous cultures, and have begun to think about different gendered and racialised cultures. But somehow issues of religion and race have often been absent in these explorations, possibly because they have been rendered invisible through being taken for granted. It might be that we can begin to explore the diversity of masculine cultures through a recognition of multiple memories and a realisation that the singular memory of the nation-state needs to be reworked and greater complexity of historical and traumatic memories acknowledged. This means resisting universalist conceptions of 'hegemonic masculinities' which can be translated into different cultural settings without being radically revisioned and their assumptions, often drawn from Protestant modernity, explored.

While acknowledging how masculinities operate in the context of structural relations of power and violence, we need also to understand relations of power within specific historical and cultural contexts. The adoption of universalist models has failed to break the silence on the formative influence of Catholicism upon gendered and racialised identities and relationships. Of course we need to be aware of secular movements, and the different ways in which Catholicism is organised in different regions and communities, but we must be ready to acknowledge the impact of the shaming of bodies, sexualities and emotional life that Catholicism can produce, even when this is disavowed intellectually. While valuing the secular traditions within the social sciences, we need to be aware of how these traditions have been shaped through dominant masculinities as well as through the secularisation of particular religious traditions.

As Gramsci recognised, hegemony is not simply a matter of power. It is crucially a matter of the legitimation of consent. This involves being ready to engage with issues of religion, culture and traumatic memories that echo across generations. If we separate power from emotional life we are in danger of legitimating the fear of emotional intimacy that often characterises a dominant masculinity. Rather than opening up ways for men to transform their lives in more equal relationships, we can be in danger of sustaining a moralism that would continue to treat emotions and desires as signs of weakness, and so as threats to male identities. As we recognised in *Achilles Heel*, it is often through honouring the point of weakness that transformations have a chance to take place.[11]

3

listening, speaking and learning

listening

How do we learn to listen to men? This question is crucial for people researching young men and masculinities, because within a positivist tradition we have assumed that no gender issues are involved in interviewing women and men; that it is simply a matter of establishing the questions we want to ask, and making sure that they are relevant to the areas we want to research. Yet where men have learnt to speak in a way that defends prevailing masculinities, this has often meant not really learning to listen. For instance, men have tended to feel that when their women partners express sadness or unhappiness, what they are looking for is a 'solution' to their problems.[1] Since this is often the way men have dealt with their own distress or anxieties, they can assume that this is what they are being asked for, and are surprised when their partners say they are not looking for solutions but just to be listened to. Often they say that this is enough. They recognise that the experience of being listened to can move a situation on, and might allow them to find a resolution when the time is right. But men often find it difficult to acknowledge this need in themselves for self-expression, and think that they instead require solutions to their problems.

In Protestant moral cultures men often grow up fearful about revelations of their 'animal' nature. They learn that they have inherited an evil nature and that only in subduing and controlling their emotions, feelings and desires can they hope to redeem themselves and gain moral worth. Traditionally this meant that men grew up identifying masculinity with self-control, meaning the domination of emotions that were deemed to be 'feminine'. In traditional patriarchal cultures, fathers were the 'head' of the household, representing God's will within the family, so their word would be treated as law. They expected to speak with authority without being questioned, and so to be listened to with respect. Within modernity, fathers learnt to speak with the authority of reason; again they did not have to learn to listen to others, but could experience questioning as disobedience deserving of punishment. In a Protestant culture the moral law discerned through reason existed to be obeyed. People learnt to silence their emotions since these might distract and interfere with their ability to hear the voice of the moral law. If they were instructed to listen to the voice of conscience, this was radically set against emotions, feelings and desires.[2] If people 'gave in' to their desires, this was perceived as a sign of weakness, proving that they were not acting out of a sense of moral duty.

In patriarchal culture fathers stood as the legislators of the moral law, and felt it to be their duty to instruct their children in its observance. Children learnt to listen to the commands of their fathers in order to be obedient. They did not listen in order to question, because they knew that to question was to challenge their father's authority and so prove themselves deserving of punishment. But they also learnt to fear the revelation of their own inner natures because they had learnt that their desires were 'bad'. They learnt not to listen to their emotions since this would involve distancing themselves from the demands of the moral law.

Young men grew up fearing their own desires and dreams. They could not allow themselves to express their emotions and desires in case they exposed publicly their 'evil' desires and 'bad' emotions. It was through learning to conceal these aspects of self that they could show themselves worthy in the eyes of others. This ethos was reinforced in the conception of masculinity as self-control. In Scandi-

navia, young men grew up feeling that they were betraying themselves if they showed their emotions to others. They felt dishonoured
in the eyes of others because it might appear that they were not
capable of dealing with their own emotional problems.

This need to be 'strong' in the face of emotions came to be seen, in
post-feminist cultures, as a sign of weakness by both men and women.
As patriarchal cultures gave way to societies that valorised gender
equality, different norms were established for men and women to
uphold. As emotional life was increasingly framed through new norms
and values, which permitted forms of emotional expression unthinkable within traditional patriarchal cultures, individuals framed their
own forms of discipline and self-regulation.[3]

guilt

Protestant cultures are often associated with feelings of guilt. Since
there is no space for confession, individuals can feel that they have to
carry their wrongdoings for the rest of their lives. These feelings of
guilt can sustain people's self-conception as sinners. As the notion of
sin has tended to give way within post-war secularised cultures, so
individuals can be haunted by feelings of guilt that are hard to place
outside of a religious tradition. Even though Scandinavian cultures
have permitted a more relaxed attitude to bodies and nakedness, so
that less shame attaches to them than in Britain, people can still feel
guilty about their own desires, and anxieties often remain unspoken.
Because they are expected to have a more relaxed attitude towards
their bodies, this becomes a norm they feel obliged to sustain. There
can be an abiding yet unconscious aspiration to shape inner emotional
life according to feelings and desires known to be socially acceptable.

Though Connell's *Masculinities* helps us to think about the relationship between diverse masculinities, it often does this theoretically
in ways that can be static and positional, framed in terms of hegemonic and subordinate masculinities. This theoretical framework has
tended to render invisible both the tensions men feel when obliged to
live up to prevailing masculinities and their actual lived experience
and emotional lives. This is partly because it is framed within the

secular terms of a Protestant tradition of self-denial that tends to think emotions as a form of self-indulgence too easily identified with the 'therapeutic'. Connell believes that men are guaranteed pleasures because of the power they take for granted within a patriarchal culture. This makes it difficult to reflect upon the feelings of powerlessness men often experience, as well as to register the transformations in gender relations that have taken place since the early 1970s. Just as emotions are deemed a sign of weakness within a Protestant moral culture, within Connell's conception of hegemonic masculinities men's emotional lives and lack of an adequate language in which to express their desires are personal issues that have little to do with prevailing definitions of masculinity. This is a 'therapeutic' issue that for Connell has little to do with 'politics'.[4]

Young men often feel guilty for failing to live up to prevailing heroic ideals of masculinity. In Norway, young men can find it hard to live up to the stories their fathers have told them about the war, while at the same time they are aware of widespread wartime collaboration. This can make it difficult for young people to know whom to believe, but it can also foster an attitude in which they learn to put the past behind them, with all its potential dark secrets, so they can look to the future. Such a denial of the past can work to shape particular masculinities in a way that can only be appreciated within specific cultural histories, and that is invisible to a universal language of hegemonic masculinity. A rationalist theory that disavows complexity in emotional life – such as an ambivalent relationship with a father who might have benefited from Nazi occupation – as 'therapeutic' can work to sustain, rather than question, a prevailing Protestant culture of self-denial.

In a secularised Protestant moral culture, men can feel that whatever they have achieved, they could have done more. As Max Weber observed in *The Protestant Ethic and the Spirit of Capitalism*, people can be haunted by a sense of inadequacy and feelings of guilt that they should have tried harder.[5] Young men can feel that they constantly have to affirm masculinities that can never be taken for granted, and that it is through showing control over their emotional lives that they prove themselves 'man enough'. This encourages men to deny whatever emotions might be emerging into consciousness in order to prove that they have asserted control. This is an ethics of masculinity that Connell unwittingly sustains. Within a framework unable to explore how a suppression of emotions becomes a way of affirming a 'hegemonic' masculinity, Connell is left to theorise masculinities exclusively as relationships of power.

In the growing culture of gender equality that has worked to replace traditional patriarchal masculinities, we need to be able to think through different gender relations rather than accepting the static terms of hegemonic and subordinate masculinities. Men, knowing that they could do more at home, might feel guilty that they are not realising their shared ideal of gender equality. They might find it difficult to give voice to the frustrations they feel and the pressures that exist in different spheres of their lives, preferring to remain silent rather than admit they have difficulties.

speaking

Men can feel that they are letting themselves down if they admit to their frustrations in meeting the demands of work and home. They can feel that they 'ought to be able to cope', so that it is preferable to remain silent than to admit to weaknesses that would cause them to 'lose face'. They prefer to leave their inner feelings unexamined, and will often be so used to not expressing them that they assume that emotions cannot really be talked about. When they are asked, they will therefore often refuse to speak about their inner emotional lives, having learnt to regard them as 'private'. Often they might say what they think an interviewer wants to hear, having learnt to shape their emotions according to what they regard as culturally acceptable.

Interviewers often have to open up a conversation in a way that builds trust. Rather than asking directly about emotions, they might ask questions about a young man's relationship with his father, and whether he thinks of his own responsibilities as a father in a different way. By opening up more neutral issues, and so helping to establish trust, a researcher might be able to move on to personal territory. Often people are brought to reflect upon personal issues through the experience of being interviewed, so that the interview can itself help men reflect upon their personal ways and the direction their life projects might be taking. Sometimes interviewing men more than once, giving time to reflect upon the initial experience, can help them to speak more openly about themselves. This procedure might be quite different from that used in interviewing women, who might have more access to their emotions and feelings, though again this cannot be assumed since there have been significant shifts between generations.

A project that looked at young women's experiences of anorexia in Sweden found that this was often the first time the interviewees had spoken about their experiences. Some of the young women felt obliged to live up to the independent and self-sufficient images portrayed by their mothers. They felt guilty about their own inner turmoil, unable show their feelings of need to their mothers, who seemed in control of their own emotional lives. With gender equality in modern Sweden, working women often assumed an instrumental relationship towards their family life, wanting everything to 'run smoothly' and not wanting to listen to their daughters' pain and difficulties. They conveyed an unconscious message that they had more than enough to deal with in their own lives, working and running the family home, so that the least their daughters could do would be to keep their emotional lives and feelings of need and dependency to themselves. Young men are increasingly feeling the same, turning their emotions into and against themselves and unable to reach for the support they need. They can also prove themselves through struggles with food, affirming a control that they otherwise feel they lack in their intimate relationships.

A vision of gender equality can mean that both men and women grow up feeling that they should be able to deal with their emotional issues on their own. Even if young women seem better able to reach out for support from friends at school, say if there is a death or divorce in the family, they can feel that within the family they should be able to keep things together, because their parents have enough to cope with themselves. Gender equality can reinforce a notion of freedom as autonomy that makes it difficult to speak about need or dependency. Individuals can feel obliged to conceal their need for contact or their feelings of dependency, experiencing these emotions as threats to their sense of identity. This can make it difficult to share feelings within intimate relationships, as they feel obliged to prove themselves self-sufficient. In Norway there is a reluctance to offer help to others, because this might suggest that they cannot deal with their emotional problems on their own. This can make it difficult for people to acknowledge that they need help, or to show vulnerability and so deepen contact within intimate relationships.[6]

An awareness of shifts in gender relations within post-feminist sexual politics can help explain a reluctance, as was often the case in the 1970s, to assume gender categories as a starting point of analysis. Sometimes men can take a 'feminine' position within families, or women can assume a position of power within families that is traditionally associated with men. Some men, wanting to break with the authoritarian patterns of fathering they have themselves experienced, find it difficult to assert authority, wishing not to threaten the closer relationship they want with their children. They may leave it up to women to assert an authority they feel shy of. This might be something they have negotiated, or else it might remain a source of tension within the adult relationship as the women feel they have been left with the difficult tasks men avoid.

learning

Researchers in positivist traditions often learn to avoid all possible sources of 'bias', which means that they have to ignore their own subjective views. They can learn to present themselves as 'neutral', as mirrors that simply reflect what their subjects have to say. But in survey research this can mean taking at face value what people say about themselves, as if it is through discourse that reality is articulated and shaped. Researchers can think that they are taking a 'snapshot' that reflects people's values and ideas at a particular moment in time. But if men are keen to answer questions in ways that show them in a good light, and are concerned not to show their 'bad' emotions or 'ugly' dreams, then they will carefully regulate their responses. The researchers will gather views that tell us very little about the different levels of men's experience or the inner tension of their emotional lives. There will be little sense of how men have come to feel about available masculinities or the struggles they have in living up to ideals they may be questioning.

Thinking in terms of hegemonic masculinities can promise a theoretical framework that stands on its own. But it often fails to engage
with the empirical research because the evidence cannot question the
theoretical assumptions. Connell's *Masculinities* givs us little sense of
how men can change, or of how they might be engaged in processes
of transformation. Though there is a continuing awareness of the
meanings that men give to their experience, there is a moralism that
suggests that as an act of will they could give up their privileges
and be different. There is little sense of where these men have come
from and the ways they have become who they are, through relating
to masculinities circulating within the wider culture. Rather, we
tend to think of them as illustrative of particular masculinities and
the relationships of power in which they are implicated. There is an
awareness of subjectivities and of the ways psychoanalytic theories
can illuminate them, but these discussions have a subordinate position
within the larger theoretical frame. Their inclusion might seem to
argue against the view that Connell conceives of masculinities exclusively as relationships of power. Yet it is difficult to accommodate
this position, given that the connection between the personal and
the political has been broken by Connell's assertion of a pervasive
opposition between the 'therapeutic' and the 'political'.

As there is relatively little connection between the theoretical
introduction to *Masculinities* and the empirical case studies that follow,
the researcher might be tempted to think that the theoretical reflections stand on their own ground. This is an unfortunate notion, given
the global interest in research into men and masculinities. It has
encouraged researchers to think that they can adopt the theoretical
framework with limited local adjustments. They may think of men's
lives as illustrative of particular hegemonic or subordinate masculinities in ways that can imply that these exist in a sphere of their own,
and thereby fail to engage with the tension within men's lives as they
attempt to live up to particular models of masculinity.

If we are to restore a sense of the lived tensions between men and
masculinities then we need to recognise the relationship between the
personal and the political, and refuse Connell's notion that a concern
with consciousness-raising in men's lives necessarily involves reducing
the political to the personal. Connell does not explore the distinction

between the personal and the therapeutic; nor does he engage with men's desire to explore more expressive forms of therapy, rather than become trapped within rationalist forms of psychoanalysis. Men's sense of their use of language as self-protection and a means of performing masculinity can produce a feeling of being trapped in their own language. They might want to reach out towards others, but somehow feel they cannot make contact. Rather than being a means of self-expression, language becomes a distancing agent.

Men have often withdrawn from an engagement with the social and political world through their involvement in therapeutic practices. They may have felt it necessary to spend time working out their own emotional issues, believing that until they have learnt how to change themselves they cannot successfully engage in transforming relationships of power. Although Connell recognises the ease with which men can get lost in these personal concerns, he tends to dismiss the therapeutic – including the contribution made by Robert Bly in *Iron John* – as a form of self-indulgence. This attitude towards emotional life reveals a disdain that is familiar within a Protestant moral culture of self-denial. Rather than engage with issues to do with power and emotions, Connell tends to assume that if men possess power then their sufferings have to be 'personal'.[7]

As researchers, men and women engaged in critical work in relation to men and masculinities must explore their personal investment in the issues they are working on. Sometimes this involves writing about their own individual experiences in autobiographical terms. This can be a way of becoming aware of what they are bringing with them into the research. Unless they become 'critically conscious' in this way, as Gramsci terms it, they are in danger of projecting their own assumptions. It is through becoming aware of their own emotional involvements that they can be more 'present' in the interviews. They will only ask questions of others that they have taken time to ask themselves, and they will not expect others to speak from a level that they have not touched themselves.[8]

Rather than treat the interview in positivist terms, as a matter of gaining information from subjects while presenting oneself in neutral terms, we can learn from feminist research methods to appreciate the interview as a relationship in which both parties are ready to share their own experience. The focus of the interview remains clearly on the subject, but researchers have to be ready to go to places that they are asking people to visit themselves, which entails having already done the necessary 'emotional work'. This brings greater depth and meaning to the interview; however, it does not make it a therapeutic encounter. Clear lines must be established, and researchers are more likely to avoid unconscious transference processes if they can also share from their own experience.

Acknowledging the range of situations that researchers may confront when interviewing men does not necessitate drawing a clear distinction between researching women and researching men, as though gender differences were clear from the outset. Gender relations have changed, and assumptions that were originally made in early feminist research about the ease of interviewing women probably need to be questioned. Young women can themselves have difficulties in emotional connection, and be caught in presenting particular images of themselves. We have to be open to exploring the significance of gender, rather than assuming it.

Yet we have to recognise the masculinist assumptions that have often underpinned traditional research methodologies. We need to investigate the relationships between masculinities and methodologies. Within interpretative traditions that have drawn from Weber we find the implicit assumption that people are free to assign meanings to their experience. It has been a critical insight of feminist methodologies to appreciate how these meanings are negotiated within relationships of power, so that some people have the power to impose their meanings on others. Those who experience themselves as powerless might feel obliged to frame their experience in terms that please those who are perceived as having power. For example, notions of female attractiveness were traditionally defined by men, until women began to dress for themselves and to feel empowered to shape their own self-image. We live in a culture where image has become almost equally significant for men.

In researching men we are seeking a language that can help them articulate an experience that they might otherwise remain silent about. It is not a matter of creating a language in a vacuum and bringing it to new consumerist masculinities, but of engaging with the everyday lives of men in a relational way that opens up language and allows them to take the next step for themselves. This also means stimulating critical discussion between the different theorisations of masculinities and exposing their methodological assumptions. We can appreciate the need for theoretically informed empirical work with young men, and the need to reflect this through a critical engagement with masculinities circulating in the broader culture. This involves developing a sensitivity to diverse cultural masculinities as well as a grasp of the ways power relates to emotions and feelings of self-worth.

Women and men are silenced if they feel their experience must conform to notions of gender equality, and they cannot voice their frustrations and anxieties. Scandinavian experience shows the difficulties that can emerge when gender equality is taken up as a rhetoric by state institutions. People can feel constrained to live up to this rhetoric in ways that sometimes mean they cannot negotiate their relationships honestly and openly. People need to develop a sense of their individual needs and desires as well as shared responsibilities if they are to learn to work effectively within a more equal gender relationship. This involves a respect for individual differences as well as a recognition of structural relations of power. If visions of gender equality are to be sustained, then they also need to be imagined in ways that include children, and allow them also to give voice to their individual needs and desires. If we define gender equality in a way that only suits the interests of adults, then it will cease to have meaning for the generations to come. We also have to be aware of how gender equality is often achieved in the middle class through the labour of poorer women, who also need to be brought into the equation.

We have to learn from the pressures and anxieties of diverse societies, cultures and traditions, so that institutional power can be negotiated and people are able to live more equal relations within increasingly unequal globalised capitalist societies. This means learning from these different contexts and resources, as well as acknowledging the new generational histories centred on gender and sexuality. The globalised worlds in which young people now find themselves offer new possibilities of relating to others which they need to learn to negotiate. Sexual politics have their own histories and genealogies in different continents; hence we must not generalise from models that have been created in the North. We need to appreciate how the discourses of gender equality, human rights and democratic civil society sustain an ethics of human development that is inherently critical of patriarchal and homophobic traditions. It is by acknowledging the complexities of diverse traditions and different voices that people will engage most effectively.

4

questioning adam: men, power and love[*]

memories/places

Where we are makes a difference to how we can think and what needs
to be said. Gathering in Puebla for the first international conference
on men and masculinities in Mexico, in the Salón Barroco of the
Edificio Carolino, we cannot avoid the shadow of the Inquisition.
The instruments of torture are not far away, being visible in the next
building, and we can imagine the fear of interrogation where people
struggle to find words in their defence. The Inquisition was carried
from Spain to Mexico and became an integral part of securing the
spiritual conquest of the indigenous peoples.[1]

People were to learn a silence and a fear of thinking differently that
would echo in the long and painful history of Mexico, and continue
to undermine creative thinking into the present. For as walls have
memories, so fears have a means of stretching across generations,
which will often have chosen to forget the traumatic histories of
the past to focus upon the present and future. This is a forgetting
often shaped by an Enlightenment vision of progress. But, as Walter
Benjamin recognised, the past refuses to be forgotten; it is only

---

* In memory of Graciella Hierro.

* In memory of Graciella Hierro.

through a willingness to face the past with all its cruelties that we can hope to think more clearly in the present.[2]

Just before the conference was due to begin in Puebla, a news conference was held in the Vatican to mark the publication of new research into the Inquisition in Europe, which concluded that of the 125,000 documented heresy trials, only about 1 per cent of defendants were actually executed. Whatever we think of these figures, the fear that was to cross the seas to 'New Spain' showed that torture was used as an instrument of political and spiritual conquest. The Inquisition had begun in Europe in 1231 as a legal procedure to root out heretics; in the fifteenth and sixteenth centuries it was increasingly directed, in a series of heresy trials, against Jews who, as *conversos*, had taken on the Christian faith. Many people were burnt at the stake. At the Vatican conference, Pope John Paul II renewed a plea for forgiveness for sins committed by Catholics in the name of Church doctrine. Yet questions remain: which aspects of doctrine are being referred to, and how are they challenged in the present to increase tolerance of those defined as 'other'? In many ways the treatment of Jews as others within a Christian Europe helped to shape the ways in which the indigenous came to be imagined with the Conquest.

Where countries share traumatic histories, there is often pressure to forget, since people fear that remembering painful events of conquest will only serve to create divisions in the present. Possibly this is part of what has encouraged a Mexican government to consider reducing the place of history within the school curriculum and to suggest that students no longer need to learn about indigenous cultures before the Conquest. It is as if history is to begin again with the Spanish Conquest, enacted by a dominant Spanish masculinity that had proved its superiority in battle. As Simone Weil recognises in *The Need for Roots*, Western consciousness has been shaped by Roman conceptions of power and greatness that assume that conquest somehow proves the moral superiority of those who have taken victory by force. Not only is history written to validate the position of those powerful enough to write history in their own image, but, as Weil realised, there was often an implicit and unquestioned identification between morality and power.[3]

Walter Benjamin also recognised that those indigenous groups that suffered the catastrophe of defeat were forced to accept the supremacy of armed power, but not the weakness of their moral values and ideals. If they learnt to remain silent in public they could struggle to sustain their values and traditions within their own communities, even as they had to be framed within the terms of a new Catholic hegemony. It was not their visions of life or moral values that had been defeated; they had simply been forced to submit to a dominating power. It was only in the eyes of the Conquest that their values were denigrated, and it was only through Catholicism's vision of a singular path towards truth that they were deemed uncivilised and their spiritual traditions unable to offer salvation. Respecting where we are in the present, we have an obligation to remember the sufferings of the past for they are also part of the present. The instruments of torture still sustain fear and silence in the present. Rather than assume the past can be put aside and no longer taught in schools, we have to question visions of historical progress that encourage forgetting and deny dignity and self-respect to 'others'.[4]

The Conquest has long taught that the indigenous were violent and their spiritual practices dependent upon sacrifice, so they needed to be saved from themselves. But this is to forget the brutal violence of the Conquest, as generations of Mexicans have learnt to appreciate it as 'shared catastrophe', to forget that indigenous peoples suffered at the hands of others who had no right to be there. Violence and torture worked to produce fears that have echoed across the generations and produced their own forms of uneasy silence. Within the intellectual cultures of modernity, and the revolutionary tradition of Mexico shaped by secular culture, it has been difficult to come to terms with history as memory. People have learnt to look towards the future to help them forget the traumatic memories of the past, making it difficult for them to grasp their gendered and racialised identities in the present.

The dominance of secular cultures in urban areas has produced a desire to separate from the past; but even if people have broken with Catholicism intellectually, it does not follow that it is not somehow formative emotionally. Religion as an object of intellectual investigation might have a place in theology and anthropology departments, but it has been largely absent within the secular discourses of gender studies. Not only does the issue of religious formation need to be opened up; we also need to make connections with issues of race and ethnicity, and with historical memory. We need to question postmodern visions of identity that refuse to acknowledge how historical memories continue to resonate and shape present identities, even if we wish to think otherwise. If individuals are to deepen their sense of gendered and racialised identities, then they will have to remember what the larger culture has often chosen to forget.[5]

This can help us understand the differences between the visions of modernity shaped within secularised Protestant cultures and the moral dualisms of good and evil, virgin and whore, that continue to shape people's experience of race, ethnicities, gender, bodies and sexualities in contemporary Mexico. While we recognise the institutional power of Catholicism in cities such as Puebla, and the morality it sustains, we also have to remember that this is also the place where the Latin American bishops came together to take a human stand for the poor and for social justice.

creations

There are many different stories of creation that help to shape gender relations in the present, even though we often refuse to acknowledge their power within secular cultures. Conquest imposes its own narratives of creation, and works to silence the diverse voices and traditions of indigenous cultures. The fact that the indigenous were the 'first peoples' does not give their creation narratives honour and respect, for they were identified with a nature that existed outside the boundaries of history and civilisation. A Western Christian colonising mission emerged from Catholic Spain to bring faith and civilisation to the uncivilised 'others', who were defined by the culture they lacked. In Spain the *Reconquista* was helping to shape the Inquisition's drive towards an ethics of purification that declared war on Jewish and Islamic differences, which could no longer live side by side with Catholicism but had to be forcibly converted or expelled. Catholicism presented itself as a singular truth that could not tolerate different traditions as anything but forms of untruth. The sword was to accompany the cross, and if people could not accept the truths they were being offered they did not deserve to survive.

Shaped through Greek and Roman power, Christianity followed a visual epistemology that devalued blindness as reflecting a moral failing. In disavowing its own Jewish sources and the Jewishness of Jesus, Christianity came to represent Judaism as a blind woman whose stick was broken, so she could not find her way. Jews were deemed blind because they could not 'see' the truths of the Christian revelation. The figure of the Jew as denigrated 'other', who had to be constantly tested to prove a conversion was genuine, became central to the Inquisition.[6] Since belief was deemed to be a matter of 'purity of heart' that was shaped through blood, there were doubts as to whether Jews could ever really convert, because of the impurity of their blood. In Europe we see the shaping of a totalitarian impulse that was to show itself again in Hitler's Germany, where people had to prove the purity of their Aryan blood to doctors if they wanted permission to marry. In Puebla at the same time that we were meeting to consider 'El Primer Sexo?' there was an exhibition in the nearby Museo Biblioteca Palafoxiana entitled 'Libros Prohibidos' that reminded us that the burning of books is soon followed by the burning of human bodies. The Inquisition set a dangerous precedent.

Catholic Europe was to bring truth and salvation to the uncivilised indigenous peoples in the 'New Spain'. Again there are questions about whether the 'natives' had souls and whether they could ever truly convert. But new Mexican identities also arose, through different stories of creation in which Cortés took the indigenous woman Malinche as his wife. This had the effect of rendering invisible issues of racial difference, as coloniser and colonised were brought together under a new ideology of mestizo. Since everyone can claim to be 'mixed', differences of colour come to be invisible and one no longer 'sees' stratifications of colour. This is also a gendered narrative: it is a women, Eve, who has to submit to the Spanish coloniser Adam to create a new Eden in the New Spain that is Mexico. The European comes later, and he is to bring religion, culture and education to the indigenous peoples. A European masculinity as the bearer of religious truth has everything to teach and little to learn.

Christianity reads the story of Genesis as a story of the Fall, which frames gender relations of power and subordination. Jewish and Islamic readings offer different interpretations, and so pose different questions to Adam.[7] How has the notion of the 'human' been shaped within masculinist terms so that men are not just the first sex but the only fully human sex? Do we assume that Adam is 'white', and the bearer of a truth that the European coloniser came to represent? Does a Christian reading of Adam see him as the bearer of a singular truth that 'other' traditions are deemed to lack? Does this produce forms of intolerance that make it difficult for men to learn how to listen and to love in both heterosexual and gay relationships? Does Adam offer us a 'queer' reading?

A recent television programme featured a man, let us call him Adam, who was learning to deal with an alcohol problem while in prison. His partner had learned all kinds of skills while he was inside, as she was looking after the children on her own. She was fearful of what it would be like when he returned, as he had always expected to get his way as the man in the house, constantly giving instructions and expecting to be obeyed. When he came out it was not easy, and she felt she did not know him any more. Whereas she welcomed some of the changes, she felt they could not really communicate with each other and she wanted something more from the relationship. Even though Adam was no longer drinking, he found it hard to be intimate and vulnerable. He still felt he had to impose his authority. Why?

readings

In *New Maladies of the Soul* (1995), Julia Kristeva returns to the Bible, to propose a particularly suggestive new reading. While she draws on the insights of structuralist analysis, she criticises structuralism for not going beyond 'specifying the profound logic' of the text as a network or encodement of differences. If we attend to 'the linguistic subject of the biblical utterance', we can recognise a biblical narrator, who is by no means 'neutral' but is, rather, a 'subject on trial', in the process of formation and susceptible to breakdown, fracture and dislocation. Like psychoanalysis, then, this approach to literature sees 'abjection as necessary for the advent of the subject as a speaking being',[8] through marking the borders of the inside and the outside, self and not-self. As Timothy Beal has noted, Kristeva's readings are very much in line with both Freud and Lacan, where

> the social and symbolic order of the Bible has as its centrepiece, foundation, and guarantor the One God, whose divine prohibition against the mother (the Law/No of the Father) is the basis for the formation of identity. In this way biblical monotheism is understood in traditional psychoanalysis primarily as 'the imposition of a strategy of identity'.[9]

As we ask questions of Adam, so we bring into question the relationship between a dominant heterosexual masculinity and the psychoanalytic vision of the father as the source of authority within the family, where his word becomes law. We trace the ways Eve becomes abject within a dominant discourse where the feminine is to be feared as the source of evil. Men as the 'first sex' prove themselves through their separations from the body and sexuality, which come to be identified with the sins of the flesh. Unable to accept the embodied and sexual desires that they learn to regard as animal, men often learn to project these disavowed aspects of themselves onto women. This helps shape the dualistic vision of women as either virgins or whores that continues to have such a strong hold upon Catholic cultures. Men are often educated to distrust women within a culture that values celibacy as an ethical ideal. This can make it difficult to negotiate sexual desires.

In 'Shifting the Blame: God in the Garden', Danna Nolan Fewell and David M. Gunn recognise that, 'For good or evil, Genesis 1–3, perhaps more than any other biblical text, has influenced the way men and women relate to each other in the Western world.'[10] Genesis says:

> And God created humankind in his own image, in the image of God, he created it, male and female he created them. And God blessed them, and God said to them, 'Be fruitful and multiply, and fill the earth and subdue it; and subjugate...' And God saw everything that he had done, and behold it was very good.

As Fewell and Gunn comment: 'And God saw that it was good.' That constant refrain speaks of discovery. This creator God is plainly not, as Christian theology would have it, omniscient.'[11] This God seems to greet with enthusiasm each new discovery of his own handiwork.

In Genesis 1 the narrator has opened up a broad and highly schematised view of creation. From 2:4b the account takes a different shape and the focus falls upon a particular category of creation, the human. In 2–3 it is gender that is under construction, and it is here that gender differences are being defined. It is here that we also discover that the binaries are less equal than they first appear. The apparent equity of Genesis 1:27 ('in the image of God he created them; male and female he created them') dissolves under closer scrutiny and we find a hierarchy in which Adam becomes subject and norm, while Eve as other becomes object. The conception of 'the human' that had included 'male and female' somehow comes to be defined in crucially masculine terms.

God forms the animals and parades them before the human 'to see what it [he] would call them'. Confident that the human will replicate God's own desire to name, God is not disappointed. Yet, as Fewell and Gunn claim,

> the experiment fails in its main purpose for a counterpart is not found. Perhaps the human is unwilling (or unable) to recognise the animals as counterparts because, like God, the human desires its own image. God reverts, therefore, to division. Man and women are created. Likeness is conjured by separation. Male and female. Opposite and like. Difference and sameness. Other and self.[12]

This means that Adam as 'queer'/trans had not as yet been 'divided' into genders, could not recognise 'himself' as part of the animal world, but was positioned in a relationship of superiority as dominion over nature. After he has formed and placed the human in the garden, God decides that 'It is not good that the human should be alone; I will make it [him] a helper, counterpart [*keneged*; 'like-opposite'] for it [him]' (2:18).

The man formed from the human claims the woman, also formed from the human, as his own. Presumably he finds in her a suitable 'helper'/partner because, as he puts it, 'This at last is bone of my bones and flesh of my flesh; this shall be called 'woman' [*ishshah*] because from man [*ish*] was taken this' (2:21–23). It is the man, not the undifferentiated human, the 'queer' Adam, who then speaks. God brings the newly formed woman before the man, as earlier (a male?) God had brought the animals before the human. But he nevertheless, as Fewell and Gunn note, 'nominates the man as still (or also?) the original inclusive being, the 'Human'. Thereby the human becomes *both* the human *and* the man. The woman is merely the woman.'[13] As Adam speaks he objectifies Eve, the woman. He does not address her as 'you', or even refer to her as 'she'. Rather, she is 'this'. Moreover, the man, like God in Genesis 1, is allowed the privilege of discovery. Though he does not pronounce her 'good', he declares that she is appropriate. He claims *her* as bone of *his* bones and flesh of *his* flesh. The direction of his claim for control is made clear in the wordplay.

Yet the woman (strictly the 'side' from which she was formed) was taken out of the human, not the man. This could seem to undermine the claims of Adam for the first sex, so 'queering' the human. The man, however, claims the past and humanity as his own dominion. This is to make universal claims for a dominant masculinity, confirmed in the claim that woman comes out of man and so is 'second', when we know that both men and woman, as Irigaray reminds us, were both born of women.[14] In this he asserts authority over the woman as a parent over a child, and this remains the way patriarchal cultures have sought to define gender relations. But what if woman had been allowed to discover and voice her own experience? Would she have recognised the man to be flesh of her flesh and bone of her bone? Would she have decided to call him 'man' because he had once been part of 'woman'? Would she have been disappointed with her partner?

These are possibilities that are alive in narratives of creation that we can discover in indigenous cultures. Within the dominant Christian discourse women are silenced and exist as the objects of male desire, and so become defined as the second sex as if she exists without desire, attachments and a past. As Fewell and Gunn conclude, 'She is simply there, waiting to be subsumed. Union with a man is her consummate purpose.'[15] They also recognise that, 'Just as relations between parents and children are diminished, so, too, are excluded relations between people of the same sex.' Human sexuality remains defined as monogamous heterosexuality.

power and vulnerability

If men remain defined as the first sex in ways that teach them within modernity to be independent and self-sufficient, love becomes problematic, as emotions are a sign of weakness. Men learn to conceal their vulnerability, even from themselves. But if they cannot allow themselves to be vulnerable, how can they allow themselves to love? Often men grow up feeling that it is women, as the weaker/second sex, who can allow themselves to be emotional and seek support. Learning to discount their own emotional needs, men often find it difficult to identify what it is they are feeling, and what they might want or need from an intimate relationship. They may learn to live as though they do not need a loving relationship, which can leave the woman feeling she cannot express her own needs if her partner seems to need so little for himself. In heterosexual relationships women may feel that their emotional needs are largely unrecognised, which can lead them to 'give up' on their partner because of the emotional distance between them.

We need to understand intimate relationships within the framework of gender power and violence. The coloniser often has the material power to demean indigenous colonised people in their own eyes; they can feel they have to hide their traditional ways of being or live a double consciousness, whereby traditional practices are hidden within syncretic Catholic traditions. Where a dominant Catholic tradition still thinks of itself as the bearer of a singular truth and as providing the only path to salvation, it can be difficult to open up a dialogue between diverse traditions. It is easy to assume that 'if only people were more educated' they would see the truth that is being offered to them. This is framed within secular traditions, as I have shown in *Unreasonable Men* and more recently in *Man Enough*, through the notion that a dominant masculinity can alone take its reason for granted.[16] This provides a secular and rationalist basis for the first sex, who can feel they alone can legislate what is 'good' for others who are deemed to be 'closer to nature'. Feminism broke the silence of women and challenged the terms of an Enlightenment vision of modernity.

As I have argued in *The Moral Limits of Modernity: Love, Inequality and Oppression*, Western visions of modernity have been framed within a rationalist tradition that has insisted upon distinctions between reason and nature, mind and body, reason and emotion, that have worked to marginalise questions of love, vulnerability and emotional life.[17] If emotions are deemed unmanly, it can be difficult for men to find the courage to love, since this would involve questioning the terms of a patriarchal culture in which women do not feel free to express their desires but learn to live in relation to husbands and children. But men often react violently to the developing independence of women, especially young women, as they feel their identity as a man is being threatened. Only through a zero tolerance of male violence and a recognition that 'real men' are not violent towards their partners can men be encouraged to change.

Young men, rather than being encouraged to reflect upon tensions between their experience as men and prevailing masculinities, learn to conform to external structures. Universalist theories of 'hegemonic masculinities' can encourage cultural blindness, as they foster the notion that gender domination can be explained exclusively in terms of power. This has made it harder to focus upon the diverse cultures of masculinity within Latin America, as it is argued that structures of patriarchal power and male violence towards women are everywhere. But unless we explore how patriarchy is shaped differently – say, according to different histories of conquest or different traditions in the Catholic Church – we will find it difficult to compare diverse Latin American masculinities.

The universalism of Connell's vision of hegemonic masculinities has made it difficult to explain the formative processes of masculinity through which boys become men. It can also encourage boys to take refuge in their status as 'first sex', and so endure in silence. They learn to prove their male identities against their own vulnerabilities, having learnt that if they have power they are not entitled to their emotional pain. It is interesting to note the implicit Protestant terms of Connell's argument that men have no right to complain about their hurts or emotional injuries as men because these cannot be compared with what women are made to suffer at the hand of patriarchy and male violence. There is little sense of how masculinities can be transformed, when masculinity is always the problem and never recognised as part of a solution.

The theory of 'hegemonic masculinities' tends to reinforce male silence; men learn to 'take it' because they have the privileges that women are denied. Often boys do not want to remember what it was like growing up in a family in which the father was alcoholic and violent, and in which they were forced to witness their mother being beaten up. They can still feel shamed by these images, unable to intervene on her behalf out of fear that the violence would then be turned against them. Sometimes they have lived with these painful memories through learning to identify with their father's power; accepting that it was his duty to discipline 'his' family. They might feel that there must have been something wrong with their mother for her to have been so brutally beaten, while at the same time feeling bereft of an alternative ethical vision that allows them to understand just how unacceptable is domestic violence. And they can feel ethically challenged as they question the Catholic morality that seems to legitimate such domestic violence.

Unless we are prepared to investigate the ways Catholicism has sustained legitimations of domestic violence and turned a blind eye to issues of sexual abuse, we cannot develop practices that can effectively challenge these sufferings. Often the therapeutic practices that have been developed to work with men who have been perpetrators remain deaf to issues of religious formation. We have been slow to recognise the religious assumptions that often underpin these secular practices. Even in urban areas where people have disavowed religious belief, young men's sense of superiority towards women, and the distrust and fears they carry, can only be understood in the context of their religious and cultural setting. Since fear is considered to be unmanly, it is often dealt with through an identification with the father. In the next generation young men might react by rejecting alcoholism, aware at some level of the devastation that it wrought in their families, and choosing drugs as an alternative means of psychic escape.

If theories of masculinities reinforce the idea that men are always the bearers of power, they can make it difficult to produce culturally sensitive ways of grasping *how* power is always entwined with emotion. Rather than thinking about hegemony as exclusively a relationship of power, Gramsci was careful to explore relationships between power and vulnerability.

love and intimacy

Within Christian traditions that assume that love can only be 'pure' if it is untainted by sexuality, it can be difficult for people to feel relaxed about their body and sexuality. The Catholic identification of the body with the 'sins of the flesh' produces an unease about bodily contact. Men in particular learn to hold their bodies in certain ways. In Mexico this tension is felt as men learn to hug each other; there is a fear of contact that could be interpreted as gay. Men's learned use of their bodies as instruments of power can make it difficult to allow intimacy within strongly homophobic cultures that still identify emotions as feminine, and thus threatening to male identities.[18]

Boys who have witnessed their mothers being beaten up by their fathers might find it difficult to acknowledge their own pain and confusion. Within a moral culture that is shaped by a Catholic dualism between good and evil they might find it hard to acknowledge the ambivalence in their own emotions. They might feel pushed to affirm a dominant masculinity in conceding to a father who says that 'she deserved it' because she was 'talking too much'. For some boys there will be ethical issues in even questioning what their father has to say, especially if they have learnt that their father, as the source of God's authority within the family, needs to be obeyed. Unable to question their father, it can be difficult to question themselves; instead they harden their hearts against their own ethical intuitions of difference, which, as Gramsci recognises in the *Prison Notebooks*, could otherwise serve as a source of a shift in ethical consciousness.

The suffering body of Christ is a constant visual reminder of the guilt that Catholics carry for 'his dying for your sins'. This is a particularly traumatic experience for young boys, who can learn to identify with this suffering. It teaches a tolerance for pain and a sense that people have to endure their own suffering, since they are 'as nothing' compared with the suffering until death that Jesus endured. A young man might learn that it is his mother's fate to suffer and that she will be given her just rewards in a world to come. Christ's tortured body is represented as a sacrifice of love; so love comes to be identified with sacrifice, and people learn that it is only through punishing the body that the soul can be purified. The animal pleasures of the body are discounted as threatening to individual spiritual status. As Eve shows, it is women who are to be distrusted most, because of the responsibility they carry for bringing evil into the world.

Within an ethic of patient endurance it can be easier to legitimate domestic violence, especially if fathers feel that they carry a moral responsibility to discipline their partners and children. This can make it difficult for younger generations to develop more open and tolerant relationships with their bodily emotions and desires, and so learn a different relationship between bodies, intimacy, love and sexuality. These issues can also be difficult to illuminate within theories of sexuality that would insist on separating intimacy from issues of sexual pleasure. If we are not to reproduce a rationalist rejection of religion as false consciousness, then, as Gramsci recognised, we have to explore the ways in which violent conquest was justified in the conviction that it was only through conversion that the soul could be saved. Within a Christian other-worldly ethic it was of little consequence what bodies were made to suffer, because what mattered was the saving of souls. Bodies were imagined as 'prisons' of earthly life; it was only through death, according to a Platonic and Christian tradition, that people could know freedom.[19]

Unable to recognise an ethics of pleasure that could celebrate the body, a dominant Catholic moral tradition saw life as a sacrifice of the present to win salvation in a world to come. The radical distinction between the earthly and the spiritual meant that it was only through a rejection of our animal natures that the human could be imagined at all. Exploring the dominant Christian tradition, Nietzsche reflected upon what it could mean to be created 'in the image of God'; rather than recognising how bodies and sexualities could be celebrated as made in the image of the divine, they were shamed as animal and so as no part of our identity as human beings. Through affirming self-control as a relationship of dominance, a traditional masculinity learnt to assert its moral authority in relation to women and children. It was for them to learn the virtue of obedience within a culture that accepted celibacy as a moral ideal. There was a radical distinction to be drawn between sexuality and spirituality, and a dualistic vision that meant sexual desires could not be sacred or holy or recognised as an expression of love.

As a Catholic culture inherits a sharp distinction between sexuality and love, so a postmodern culture that has wanted to treat sexuality as pleasure has found it difficult to think about intimacy, contact and love. As long as we identify sexuality as animal it cannot be recognised in its diverse forms as an expression of human love. It is possibly only through 'queering' this distinction between the human and the animal that we can refuse a categorical difference and recognise the need to bring sexualities, desires, bodies into complex relationships with identities and spiritualities. This is not only to recognise distinctions between religious and spiritual traditions but also to imagine alternative ethical visions that can enable us to assess critically the moralisms of traditional religious practices. Hence the 'queering' of Adam allows us to accept that often no sharp distinction can be drawn between masculine and feminine, and that within a postmodern culture we need to value ambivalence and uncertainties, whilst we also appreciate the need for moral deliberation about complex issues of histories, identities, bodies, genders, 'races' and sexualities.

In cultures that have denigrated and shamed bodies and sexualities, it is important to conceive of intimate and sexual relations in ways that are affirming of sexualities. In a new summer programme to help teenagers in Camberwell, a fairly deprived area of inner London, they are asking young men like Adam how they see the opposite sex, and what they feel about relationships. Teenage girls have thought about these issues endlessly, whereas boys have not done so at all. In the Western world, as Raj Persaud has argued, physical attraction and romance are seen as the most important factors, at the expense of compatibility.

As we watch the transformation of gender relations of power in urban and rural settings, we need to think about diverse cultures of masculinities within the context of global relations of power. New inequalities are being produced within globalised relationships, particularly through access to new media technologies. Yet these have also facilitated the circulation of new images of masculinity and new forms of emotional support across space. We need to ask Adam different questions that show him what is to be gained through open and loving relationships. Rather than framing masculinity exclusively as a relationship of power, we have to explore the tensions between men and prevailing masculinities. As we understand the significance of exposing relationships of power and violence, and the ways they express themselves both locally and globally, we also need to be able to present new forms of intimacy and love as part of a process of transforming masculinities.

5

rethinking fatherhood

histories

Western culture has in different ways been conceived through a relationship of fathering. We are still haunted by a sense of 'God the father' and religious traditions still think of the relationship to God as a relationship of obedience due to a father. How do different religious traditions in the West think of creation in the book of Genesis as the creation of God the Father? How do they continue to shape visions of authority within secular cultures, and how do they help illuminate differences with Eastern traditions that sustain diverse secular inheritances?

In different ways, Judaism, Christianity and Islam all think of Abraham as the 'father' of their religious tradition, and each has its own reading of the story of Creation in Genesis. In each tradition the notion of God the creator, who brings the world into existence, imagines God as 'fathering' the world, bringing it into existence and forming it according to his will and intention. These different 'Abrahamic' traditions imagine a direct line that stretches back to Abraham, and through him to the discovery of a singular God who can speak directly to Abraham to set the terms of monotheistic traditions.[1]

Yet the traditions differ in their recognition of whether people have a direct line of communication with God, listening to what he has to say and disagreeing with him if necessary. The Jewish tradition gives priority to hearing the voice of God, and so to a sense that God speaks directly, even though people often cannot hear or do not want to hear what God has to say. There is the possibility of a conversation, and at crucial moments in the Jewish texts human beings question the wisdom of what God is instructing and encourage him to think again about what he is advising. These religious traditions have been interpreted in different ways, and the ways people have conceived of their relationship to God have often reflected their conceptions of fathering. It is important to attempt to trace the ways in which a dominant Christian tradition in the West came to disavow its Jewish sources and the Jewishness of Jesus, wanting to define itself in opposition to what it imagined as 'carnal Israel'. Christianity learnt to reimagine itself, partly through Paul, in Greek and later Roman sources. This involved a radical shift from hearing as a source of knowledge towards the eyes and sight as the vital sense that could alone be trusted.[2]

Within a dominant Christian tradition, revelation became a matter of 'seeing' the Virgin Mary and so being reminded of her purity. The Virgin Mary vitally came to replace the image of Eve. In the narrative of Genesis, it was Eve as a woman who could be blamed for bringing evil into the world, through being unable to resist her own bodily urges and 'giving in' to temptation. The narrative gives little space to the possibility that Eve could have made a decision for herself, because of her desire for the apple. Her decision was interpreted not as an expression of her love, but rather as a sign of her disobedience towards God the Father. This critical moment is interpreted in different ways in Jewish, Christian and Islamic traditions, reflecting their visions of authority over different historical periods. We are encouraged to believe that 'evil' had no presence in the Garden of Eden before Eve showed her weakness in giving into temptation that she should have been strong enough to resist.[3]

The story of Genesis, however it is interpreted, remains crucially a story about gender, because it places the responsibility for bringing evil into the world on Eve's shoulders. If it was not for her actions,

Jesus would not have had to 'die for our sins', Christians still learn. It is only through the narratives of Genesis that we can understand how Jesus is to be imagined as a second Adam, and Mary as an Eve who has supposedly learnt her moral lesson. It is through witnessing the sufferings of Jesus and his tortured body – through 'seeing' this suffering for herself – that Mary supposedly learns the significance of resisting her own bodily inclinations and the 'sins of the flesh'. She watches silently, unable to speak. She sees what she needs to know, and there is nothing that she can say. As Simone Weil recognised, Jesus cries out against his suffering, for he does not understand why he is being made to suffer. His cry comes to symbolise the sufferings of innocence and the pain that is caused when people are made to suffer without being able to explain this suffering.[4]

Often children cannot understand the suffering they endure at the hands of their fathers. Within dominant Christian traditions children have traditionally learnt that they have to be obedient and learn the virtue of silence. There is a singular authority within the family: the father is imagined as representing God's authority and his word is law. The Christian notion of God as omnipotent Father implied that the father was also to be recognised as omnipotent within the sphere of the family. It is paternal authority that is deemed natural, not maternal instinct. Women cannot be trusted because of their instincts; because they are 'weaker' through being 'closer to nature' they are unable to resist temptation. As Eve could not be trusted to obey, so women cannot be trusted to make decisions for themselves. In Catholic cultures boys are still often brought up to distrust their mothers and sisters, as they learn to identify with their father's paternal authority. Often they are taught that it is up to them to protect their sisters, and if their father dies it is the eldest brother who is expected to assume his position as 'head of the family'.

The 'head' of the family is entitled to expect that his word will be obeyed without question. So fathers inherit a responsibility to keep the body of the family – women and children – under control, as they cannot be trusted to know what is good for them. Within a Protestant modernity the head comes to be identified with reason, mind and consciousness, and so with culture that is framed within masculine terms, while women and children exist outside the sphere of culture, within the realm of nature. They cannot help but be more influenced by their emotions, feelings and desires. They cannot expect to be able to control their behaviour, and it is only through accepting their subordination to the father and believing that he alone has a strong enough inner relationship with reason, as Kant frames it, that they can share in freedom and autonomy. This produces a crucial tension whereby it is only through learning obedience – and so silencing their own desires and feelings – that they can achieve a degree of freedom and autonomy. This means, as Kant explains, that women and children need their husbands and fathers in ways that men do not.[5]

This shows the ways men as fathers can take on God's authority within their own families. It also means that the vision of 'being human' is shaped within the terms of a dominant masculinity. Within different humanist traditions, it is man alone who represents the human; women are crucially defined through what they lack. What separates Erasmus and Kant is their conception of nature in relation to ethics: Kant insists upon a radical split between reason and nature within a secularised Protestant tradition; he does not recognise, as Erasmus is more inclined to do, that it is through a realisation of our natures that we shape ethical identities. Rather, Kant insists upon an antagonistic relation with nature that is more identified with bodies, sexualities and the 'sins of the flesh'. This reflects a sharp gender division and an insistence that women, as 'closer to nature', cannot be trusted to know what is good for them. Men alone possess the reason that can legislate what is good for their wives and children. Sometimes they will have to resort to violence: since women and children cannot be reasoned with, the only language they respond to is a language of power. But since, in producing order where there was a threat of disobedience, this is violence exercised 'for their own good', they should feel grateful. They might resent it in the present, but in the future they will surely recognise that they deserved the punishment.[6]

The sacred authority of the father is sustained through a discourse of 'natural rights' within which patriarchal privilege has traditionally been framed. In the patrilineal system of inheritance fathers had absolute control over their property; this property effectively included a man's wife and children. The divine legitimation of paternal authority gave fathers primary responsibility over the religious education and moral guidance of their children. Fathers were expected to enforce high standards of ethical virtue and to set an example of emotional restraint within family life. Within the Protestant tradition there was a fear of emotions, defined as 'feminine'. Men learnt that they had to be dispassionate and objective in their exercise of rational judgement, which meant that they had to remove themselves from emotional involvement with their children. Unless they could detach themselves emotionally, they could not expect to be impartial in their judgements.

As God existed above the world as a source of authority and judgement, so fathers were expected to exist 'above' the family in some way. They were the source of authority, but learnt within a Protestant tradition that this authority came at the price of emotional involvement. This meant that fathers were 'in' the family but not really 'of' the family. They existed in a space of their own, and even if they were often concerned with the moral well-being of their children they had to be careful to sustain a detached position.

traditions

The model of the father as a dispassionate and objective observer of what is going on in the family, ready to give judgement and exercise his authority when needed, is sustained within the Protestant tradition. This fear of the personal and the emotional was particularly strong within middle-class families. Though this model was challenged within a feminism that recognised that 'the personal is political', this insight proved difficult to sustain within post-structuralist currents that allow us to investigate the instability of identities, but tend to place people outside what they are investigating.

As people explore the range of discourses around fathering and the kind of assumptions they make about the symbolic presence of fathers in different disciplines, it can be difficult to explore tensions between the assumed power of fathers and the absence of men's experience of fathering. This is partly because an emphasis on discourse tends to assume the terms on which fathering can make itself visible, and so makes it difficult to explore unspoken tensions between discourse and the lived experience of fathering.

We need to move beyond strategies that seek to make visible the ways in which fathers set the terms by which others evaluate themselves, by listening to what fathers have to say for themselves. But this involves researchers becoming clearer about their own ambivalences. Sometimes it is only through a more engaged relationship with our ambivalent feelings towards our own fathers and stepfathers that we can become aware of our investments in the research we are doing. This can help provide a focus that may be lacking in a more neutral and dispassionate consideration of the discourses around fathering. In this way we also recognise how Protestant modernity has helped shaped intellectual traditions, fostering a fear of the personal that makes it difficult to explore sexual politics in any depth, because it tends to foreclose the kind of issues that can emerge. Often it is the concerns that we bring into our research that allow for a more complex analysis. More impersonal modes often tacitly reflect a dominant masculinity and its unacknowledged fears.

A Protestant modernity tends to reinforce more impersonal and impartial styles of research, and it inherits a fear of embodied knowledge. The radical split between mental classifications, as ordering visions of the social world, that emerges from Durkheim's reading of Kant makes a tacit identification between culture, knowledge and masculinities. For it is through a disavowal of the body and emotional life that culture can be radically separated from nature. Not only is culture defined in masculine terms; it is the creation and production of a dominant rationalist masculinity that was structurally shaped through the separation between domestic and occupational spheres that was born with capitalist industrialisation. The family became identified with the female space of nature, while labour came to be identified with masculine culture. The father was physically separated from the family, and came to be separated as breadwinner and provider. The great divorce of labour from the home has been a defining feature of Western capitalist societies. But, as Leonore Davidoff explores, the assumption that labour was removed from the home conceals the fluid boundaries between these spheres, through the work of domestic servants and the unpaid labour, female and male, that was required to maintain middle-class family life. However, the image of the father as remote breadwinner was to hold sway until the middle of the twentieth century.[7]

As Tabitha Freeman writes, 'The rise of the ideal of the father as exclusive breadwinner therefore marked a significant diminution in men's parental responsibilities, with a coalescence of cultural, economic and social forces underpinning the displacement of the traditional importance attributed to men's involvement with their children's upbringing.'[8] As she frames it, 'the glorification of paternal authority was seen to give way to the celebration of maternal love.' As the primary responsibility for the upbringing of the children shifts to mothers, fathers can feel increasingly alienated from family life. As John Gillis observes in *A World of Their Own Making: Myth, Ritual and the Quest for Family Values*, 'historically, motherhood and fatherhood have switched places in our symbolic universe.' As Alexander Mitscherlich argues in *Society without a Father*, there has been 'a progressive loss of the father's authority and a diminution of his power in the family and over the family'.[9]

Yet we have to be careful about how we interpret these changes. We need to recognise that in the late nineteenth century fathers were still regarded as the principal parent, and were invariably awarded exclusive custody rights in the case of divorce and marital breakdown. We need to trace the processes through which the father's custodial claims over children were gradually contested, as legal discourse became more concerned with the interests of the child and the idea that the mother was more naturally suited to a caring role gained dominance.

The intervention of the law was part of a wider process through which state regulation and legal control sought to protect children's welfare by curtailing instances of abuse, cruelty and exploitation at work, thereby implicitly limiting a father's authority and position within the family. This was part of a process through which children were to be recognised as the bearer of rights, so limiting the notion that children belonged as property to their fathers. As Philippe Aries recognises in *Centuries of Childhood*, the cultural shift from viewing children as 'miniature adults' towards conceiving childhood as a special stage of life is illustrated by the decline in child labour and the introduction of compulsory elementary education. These changes helped to refigure the responsibilities of fathering, as children could no longer be seen as economic assets contributing to household productivity.[10]

The rise of romantic ideals of companionate marriage shifted motivations for middle-class marriage away from practical advantage towards a greater recognition of love and emotional compatibility. As Alexis de Tocqueville observed on his visit to America during the 1830s, 'a species of equality prevails around the domestic hearth', within which 'paternal authority, if not destroyed, is at least impaired'. But, rather than view this as a decline in paternal authority, we could recognise the gains this promised for men's emotional lives and the possibility of more equal conversation and support between the sexes. Those who are concerned with reasserting traditional fathering duties and responsibilities can only recognise a discourse of decline. As Blankenhorn has it, in *Fatherless America*, 'today's fragmentation of fatherhood represents the end point of a long historical process: the steady diminution of fatherhood as a social role for men. Over the past two hundred years, fathers have gradually moved from being the centre to the periphery of family life.... Not to be overly gloomy, but in some respects it has been downhill for fathers since the Industrial Revolution.'[11] Yet this is to ignore what fathers have to say themselves about their private behaviours and feelings.[12]

In Catholic tradition there is less concern with the father's neutral position of authority. Instead there is a stress on the respect and deference due to fathers because of their position. The need to inculcate in children behaviour that upholds the honour of the family – not behaving or dressing in ways that could shame or bring dishonour on the family – can allow for a more personal relationship between father and children. Even though parenting might largely be seen as the responsibility of mothers, fathers can be expected to assume particular responsibility for their sons. If children are perceived as inherently sinful and prey to unruly and wilful desires, the civilising influence of a strong and authoritarian father can protect them from the contaminating influence of a sentimental mother. Women are seen as more indulgent towards their children and, because of their sinful nature, less able to discipline children when necessary.

In diverse religious traditions women have often remained economically dependent on their breadwinning husbands, often confined within the domestic sphere and deprived of a public voice. Within Catholic cultures women were often expected to remain unseen in public, so that they had little presence within the public sphere. In this way the breadwinner role can easily represent a continuation of patriarchal power, rather than its erosion as traditionalists have suggested. The breadwinner father commonly remained the final source of authority and discipline until the 1960s and beyond, when mothers still commonly threatened 'wait till your father gets home.' In many families the father remained a feared figure. Children had to be careful when he was around, as if the family somehow became his space and their lives were suddenly organised around his time. These tensions need to be explored in relation to diverse class, 'race' and ethnic cultures, so we can identify transformations in paternal authority. There are many reasons to think that paternal authority may in fact have been enhanced by a man's material absence at work, but we have to be careful to specify the forms of paternal authority and its relation to everyday emotional contact and relationships with partners and children.

As Tabitha Freeman argues, 'a more subtle analysis is required to understand the impact of the separation between the workplace and the home on paternal authority which reflects both continuities and changes within men's capacities and desires to exercise power over their dependants.'[13] She quotes B.E. Carroll: 'Scholars are now beginning systematically to argue that fathers' family status and involvement did not necessarily decline.... Absence did not necessarily mean diminished authority; rather, fathers' breadwinner role tied them to their families and became a new basis for economic leadership.'[14]

John Gillis has explored the ritualisation of a father's time within the home, and the significance given to his homecoming. An attentive welcome was expected from all other family members, marking the father's return from work as a special moment within the family's day. While women were contained within the passive domestic role, middle-class fathers shared a patriarchal prerogative in their relative freedom to move between public and private spheres. This prerogative, as Davidoff and Hall explored in *Family Fortunes*, was generally concealed within orthodox historical narratives by the re-production of the doctrine of separate spheres. Men alone had the freedom to move between them, so when things got uneasy in one sphere they could always escape to another.

As Gillis recognises, whilst the home was for men a refuge from work, where they could expect support and draw upon the emotional labour of their wives, for women the domestic sphere remained a place of work and routine. The sanctification of the home as a moral and emotional retreat from a potentially corrupt and competitive public sphere of work and politics can be seen as a masculine ideal. For women this confinement within the domestic sphere involved a burden of responsibilities that were rendered invisible within this idealised account. Similarly, the self-conception of masculinities as self-sufficient, in contrast to the dependence of women, rendered in-visible men's emotional dependence on their wives. The emotional labour that men relied upon was thus devalued, and women were deprived of recognition for the support they provided. The extent of women's emotional labour within patriarchal cultures became publicly visible only through the second-wave feminism of the 1970s, when women withdrew their emotional labour and insisted that men deal with their own emotional needs.

emotional lives

Often men, regardless of class and ethnic background, resent being reminded of their emotional dependency on their partners, because this threatens their autonomous and self-sufficient self-image. Rather than acknowledge the support they receive, they can often respond with a certain hostility as if to wipe out its threat. This is a tension that John Tosh explores well in *A Man's Place*:

> The greater a man's dependence on his wife for counsel and comfort, the greater the strain on his sense of masculine self-sufficiency, and the greater the temptation to compensate for this by the arbitrary exercise of domestic authority. Husbands negotiated this contradic-tion between dependence and dominance by relating to their wives in quite distinct modes. When asserting his authority the husband acted as patriarch; in turning to his wife for support his conduct was more like that of a child towards its mother.[15]

The authority that men could take for granted within the family allowed them the freedom to move between these different registers. They could reassert their authority by assuming the voice of 'head of the family', so repairing whatever damage could have been done to their egos by showing their need for support. It is partly because men had such limited experience of expressing vulnerability that they could only show this as children. This is something that could hardly have been satisfying for their partners, who would have had to deal with the disappointment of not having an emotional equal to relate to.

J.S. Mill in his *Autobiography*, reflecting on his own education, recognised how his Victorian education allowed him to develop intellectually while blocking his emotional development; though he understood the world intellectually, he had slowly to learn to relate emotionally within a more equal relationship. He might be able to dictate to others or assess the validity of their argument, but he could not emotionally discern their needs and what they were really asking of him.

Victorian fathers could experience an acute conflict between maintaining their paternal authority and being able to share emotions of loss or grief, say at the death of a child, since they had often learnt to identify emotions as 'feminine' and so as a threat to male identities. If a man allowed himself to cry, it had to be in private. These emotions could not be shown to others, as they threatened to undermine a father's teachings of emotional control and self-restraint. Sometimes it was difficult for men to switch from their identity at work, where they might be able to exercise power unproblematically, and exercise control within the family. Their partners might be forced to live with different levels of resentment, envy and hatred that could find no open expression, and were therefore productive of emotional distance within relationships.

Finding it difficult to deal with emotional intensity, men may withdraw and take refuge at work. Since male identities are often affirmed through achievement and success at work, this can seem preferable to giving attention to the family, if this might mean jeopardising the chance of promotion. Fathers could take refuge in the notion that in being a good provider they were showing their love for their children and their dedication to their families. Being seen to be a 'good family man' could also become an important constituent of a man's standing among his peers. By exploring these tensions within conceptions of fathering, we can also illuminate the patriarchal relationships that were exported and reinforced through empire and colonialism. In India and Pakistan we can still witness these authoritarian forms of childrearing, which also feature within migrant communities within the UK, creating an emotional distance between generations.

Historians have questioned the notion that a father's engagement with family life was radically diminished due to the separation of work from family life. As Davidoff and Hall point out, 'There is scattered evidence that some men exercised their power in a direct and domineering manner. But the local sources more often point to an intense involvement of men with their families, and a loving interest in their children's lives.'[16] We should reflect before concluding with Freeman that 'The dominant image of the emotionally detached Victorian father thus negates the growing weight of substantive evidence pointing to men's active involvement with their children.'[17] Freeman readily supports Griswold's observation that 'surely the stereotype of the distant, uninvolved father of an ill-defined past can be laid to rest for ever.'[18] Careful consideration needs to be given to how we think of 'men's active involvement with their children' and the kind of relationships this implies. It is important to acknowledge fully the poignant accounts in the literature of paternal bereavement and the deep anguish experienced during a child's illness. And Freeman is right to say that 'Perhaps more compelling, however, are everyday instances of men's loving concern for, and engagement with, their children, with the mutual enjoyment of recreation and play between father and child emerging as a frequent theme across the historical literature.'[19]

confusions/promises

In a 2004 *Observer* article, 'How New Man Turned into Distant, Confused New Dad', Ruth Hill writes that losing their traditional role as head of the family has left today's fathers in Britain feeling like failures. She reports that, according to a survey of 2,100 British adults, 'Fatherhood is in crisis, with men admitting they are worse parents than their fathers, that they shy away from emotional involvement with their children and use the office to avoid the stress of home life.'[20] Trendspotter Marian Salzman is quoted as saying that 'Fatherhood is becoming a mild form of depression for modern-day man, there is a grey cloud that hangs over it.' As she frames it, probably too generally, 'These men were New Men until they became new fathers, which is why they are all the more disappointed when they fail to be the sort of dads they expected and hoped to be.' Salzman admits that 'Celebrity dads demonstrate a completely engaged, celebratory and unstressed model of fatherhood but society offers no realistic role models for real men trying to do their best.'

Within a celebrity culture, young fathers might identify with images of David Beckham and Coldplay frontman Chris Martin, without realising that these men's childcare is underpinned by the paid labour of poorer women. They compare themselves to this ideal, and can feel that they have only themselves to blame when they find things difficult in their relationships. Visions of gender equality are easier to maintain in relationships where both parties are earning, and dividing household expenses equally. Men might assume that life 'will return to normal' soon after the birth, only to discover that nothing has prepared them for the fundamental changes that a new baby brings. They want the freedom that they now take for granted, but want to be able to think of themselves as a 'good father' too. The balance they have enjoyed in their intimate relationship might have depended upon sustaining separate friendships and a certain degree of emotional distance. When these tacit foundations give way to the emotional intensities of birth, young men can feel unprepared for the unresolved emotions that surface, tracing back to their own early experience of being parented. Having connected to their babies through being present at the birth, and having resolved to 'be different and more involved' than their own fathers, they can find that the dreams soon fade.

As Salzman interprets the data, 'The disappointment and feeling of failure is resulting in men shutting down emotionally because they no longer have the old central role in their family and don't know what other role is available to them.' But there is little sense that men want the position that their fathers had, and they are often clear that they want to be closer and more involved with their children than their fathers were. The notion of 'role' can be misleading here. We have to conceptualise the issues that arise between the parents and in relation to a child, and how they affect new fathers' feelings about themselves and their relationships.

Though fathers questioned for the survey admitted to being depressed and pessimistic about their parenting skills – with one in five feeling strongly that they were worse parents than their fathers had been – this could be interpreted in very different ways. For instance, young fathers might blame themselves for splitting up with their partner, and feel they have failed themselves and their relationship. The comparison with their own father might only arise on questioning, and could be interpreted in a number of ways. It is revealing that men also reported feeling swamped by the multiple duties of work and home, with three out of four saying they were not in control of their lives and one-third feeling desperate to 'declutter' and reduce stress. This sense of being overwhelmed reveals significant changes in notions of male identity and the new forms of individualism that both men and women aspire to within a post-feminist consumer culture. It reflects the difficulties individuals experience in sustaining a sense of self, and the risk of losing direction and feeling out of control.

People can feel increasingly uneasy about *how* to sustain a sense of self while being in a relationship. Men no longer have a shared sense of who they are through the roles they are supposed to perform. It is no longer enough to define themselves as providers and fathers: not only are the expectations that define these roles within contemporary society unclear, but men and women within postmodern culture tend to need a more individualised and reflective sense of self. This contrasts with earlier generations of men, who just assumed that they would get married and have children because 'that was the way life was', and you learnt to 'get on with things'. Possibly they learned to ask themselves fewer questions.

Men who grew up in the 1980s within the industrialised societies of the North were often uneasy about the intense emotional reflexiveness of an earlier generation of men, who had been challenged through feminism. They aspired to notions of gender equality but they also accepted notions of gender difference more readily. Women who had benefited from the struggles of women's liberation did not necessarily identify with feminism themselves. They had learnt a different relationship with their femininities, and relished the possibilities of fashion and consumer culture. Even though they might be politically aware, politics often existed as one remove from their own everyday lives. They accepted that there were limits to the differences they could make as individuals, and, while aware of inequalities and sufferings, they wanted to enjoy their own lives and put difficult challenges aside. But this also meant that as a generation they were less prepared for the emotional demands of childbirth, and often less skilled emotionally in dealing with issues that emerge in relationships.

According to Salzman, 'Modern fathers feel pride but no joyousness in their role as family man and dad, with a sense of duty becoming their most overarching emotion.' The greatest desire of men, the survey suggests, is to simplify their lives after having children. They attempt to escape the demands of their families by hiding in the workplace. Almost one in four surveyed wanted *less* holiday time than before they became fathers. As Salzman suggests, 'This may be because their desire for a holiday is tempered by thoughts of the cost and effort of taking the family on holiday, or because staying home is anything but relaxing.' But research shows that it is not only men who seek escape; women would also prefer to take refuge within the orderly space of the office. Possibly it is the fact that men seem more able to escape that can create resentment in the relationship.

People can find the transition to parenthood difficult because they are used to a greater sense of order and control in their lives. When the baby has colic or refuses to sleep at night, they find it hard to cope: life can feel constantly in the brink of chaos. When a man returns to work soon after a baby is born, his partner can feel a sense of betrayal if they had imagined a more equal experience of parenting. If the relationship has previously tended to be 'cool' and in control, it can be difficult to deal with the deep emotions that emerge with a new baby. Men can feel that it falls to them to 'make their partner happy', when all she might want is to communicate her feelings. If men feel that they need to offer a solution to difficult or negative feelings, their partner's depression can lead them to feel that they have failed.

Salzman thinks that 'the result is that dads are slipping into a tail-spin of a more distant, conservative role that is more about discipline and the sterner expression of love, such as that expressed through helping with schoolwork.' This might follow from the difficulties fathers can experience in dealing with children as they get older. Fathers who identify the assertion of authority with being authoritarian may fail to set clear boundaries. They might find themselves slipping between being liberal with weak boundaries and falling into older patterns when young children react by acting out, in which they are shocked to find themselves responding as their fathers did to them. If they have not really dealt with their own emotional history in relation to their own fathers, thinking that it can just be put aside, new fathers can feel ill-equipped to deal with behaviour issues with young children. They might feel disappointed when they hear themselves getting angry and screaming at a child for misbehaving, feeling both desperate to gain control and powerless to provide appropriate boundaries. This might be part of what Jack O'Sullivan, director of Fathers Direct, means when he says, in relation to the survey, that society's definition of fatherhood is filled with contradictions. He believes that 'Society is alienating fathers from their children.... While there are clear demands for fathers to be more involved in family life, there is an absence of roles for them.'

Is it, though, a matter of 'roles' or rather of accepting fatherhood as a relationship in which men have to learn to deal with their own emotional issues if they are to be more honest and clear in relation to their children? It is partly because of the intense demands and the need to be 'constantly there' in the modern workplace that men can find it hard to find a balance between the different areas of their lives. Sometimes they can feel as if they are 'falling into a void', unable to articulate their experience and wary of acknowledging that they need help because this still threatens their sense of male identity. They do what is required of them but feel unsure of how to be with their children and also with their partner.

The survey found that modern fathers increasingly avoid emotional involvement with their children, feeling that they have failed to fulfil their role. This might reflect something more general about contemporary masculinities that needs to be related to issues of new fathering.

Given that a quarter of respondents said they never talked about personal issues with their children at all, it is important to know about the class, race and ethnic background of the men, and to understand their feelings about emotional expression. If they regard emotions as feminine and as reflecting a lack of control, they will feel obliged to be strong so that they can provide an example of masculinity to their children. It is difficult to interpret results unless we are clear how interviewees are understanding the question. Some men feel that it is through providing their children with the toys they never had as children that they demonstrate their love, and it never occurs to them that their children might prefer regular time together playing football or going swimming. If this is a contact they have never allowed themselves to miss, in relation to their own absent fathers, it can be difficult for them to negotiate the needs and desires of their children.

Laurie Taylor, who wrote *What Are Children For?* with his son Matthew, believes that the status of fatherhood in the West has been undermined by modern life; he thinks that fathers are more distant from their children than ever before. As he explains it,

> In the past, sons duplicated their own father and looked to him to emulate his job and his wisdom. Now, however, fathers have nothing for their children to inherit – the world is changing too quickly and, instead of sitting at their fathers' feet listening to their stories about the world, children are closed up in their own rooms on the Internet, finding out about it first. It is difficult to know how to reassert the role of fatherhood. There is nothing obvious for him to do or be.

However, Matthew disagrees. 'This is a difficult time for fathers, as the old model of fatherhood shifts into the new.' But, he says, 'As men stay younger in their lifestyle longer, the capacity to become mates with their sons has transformed. In addition, children have their teenage crisis earlier, which means they relate to their fathers as adults earlier.' He thinks 'we are on the cusp of a great time for fathers.'[21] It may be that boys do not want their fathers to be 'mates', but they do want to feel that their fathers will be there for them emotionally, when they need it.

In an *Observer* article of 2004, Cristina Odone welcomes 'the new dad'. She thinks that the new good father is not just a fiction. Today's father really does see more of his children than his predecessors ever did. Twenty years ago, fathers of children under five devoted less than a quarter of an hour a day to child-related activities, compared with two hours a day now. Despite the nuclear family continuing to fray and one in five children born into a family without a father, British dads are currently responsible for approximately a third of all childcare.

She argues that 'Those who relish fathering are supporting their partner's efforts at mothering. And once the home dynamics are better, the office must surely follow suit.'[22] Odone is writing from her own experience here, and seems to relish the fact that her partner's office screensaver is their baby's smiling face. Somehow it has become more acceptable for him to request time off for parent–teacher meetings than it is for her to talk about her baby. To do so is to break a universal office taboo. She recalls one male Fleet Street editor advising her a few years ago, 'If you want to climb the career ladder, don't ever mention your children in the office.' As she admits, 'Children continue to be the working mum's dirty little secret. But on Father's Day we can celebrate the fact that children are now the working dad's very visible trophies.' Odone also knows that 'True, long hours, a measly two-week state paternity leave, taken up almost exclusively by white-collar workers, and the dearth of in-house crèches continue to challenge working fathers who would like to do a bit more fathering and a little less working.'

Crucial questions remain about how to evaluate these different experiences and reports of fathering, and the ways we can illuminate diverse generational experiences across class, race, ethnicities and sexualities. With complex transformations in intimate relationships and with men often looking after children who are not their biological offspring, sharing responsibilities across the boundaries of different families, we can recognise that fathering will remain central to the revisioning of contemporary social life. It will challenge us to rethink the intellectual traditions that have failed to recognise the centrality of fathering experiences, if we are to foster and sustain more equal, just and loving relationships.

6

masculinities, bodies and emotional life

This chapter investigates the ways in which an Enlightenment vision of modernity still works within a postmodern culture to make it difficult to examine relationships between men, bodies and emotional life, and to explore diverse cultures of masculinity and the ways men's bodies and emotional lives are shaped. This entails questioning certain ways of thinking the relationship between men and masculinities, as well as drawing upon a diversity of sources to understand men's embodied emotional lives. Our dominant Anglo-American culture privileges universal models that echo the idea that a dominant white European masculinity can alone take its reason for granted.

Identifying with mind, reason and consciousness, dominant masculinities have within the Cartesian tradition learnt to disavow bodies, sexualities and emotional lives as elements of an 'animal' nature that needs to be controlled. Within colonial discourses, bodies, sexualities and desires come to be identified with the uncivilised, who can make the transition from nature to culture only through accepting subordination to their colonial masters. Through a widespread identification of masculinity with self-control, men learn to relate to emotions as threats to their male identities. If we are to open up space to explore within particular cultures the diverse ways in which men's gendered and sexed bodies come to terms with their emotional histories, we need to think in new ways about transforming masculinities, and about how power works across diverse bodies and emotional fields. We need to be able to engage with the new experiences of men who are challenged by issues very different to those that shaped previous generations. The complex male identities that have emerged through diasporic and transnational migration also call for new ways of thinking body cultures and emotional lives.

masculinities

Feminism understood the relationship between power and emotional life, recognising through the practices of consciousness-raising that women's individual emotions need to be understood in the context of gender relations of power. But it was harder for men to appreciate the implications for their own self-understanding of the radical and transformative notion that 'the personal is political'. As the bearers of power they could not, as Bob Connell argued in *Gender and Power*, also suffer emotionally.[1] Somehow it was difficult to reconcile the power that men inherited within a patriarchal culture and the individual feelings of powerless they might experience, especially as gender relations were redefined. Within the conception of power that Connell later develops in *Masculinities*, consciousness-raising for men could only mean developing an awareness of their role within gender relations of power.[2] This was part of a distinction that Connell draws between the 'therapeutic' practices of the 1970s and what he identifies as the 'real politics' that emerges in the 1980s. But this distinction between the therapeutic and the political not only served to disavow the history of men's relationships with feminism – for instance the existence of *Achilles Heel* magazine in Britain – but also served to block reflections upon the relationship between the personal and the political in men's lives.[3]

This distinction made it difficult to understand the ways in which young men grow up to become men, and tended to reproduce a politics of guilt that did not allow for the possibility of change. Rather, it tended to reproduce an anti-sexist men's politics that was helpful in making men aware of the violence and suffering experienced by so many women, but left them feeling that masculinity, conceived exclusively as a relationship of power, was the problem that needed to be deconstructed and could be no part of imagining a solution. This tended to block understanding of how men could change, and made it difficult to work creatively without merely inducing guilt in younger men.

Connell's work has proved invaluable in questioning essentialist notions of masculinity. But he tends to frame the relationship between, say, straight and gay men as a matter of power that somehow mirrors the power between men and women. He also tends to reproduce a distinction between women's 'structural' oppression and men's merely 'personal' pain that is too generalised and that fails to show how men's emotional lives are also structured through relations of power that work through differences of class, race, ethnicities and sexualities. It is important not to imagine these structures in similar ways to the intersectional discourses that have often served to silence investigations into men's emotional lives. Thinking masculinities in terms of a hegemonic model has itself become hegemonic, since its very universalism has appealed to international agencies wanting a model that can be translated across cultural differences. Rather than thinking that, aside from minor adjustments made for cultural context, violent practices resonate right across patriarchal cultures, we need to explore the diversity of cultures of masculinity.

Connell's vision of 'hegemonic masculinities' carries an implicit universalism that shows its inherent rationalism, and obscures the ways a dominant white European masculinity has alone been able to take its reason for granted. This rationalism sustains Connell's distinction between the therapeutic and the political, and informs the universalism that in the West has been so crucial to a modernity which is continually reshaped – even in the Marxist terms that have contested the power of global capitalism – in terms of a dominant masculinity. The discourse of modernity has the effect of silencing diverse cultures of masculinity, as men are caught between their own masculine experiences and the theoretical framings of the West that offer academic credibility.

This does not mean that we cannot still learn from Marx, but it does mean engaging, as I argued in *Recovering the Self*, with a univer-

salism framed in rationalist terms.[4] The disdain for the therapeutic
– which reflects a more general unease about the personal and the
emotional that characterises post-structuralist and deconstructive traditions – echoes an ethics and politics of self-denial that I attempted
to deconstruct in *Recreating Sexual Politics*.[5]

vulnerabilities

In *Rolling Thunder Logbook*, Sam Shepard's 1977 chronicle of Bob
Dylan's 1975 US tour, he writes: 'Myth is a powerful medium because
it talks to the emotions and not the head. It moves us into an area
of mystery.' This is something Robert Bly recognised in *Iron John*, as
I explored critically in *Man Enough*.[6] Bly is exploring myth as a way
of reaching men emotionally, but he says less about issues of class,
race, ethnicities and sexualities. Communication operates at different
levels, and a postmodern culture that recognises the fragmentation
of identities can open up new spaces. But we also need to question
postmodernities that suggest identities can be easily constructed, and
conflicts between different spheres of life easily handled.

Richard Hoggart helpfully reflects on the construction of identities when he talks of the hurt he unwittingly caused his uncle John
through writing about his drinking. John was the youngest and most
tenderly loved of his mother's ten children, and his drinking upset
her. She knew that he was clever and might have gone far but for
his boozing. His sister labelled him a 'good for nothing' who would
certainly 'come to a bad end'. As Hoggart recalls, 'His ways ran
like a constantly recurring, upsetting thread through our lives; they
threatened our respectable, Primitive Methodist working-class status,
for of course, the neighbours knew.' Hoggart asked his brother what
their uncle felt about being written about in this way. His response
was unequivocal: 'Of course Uncle John was hurt. He had probably
never faced his own drunkenness. He would have hated being told
about it; and worse, seeing it in print; worse still, to think of it being
read and gossiped about "all over the place".'[7]

Even though it was he who had caused the gossip, Hoggart realised
he did not like the idea of himself and the family being 'shown up'.
Within the culture in which he had grown up, judgements about

people did not take place on an abstract level. As Hoggart recognises, 'They had a great many words and phrases, concrete and metaphorical, for their purposes. They would say: "E's right mean" but also "She'd give away 'er last penny".' As Hoggart understands this class experience that he first explored in *The Uses of Literacy*,

> To capture a character in abstract language could seem belittling, reductive and not true to the rich reality of the person behind it, whom they knew better. They seemed to feel at the back of their minds, indeed probably without being conscious of the roots of their unease, that there was behind him or her 'much more than that', more than cold, abstract words could capture. Again, they did not themselves put this in a generalised way; they used metaphors or oblique criticism: 'It's not him', 'not a good likeness', 'not the woman I knew'.[8]

Understanding of class needs to reflect an appreciation of these vulnerabilities, and of the complexities of power and emotions that so easily get lost within the individualism of postmodern theories. Psychoanalysis also carries a blindness, in its assumption that emotional suffering needs to be explained within the universal framework of early family relations. Not only does it tend to seek refuge in past relations, but it also finds it difficult to explore vulnerabilities of class, race and sexualities, as it is so often trapped within its own normalising discourse. Hoggart's uncle John did not like the idea of being 'shown up'; he did not want the gossip to 'get around'.

As there are different masculinities, so there are different ways of relating to emotional lives. As we have seen, men often feel that they have to conceal their vulnerability so as not to 'lose face' in front of others. Young men sometimes find it easier to take their own lives than to reach out for help to those around them. They do not want to share what is troubling them, or the source of their depression; indeed they might not know it themselves. They feel so bad about themselves that daring to show this to others could only make it worse. With suicides, those who are left are often shocked that they had so little idea of what was in the mind of the young man they loved as a friend or part of the family. Often men feel that it is harder to lift the phone when they are down than when they are feeling good about themselves. This seems to be true across class. Masculinities become performative often as a way of concealing inner emotional turmoil from others. If young men are afraid about how they will cope, this is often a fear they hide from themselves. They can take refuge in the notion that as long as these emotions remain unspoken and others do not know about them, they are not 'real' and might disappear just as they arrived. Vulnerabilities are hidden, as men feel they should handle their own emotions so as not to experience more shame. They might feel that their masculinity is all they have left.

bodies

Within a tradition of Enlightenment modernity, men learn to relate to their bodies as machines that they need to control. As the gym has taken the place of the cathedral as the spiritual home of masculinities, so men learn to endure pain in order to build bodies they can proudly show to others. A younger generation has learnt a relationship to their bodies different to the working-class cultures of 1950s' Britain that Hoggart reflected upon. Yet, if there has been a shift in gender relations, there has also been a tightening of male bodies which can make them react with greater inflexibility and violence if they do not get their way. Unless young men learn to develop an easier relationship with their bodies and to be more accepting of emotional ambivalence, it can be difficult to communicate their emotional needs in relationships. This often means coming to terms with their own emotional histories and exploring means of expression that shake the boundaries of traditional psychoanalysis. Sometimes it means naming a Protestant inheritance and the ways it has left one feeling bad about oneself, and the compulsiveness it has fostered in relation to the body as a way of redeeming troubles of the soul.

In an interview that D.B.C. Pierre gave on winning the Man Booker prize for his novel about the eponymous *Vernon God Little* he talks of just such a compulsiveness in the formation of identity. As with his 15-year-old hero, Pierre knows what it is like to experience '90 flavours of trouble riding on his ass', having been addicted to cocaine and run up such huge debts that he ripped off a friend to the tune of £30,000. Born in Australia to English parents, he was brought up in Mexico, where his father moved the family to pursue his career as a scientist. He had a transcultural childhood, and speaks of the difficulty of creating and sustaining complex identities. 'I grew up with a real sense of cultural homelessness,' he tells Emma Brockes. 'I haven't been successful in fitting in anywhere. I clearly wasn't Mexican, although I could move in that culture as easily as anywhere.... As a kid it was really fucking difficult to know which crowd I belonged to. I changed accents a hell of a lot.... There's nothing I love more than just to be part of something, for someone to pay you a hello.'[9] Emmanuel Levinas, in his essay 'The Proximity of the Other', says

> All encounters begin with a benediction, contained in the word 'hello'.... This greeting addressed to the other man is an invocation. I therefore insist on the primacy of the well-intentioned relation towards the other. Even when there may be ill will on the other's part, the attention, the receiving of the other, like his recognition, mark the priority of good in relation to evil.[10]

D.B.C. Pierre (or Peter Finley as he was then), from a childhood lived in luxury and security, and little understanding of 'how the mechanics of life worked, or a concept of reality', was plunged into chaos at the age of 16 when his father was diagnosed with a brain tumour. Pierre was left largely on his own.

> 'There came a time,' he says, 'when my mates moved into the house and we had all this money and we started experimenting with things [drugs] and there was no one to oversee it. My father eventually died when I was 19.' He pauses painfully. 'That was a great shock.' He pauses again, folding in on himself. 'In a way.'

Pierre felt he had to support the family but was clueless about financial responsibility. He started borrowing and lying and kept telling himself that maybe tomorrow something would come up. He speaks of his twenties as 'a fully fuelled jumbo jet just reaching take-off point and having to slam on the brakes. You've got this enormous bloody thing careering off the end of the runway, through the fence, through the house next door, bursting into flames and me crawling out and scraping my wounds for 10 years. I won't be flying that one again.' According to Brockes,

This is not a glib compression. The lesson of those years Pierre spent despising himself, toying with suicide, and eventually coming down on the side of life, if not happiness, was that he was 'nothing', a total shit, unworthy of feeling good about any aspect of himself. Pierre stands uniquely at odds with the cultural consensus that everyone, however rotten and devious, has a right to a basic level of self-esteem. 'But it needs to be "based" on something,' he rages. 'We're prompted to hold strong opinions and act on them and big ourselves up and think that we're worth it and, shit, where I'd just been showed me that I wasn't worth it, my judgment was poor, I was basically nobody. But the culture around me had gone the whole other way. It didn't matter what the fuck you were doing as long as you looked good doing it. I finally came to a point where I thought I'll proceed by being humble, straight forward, very cautious. My default position is one of doubt.'

Humility is often difficult for men, who can feel that they ought to know. It can be difficult to admit to doubts or to feeling unsure of what is going on. Somehow the instrumental relationship men are encouraged to adopt in relation to their bodies can make it difficult to acknowledge how uneasy, awkward and estranged they often feel. Within a Cartesian modernity, men have learnt to assume an external relationship with bodies that are not part of us as rational selves but belong to a disenchanted nature. Rather than recognise how our bodies carry our emotional histories, postmodern theories often view the body as an external space onto which cultures inscribe prevailing representations. This fosters its own forms of cultural displacement, making it difficult for men to recognise ambivalences in their lived relationships with their bodies. Rather, the body as performance and display sustains an instrumentality that remains beyond question.

As the body becomes an instrument that can be shown off proudly to others, so muscles can be hardened against feeling. Even though men recognise bodies as possessions, it can be difficult to acknowledge how little they know them. As men explore the emotional histories carried in their bodies, so they can learn to develop more of a relationship with them. This is not something that they can achieve as a matter of will, but involves a process of self-recovery. These practices of care for the self have been developed within the various traditions of body psychotherapies that have developed since Reich argued with Freud about the status of the body within psychoanalysis. Rather than acknowledge feelings of sadness or vulnerability that are experienced as signs of weakness or femininity, men split from their inner emotional lives or else unknowingly transform the sadness into anger or violence that still works to affirm otherwise threatened male identities.

Foucault in his later work was concerned with technologies of the self. He appreciated the need to explore the spiritual and philosophical traditions that informed Western conceptions of individuality and ethics, as well as counter-traditions that could sustain alternative visions. He identified the importance of uncovering and naming the religious traditions that help shape peoples' relationships to their bodies and emotional lives. If men are constantly struggling against feelings of inadequacy they cannot name, and feel their traditional identities as providers undermined within a globalised economy, the body becomes an exclusive site to affirm threatened male identities.

emotional lives

As long as a dominant masculinity within Western modernity defines itself as independent and self-sufficient, it will be difficult for men to acknowledge their emotional needs. Having learnt to identify happiness, within a Protestant moral culture, as a reward for individual success and achievement, men can still find it difficult to feel entitled to a sense of emotional fulfilment. Even if they have traditionally expected their sexual needs to be given priority, this has often sustained a vision of sex as performance. Traditionally sex – for instance in the working-class communities Hoggart describes – was an obligation that women owed to men. Feminism was revolutionary in its claims that women were equally entitled to sexual pleasure and that sexual desire was an expression of human love. The Christian West had inherited a deep fear of bodily desire as a threat to human spirituality. Disavowed, it was projected in the discourses of Christian anti-Semitism onto Judaism ('carnal Israel', as Daniel Boyarin has termed it), which was identified with the body and the 'sins of the flesh'.[11]

Freud, himself within Judaism, identified the suffering that was created within the West with the repression of sexuality. Psychoanalysis was to produce a space in which people were able to name their own desires, no longer shamed as animal. But this remained a masculinist tradition, in that sexual energy was identified with activity and so with masculinity, thus echoing an Aristotelian epistemology. Women became instead the primary object of the psychoanalytic gaze. Often men have felt a need to break with psychoanalytic rationalism, in order to explore emotional lives in more expressive ways that are not confined within a transference relationship. It is often through engaging with their bodies that men can give voice to emotions that would otherwise remain disconnected. Sometimes this is a process through which men are able to differentiate between emotions and feelings, opening up to a deeper connection with themselves.

Within a globalised economy, men can no longer expect to identify with their work in terms of a lifetime career. The future is uncertain, and both men and women have had to learn to live with these uncertainties. Often this means that young people assume a more instrumental relationship to their work, even though work tends to define their identities. People often fear taking time off work because they will not be there to protect their position. Working long hours produces tension when both partners return home exhausted and unable to relate to children, let alone each other. As emotional distances grow, people find it harder to communicate, and both men and women can find themselves locked into dreams and fantasies that somehow sustain them through everyday routines. Even if there is a shared commitment to gender equality, there is less sense of how it works in relation to children and family life.

It is only as men and women learn to communicate more honestly in relation to their emotional lives that differences can be appreciated and compromises sought. This involves listening to children and responding to their needs differently. But in order to rethink gender equality we need to engage in new ways with masculinities and emotional lives.

language, power and emotions

Thinking the relationship of language, emotions and power challenges us to think about the implications of men's transference of feelings of vulnerability or fear more or less automatically into an anger or violence that affirms their male identity. What kind of claim is being made, and how does it relate to Wittgenstein's notion in his later work that emotions are not 'inner states' but can only be known through their outer expression? How does this questioning help us to rethink the relationship between inner and outer, and so between psyche and social, since this is very much at issue in the ways we think relations between men's bodies, cultures and emotional lives.

In the early 1980s in a review of Martin Scorsese's film *Raging Bull*,[12] I reflected upon the ways in which men sometimes learn to punch their way through life. Young men within an Italian immigrant community in New York can grow up feeling that they are owed respect, and they learn to demand it from those around them. But this can make it difficult to experience fear or vulnerability, as these are seen as threats to male identity. Sometimes there is not the 'emotional space' for men to become conscious of these emotions, and it is often through therapy that they are able to find it. This interrupts their learned responses, and can make them aware of a vulnerability that they would otherwise not recognise. In this way emotions can be grasped as processes that are implicated within structural relations of power.

It is not a matter of legislating what men 'should' be able to feel; it is not possible to determine in advance whether anger and violence are indeed reactions to feelings of inadequacy and vulnerability. This is not to excuse male violence, but to suggest that we need to think in different terms about the relationships between power and emotional life if we are to be able to engage effectively with the issue. Of course men should become responsible for their violence, but it is not simply a matter of triggering guilt and shame, even if this might be part of the process. We need also to be able to engage with the emotional processes through which boys have grown up to be men, and which have shaped their emotional bodies to affirm dominant masculinities.

Wittgenstein's later work is engaged in questioning an essentialism that would treat emotions as 'inner', as if individuals alone are the authority on their own emotions. In this way Wittgenstein questions the prevailing Protestant tradition in the West that has shaped a rationalist modernity. The distinction between inner emotions and outer behaviours is also sustained within the structuralist opposition between nature and culture that underpins discourse theory: because we cannot know 'what is inside someone else's head' we can only use what they say, discourse, as establishing the terms of 'reality'.

This distinction between inner emotions and outer behaviours also underpins Connell's structural analysis, which tends to treat emotions and feelings as 'therapeutic'. This fosters a conviction that men can change through an act of will, and so sustains a Protestant conception of human action. Within Protestant cultures men are often haunted by the question, why should one share one's emotions if we know that emotions are 'bad' and dreams are 'ugly'? It is understandable that men conceal their emotions if they know that they are going to be judged negatively if they reveal them. This question shows the continuing grip of a moralism within a secular culture still shaped by religious traditions whose influence remains unnamed and unacknowledged. People learn to regulate their emotions, showing to others only what they know in advance they can defend rationally. For example, men may only show their anger if they know in advance that it is 'rational'. This is in line with Connell's conception of masculinities, which enforces its own vision of self-denial and allows men to adopt a theoretical position without exploring their own emotional lives and experiences.

Sometimes it is difficult to explore our emotional histories or acknowledge the hurt and injuries we carry. People can live their whole life with a sense of loneliness and isolation that they feel unable to break. They might have been born into power and privilege, but this in no ways guarantees them the capacity to love or the possibility of fulfilment.

Stevie Davies opens her review of Jane Gardam's novel *Old Filth* with the observation, 'Once a Raj orphan always a Raj orphan.'[13] She describes Sir Edward Feathers, a retired judge, as one who

> enters extreme age carrying his secret wound coiled inside him like a baby. Born in Malaya to a mother who immediately dies and a father whose heart has been petrified by the first world war, Eddie is expelled to the loveless mother-country. He is alone, with the Raj orphan's stiff-upper lipped anguish as to where 'home' is. Shuttle-

cocked to and fro between institutions and colonies, Eddie's odyssey is a sad mock epic version of the wanderings of the children of the British empire, partly based on the early life of Rudyard Kipling.

Because he is unable to give his wife Betty the love she needs, she has an affair with a colleague, Veneering, who is able to offer her 'the sensual tenderness missing from her Raj orphan husband'. Edward is not able to intuit what has been happening. But there are flashes of insight, for as Davies describes it, 'An aged man is a babe-in-arms; his childhood is still quick within him and he remains capable of flashes of insight, quirks of impulse.... he dies on a final journey "to Malaysia, then up to Borneo. Kotakinakula. Where I was born."' Lawyers gather as the bells toll at Temple Bar in London for his death. They look at the inscription on an monument in the Inner Temple Gardens that serves as an epigraph for the novel: 'Lawyers, I suppose, were children once.' A pair of lawyers agree that he deserved no more than a brief epitaph: 'Laughable... Good judge.... Travelling alone. Quite alone.'

If we are to heal the splits that have developed between the personal and the political, when it comes to reflections on men's lives we need also to question a structuralist vision of language that works to deny the tension between language and experience. This is a tension that Wittgenstein can help sustain, through his appreciation that others might well know what we are feeling better than we do ourselves, at least initially. If someone says 'you are looking sad', I might initially reject the suggestion because I feel somehow threatened. I resist the notion that someone might have recognised what I was feeling before I did myself. In that rejection I create a defensive space, in which I can tune into myself and explore in relative safety what I might be feeling. I might only days later appreciate that there was indeed something troubling me. There is no automatic authority; it is a matter, as Wittgenstein explores it, of establishing a different relationship between 'inner' and 'outer'.

Stevie Davies speaks of the memorable scene in *Old Filth* where,

putting up at the garish hotel that has replaced The Old Judges' lodging, this most ramrod backed and disciplined of elderly men sees his wife's obituary whilst doing his stately breakfasting. He 'wept silently behind his hands, sitting in this unknown place', the sole figure in the vastness of the dining room. He weeps on and on. Round him the staff clear the table, change the cloth. 'They said not a word.'

Reminding us of a distant colonial world, this shows how empire remains resonant within post-imperial Britain. It can also help us to identify the ways in which each generation, including our own, remains marked by a particular cultural moment. The sexual politics of men and masculinities in the 1970s' generation was shaped through the experiences of the Vietnam War, and the challenges of feminism and gay liberation. Young people now grow up into cultural worlds shaped by new technologies and global communications, and within different kinds of gender relations and new relationships of gender power. When thinking about diverse cultures of masculinities we need to appreciate the generational transformations of patriarchal cultures, which can otherwise become fixed through notions of hegemonic masculinities.

Young people across the world are growing up in new relational and sexual worlds in which global images often have enormous power. Within globalised consumer cultures sexualised gender images are constantly circulating, and young men and women can feel that they are caught in comparing themselves with these images. They can feel themselves inadequate and guilty; bereft within a secular culture of moral language that might allow them to question the power of these images.

The events of 9/11 and the fears of terror that have gripped urban spaces in the West have sparked new uncertainties in relation to the global religious traditions that still shape contemporary subjectivities. There is a widespread recognition that we need to rethink the oppositional ways in which secular modernity has shaped religious beliefs as forms of irrationality that will inevitably give way to the advance of reason, science and progress. This is an expression of the arrogance of modernity that sustained colonial relationships of white superiority towards 'uncivilised' others.

How is the West to relate to the emergence of Islam as a global force? What are the cultural sources within contemporary theorisations of men and masculinities that allow us to engage with diverse and troubled masculinities? It is notable that Foucault felt the need to abandon his investigations into truth and power in order to open up concerns for ethics and subjectivities, showing the inadequacy of discourses that exclusively relate to power and knowledge. Somehow we need to bring these concerns together, by thinking about the transformation of diverse cultural masculinities in ways that can heal unsustainable splits between men's power, bodies, emotions and pleasures.

7

bodies, desires, pleasures and love

thinking young men

In conceiving of young people as 'adolescents', we are defining the teenage years as a stage in the life process on the way to becoming adult. We think of this as a 'phase' that they will 'pass through', because we tend to view young people from the point of view of adult life. In terms of psychological theory, we tend to think about the interface between biological processes and the social worlds that young people confront. But this vision can be misleading, even though it presents itself 'scientifically', because it abstracts from the particular historical and cultural moments through which young people are living. What is more, we can unknowingly reproduce cultural assumptions that in fact need to be questioned.

As adults we can assume that 'adolescence' is a problem that needs to be solved, in order to minimise the risky behaviour that young men, in particular, are likely to engage in. We readily assume that to be young is to be 'guilty', as if young people are waiting to be blamed for whatever goes wrong in their lives. Implicitly we theorise as adults who 'already know', through a reason that a dominant masculinity alone can take for granted. In an Enlightenment vision of modernity shaped by a dominant masculinity, reason as the source of knowledge is separated from feelings and desires, which are framed in Kantian terms as forms of unreason and determination.[1] So 'adolescence' as a category within a rationalist tradition is framed as the object of a scientific gaze. As a biologically defined stage of development, we come to know 'adolescence' within rationalist terms according to which, as social scientists, we have everything to teach and little to learn.

There is no need to open up a dialogue with young men and women; we 'already know' what 'stage' they are living through, since this has been fully mapped out within the realm of scientific discourse. Since this is also a stage that we have 'lived through' ourselves, even if in a different moment of time, we can assume that we already know it from the inside, even though many of us have lost connection with these years and remain unprepared to do the emotional work that would allow us to re-create a connection. A rationalist current within psychology and sociology devalues and fails to appreciate this emotional work, especially given a positivist tradition that can only recognise it as a source of bias within an otherwise objective practice. Rather than being neutral and impartial, these paradigms of scientific practice already encode a dominant European masculinity. It is no accident that the seventeenth-century scientific revolutions presented themselves, in Bacon's terms, as a new 'masculine' philosophy (see my *Unreasonable Men: Masculinity and Social Theory*).[2]

Within the structural framework of scientific rationality, culture is radically separated from nature as reason is separated from emotion. As Kant makes clear, it is only to the extent that we have reason and are rational that we can be human and so civilised. Within these terms the body remains uncivilised and identified with sexualities, and so exists as a threat to our status as human beings. As we have seen, this was crucial in defining Europe as the bearer of science, progress and Christianity, and so legitimating the project of conquest. An uncivilised nature needed to be dominated if it was to cut the path from tradition to modernity.

Within this framework it can be tempting to treat 'adolescence' as an incomplete state – if young people do not lack reason, then they are at least imagined to have temporarily lost connection with it. In taking unnecessary risks with their lives they are in the grip of their emotional nature. Like the 'uncivilised', they cannot be communicated with because they lack reason. The only language they can appreciate is the language of force. Within a rationalist tradition that treats adolescence as an object of scientific investigation, there is no need to communicate with or listen to what young people have to say for themselves.

Yet positivist traditions within the social sciences also serve to silence the people we are investigating. As 'objects' of knowledge they are expected to respond to the questions we ask but not to ask questions themselves. Instead of thinking about men and masculinities as objects of social-scientific research – as though traditional positivist methods can unproblematically be applied – we have to recognise the ways in which traditional methodologies already encode masculine assumptions. Researchers must learn that they can only ask questions of others that they have already asked themselves, so that they are able to share their own experiences when it is appropriate. Carol Gilligan discovered in her work with adolescent girls that she had to question the notion of ignorance that is so often assumed, and recognise how much her subjects already knew.[3] They were not ready to share their knowledge about their experience unless she was also ready to share herself. This was part of creating a relationship of trust.

Feminism challenged the rationalist terms of modernity through its refusal of the distinction between reason and emotion, minds and bodies. This broke with the dominant Cartesian tradition that traditionally devalued bodies as part of a disenchanted nature, and insisted instead that bodies should be recognised as part of our identities as human beings. In creating spaces to explore hidden relationships between emotions and power, the recognition that the 'personal is political' enabled feminist researchers to analyse the play of power relations within intimate and familial relationships. However, unfortunately, when it came to the analysis of men, the adoption of a structural analysis of hegemonic masculinities in terms of relationships of power meant that some of these insights were lost.[4] This has meant that, when it comes to men, we assume again the impersonal 'view from nowhere' that comes from the rationalist tradition. We assume that when men come together it is simply for the benefit of their personal lives, and not to reveal the workings of structural relations of power by reflecting upon their experience.

We can learn from postmodern theory, echoing an early (if disavowed) feminist insight, that we always theorise from particular historical and cultural moments that we need to acknowledge. Otherwise, not only do we find ourselves talking about young people without listening to what they have to say, but we find that our thinking abstracts them from their particular historical and cultural settings. We find ourselves talking in general terms about the interface between young people and the institutions of the adult world. We can also find ourselves legislating for them through the use of reason, rather than learning about the very different worlds they are growing up in. In this time of mass communications and new technologies, it is unhelpful to generalise across generations; rather, we must focus upon the particular troubles and pleasures that shape young people's lives. But to do this we need to break with a rationalist tradition that can talk of power but not of love, and explore new ways of understanding how power operates through these different spheres of life.

generations

Young people grow up in particular worlds with their own histories and cultures. A young man in the outskirts of Santiago in the early years of the new millennium has questions, concerns and dreams different to those of the late 1970s, when the shadows of that earlier 9/11 were part of the everyday struggle for survival in Pinochet's regime. In the silence that fell, it was often difficult for mothers and fathers to share with their children the painful experiences they had lived through. In other countries in Latin America there were different silences, as military governments took hold and popular movements were crushed. Parents felt they needed to protect their young children from the painful experiences of the past. Often it was too dangerous to remember, and easier to forget.

Such a silence can stand in the way of communication between parents and children. Parents can be too anxious to look to the future and away from the past, and children soon learn what they are not supposed to ask about. Children can unknowingly carry the unresolved feelings of their parents. Sometimes they find themselves dreaming about horrors they cannot place, which have come from somewhere they cannot name. With the closing of the public world parents may feel more focused upon their relationship with their children, but at the same time wish to protect them from a painful history. Boys feel a particular responsibility, especially when they have grown up without fathers. Within a patriarchal culture they can feel they should not add to their mother's burden. Sometimes there is the painful experience of separation following exile, where children can feel anger that their parents have not 'been there' for them emotionally. The shadows of these 'difficult histories' fall unevenly across families. Boys might find it difficult to share their uncertainties about their bodily desires and emotions, feeling they have to sustain a silence across the generations.

Listening to parents talking about their teenage children in Santiago today, one hears them voicing concern about the depression they feel their children carry, about which they cannot speak. Amid widespread mental illness and use of antidepressants, it is still difficult to open up conversations about the experience of adolescence after the coup, given the years of violence and terror that followed. It is difficult to know when the time might be right for such a conversation. Sometimes adults are concerned not to burden their children further; at other times they feel their teenagers are not really interested, because the world they are growing up in is so different. Yet often young people already know much more than their parents give them credit for. They may be maintaining their silence because they have grown up silently protecting their parents.

Such traumatic histories are inflected differently within different Latin American cultures. A young person in Chile might reflect that they have never really talked to their parents about their experience after the coup. They know that their parents suffered but, through the years of exile, they never felt that they could talk about these painful memories. Chilean culture is sensitive to not hurting others, to the need to adapt to the expectations of others, and is wary of the expression of feelings and thoughts lest others be offended, and so a silence is easily preserved. People are reluctant to bring painful experiences back to the surface, especially if the culture fosters a belief in the future and encourages a forgetting of the past. At the same time people are themselves aware of carrying an unspoken burden from the past, as if somehow they cannot get on with their lives in the present because of a silent depression.

different worlds

Often young men feel they are growing up in a world that is different to the one their parents knew. As they begin to define their identities in opposition to their parents it can be difficult to sustain communication. This is especially true when emotional communication has not been established between father and son in the early years. There can be a critical moment when a boy is about 7 or 8, when a father feels he can no longer hold his son's hand in public. The son might reach out for his father's hand, only to feel rejected. If no explanation is forthcoming an uneasy distance within the relationship can be created that is difficult to repair.

Emotional bonds are created if fathers are involved in the everyday care of their children. The days after a child is born can prove crucial, if fathers learn the skills of bodily care for the baby at the same time as the mother, rather than having to defer to her. It is this early investment of time and attention that allows for connections to be sustained through the difficult years of adolescent withdrawal. Sometimes boys have to 'find their own way' though these years, wanting parents to 'be there' for them but allowing them to make their own mistakes. In their later teenage years they are able to return.

We have often failed to recognise the ways in which adolescence is gendered. This has made it difficult for us to appreciate how the gender separation that takes place in schools as early as 7 can isolate those boys who – possibly because they come from families which value emotional awareness or greater gender equality – prefer playing with girls.

Early feminism focused upon issues of gender equality in ways that made it difficult to give equal recognition to the emotional needs of children. Sometimes children wanted more contact with their working parents, and resented being left with the poorer women who enabled this middle-class couple to have greater gender equality. This is a generational experience that partly explains why the children who were brought up by feminist parents in the 1970s and 1980s seem to be making different decisions for themselves. Men could be slow to respond to the challenges of feminism. Feeling they needed to be 'role models' for their sons, they would often conceal their own feelings of fear and humiliations at school. But this can leave young men feeling more alone and isolated, unable to recognise their fears as 'normal', and interpreting them as a sign of weakness and so as a threat to male identity.

Young men might look towards the Internet as a virtual space where they can explore feelings that they are unable to share in person. They might even find that they can say things to their friends on the Internet that they would not risk saying face to face. Young people might feel that they can only really acknowledge and explore some desires through virtual reality. A young man who is interested in same-sex relations can discover that he is not 'abnormal' for having these desires. On the Internet he can find chatrooms in which he can own up to feelings that he might feel he has to silence in everyday life. The Internet is a space in which people can explore a range of gender and sexual identities. Young people who feel ambivalent about their gender or sexual identity might use it to perform and act out these diverse identities. In learning how they feel through these diverse performances they can gain information about themselves that could make a vital difference to the relationships they choose. They can discover others who are dealing with similar issues in their own lives and so feel less isolated and alone.

It would be wrong to draw too sharp a distinction between the 'real' and the 'virtual', for young people move easily between these different realms. They can learn from the virtual in a way that changes how they feel about themselves and so also how they act in their relationships. Rather than viewing the virtual as an escape from the dilemmas of the real, we have to recognise how it can also act as a space of exploration. The anonymity of the virtual can allow young men to dare to name their own emotions and feelings. Rather than feeling they need always to have the answers, which can be a particular pressure for young men who have learnt to fear their own vulnerability as a sign of weakness, men can own up to their own ambivalence. They can also explore the distance between what young men feel they have to say, especially in front of other men, and how they feel themselves. They can allow themselves an honesty of expression, perhaps through assuming a new identity on the net.

In this way young men can begin to acknowledge how their bodies have been shamed, and so understand the tension between what they would like to feel and what they actually feel about contact, sex and intimacy. Possibly they still feel unconsciously shaped by Catholic doctrine regarding the untrustworthiness of young women and the threat they present to male spirituality, even though they have broken with these beliefs rationally. They might feel torn between dualistic notions of good and evil, so that at some level they feel femininity represents an 'evil' that needs to be resisted. This might also make it difficult for young men to come to terms with their own embodied feelings, particularly with their own vulnerability, tenderness and fear, which they have learnt to identify as 'feminine' and so exist as a threat to a heterosexual male identity.[5]

bodies

As we rethink Freud's theories of latency, so we think in different terms about how boys become men. When 7-year-old girls and boys separate into different worlds, boys can feel stranded and exposed as they are absorbed into a masculine world of football they might not feel comfortable with. This is a time when boys can get bullied. The emotional sensitivity of boys brought up in anti-sexist ways can seem like a handicap, giving other boys grounds to reject them. In these years it can be dangerous for boys to show any vulnerability, especially in school. It is only when they are outside the school gates that they allow themselves tears, as they retell the events of the day. Boys take on particular bodily disciplines where they learn to conceal their inner emotional lives. Bodies get tightened against experience, and the gap between how they feel inside and what they can risk revealing to others widens.

As a form of self-protection, boys often assume an instrumental relationship towards their bodies. Not wanting to acknowledge their fear, sadness or vulnerability they learn to deflect these emotions into anger and violence, which affirms their male identities. It is here that we can recognise the weakness of notions of 'hegemonic masculinity' that effectively define masculinities as relationships of power. Rather than exploring what it means to say that men often lack an emotional language, Connell prefers to insist that men have power and privileges that should be more equally shared. His disdain for the 'therapeutic', set in opposition to the 'political', makes it difficult to think creatively about the relationships of power and emotions.[6]

In Connell's *Masculinities* there is a tension between this theoretical framework and the case studies of particular masculinities. But even with the case studies we are left unsure about how these men have *become* who they are, and about the tension between the men and the diverse masculinities they have grown up to identify with. It is partly because of the abiding split between emotions, feelings and desires, which are regarded as 'therapeutic', that we are left with a somewhat rationalist conception of power, conceived in zero-sum terms as if the power that men give up can be assumed by women. This vision of power not only locks men into particular masculinities, identified as they are with particular relations of power, but it makes it difficult to explore the tensions between men and the masculinities they can feel obliged to identify with.

This rationalist vision makes it difficult to explore the workings of relationships of power, and the ways in which they can undermine self-worth and devalue experience. It is a vision of power separated from bodies, experience and emotional life. It was partly because Foucault, in the essay 'Technologies of the Self', discerned the weakness of his vision of power/knowledge, yet could not find a way through the impasse, that he felt he had to start again through his explorations of ethics and subjectivities.[7] This shift of focus did not mean that he abandoned his understanding of the centrality of power, but that he had to leave it for a while to analyse power through its relationship with identities and experience.

Foucault's discussions in *The Care of the Self*, the third volume of his *History of Sexuality*, have a particular resonance for understanding the experiences of young men.[8] Foucault was concerned with questioning prevailing traditions that teach a disdain for the body and sexuality, and so an abuse of the self, by looking for alternative sources within ancient Greece that could foster a different kind of caring for bodies, emotions, sexualities and love. He wanted to question the heterosexual framework encoded within a secularised vision of modernity in the West, which too often has taught that white heterosexual masculinities provided the norm against which women, people of colour, gays and lesbians were to be found 'lacking'.

A universalist theory that tends to think about hegemonic masculinities exclusively as relationships of power makes it difficult to theorise diverse cultures of masculinity. Locked into thinking the relationship between masculinities in terms of power, it becomes tempting to apply a universal theory to a broad range of cultural settings. This produces its own forms of blindness, even if it is tempting to international organisations, who can make only minor cultural adaptations to their practice. Within an increasingly globalised world economy this can serve to circulate particular masculinities, rather than critically engage with them. We still need to explore how, say, in different countries in Latin America, Catholicism has shaped the ways people still unconsciously feel about their bodies, emotions and sexualities, despite a growing secularisation.

The idea of the body as a site of sin and temptation produces its own silences between the generations. The bodily experience of young men who go to prostitutes for their first sexual experience is not a matter of the 'meanings' they assign to that experience, as an interpretive tradition might suggest. Rather, it can lead them to overvalue performance, and disrupt connections between sexuality and feeling, sex and love. In Latin cultures where the family remains a significant institution, there is a different modulation between private and public. The Catholic emphasis upon sustaining public appearances can open up a particular split between people's inner emotional lives, which do not expect to share, and the ways they present themselves to others. This can be a particular issue for young men, who in their early adolescent years have to deal with powerful stirrings of sexual feelings and emotions.

While the onset of periods is recognised as a rite of passage for young women, there is no equivalent awareness of the significance of the first wet dream or masturbation for young men. Such experiences can be overwhelming and, unless there is dialogue between fathers and sons, a source of shame. Where young men discover they have sexual feelings for their own sex the discovery can be disturbing and shaming, as it can threaten their sense of masculinity. They can feel isolated and alone, unable to appreciate their own desires. In the difficult years of early adolescence, when young men are coming to terms with their sexuality, they often look to their peer group for support. Unsure of their own desires, and often trapped within traditional conceptions of masculinity which insist that men are active in their desires, while women are the objects of male heterosexual desire, it can be difficult for men to sustain a balance between 'activity' and 'passivity', giving and receiving love. A pattern may be established in which men feel it is easier to give than to ask for affection, offering to others the love they really desire for themselves.

sexualities

It is sometimes easier for men to give than to receive love. Other men might feel quite different, more able to receive than give. If emotional needs are understood as a sign of weakness, men learn to deny their own needs for contact and intimacy. As I explored in *Rediscovering Masculinity*, and in more detail in *Man Enough*, there is often a fear of intimacy.[9] Young men can use sex as a channel for diverse needs and desires, uneasy about their need for contact. Sometimes men initiate sex when, if they were more sensitive to their own needs, they would realise that what they want is to be touched.

Since their dependency is often denied, young men learn to speak of sex as performance. They might desire sex, but feel unsure about intimacy because this can seem to threaten the boundaries of self. Because of the identification between masculinity and self-control young men can feel threatened by the uncertainties of desire, which seems to have a momentum of its own, beyond conscious control. This can make 'falling in love' very unsettling. Often there is a confusion between sex and love that needs to be carefully explored. Moreover, as women learn to demand independence, men can feel threatened in their traditional male roles. As women connect to their own sexual desires, and reject the traditional sexual contract based on obligation, they seek greater negotiation over desires. This can be experienced as a threat to male power, and men can respond violently to affirm their identities.

Even in urban contexts, where there is a movement towards greater gender equality, young people can feel uneasy about the negotiation of their sexual desires. They can assume that if there is love, then their partner should know what they need. Young men may experience themselves as trapped within a male identity that no longer resonates with their experience. They may feel that they can show tenderness in private, but in public need to sustain a more traditional masculinity. Young gay men might feel they have to sustain a certain image within their family. Often people express a double identity through indulging in affairs, thinking that if their partners do not know then they will not be hurt. Within an inherited tradition of confession, there is an unspoken expectation that people can be forgiven and that people can begin again in their relationships. Often men learn to use language as a means of self-defence, wary of exposing their inner emotions and desires to others for fear of rejection.

Within Latin American cultures that are still shaped by Catholic traditions, as we have seen, there is commonly an unconscious fear of the body and sexualities. It is one think to forsake these traditions intellectually and quite another to 'work through' their unconscious imprints. There is often an implicit connection between love and self-lessness which treats 'pure' love as untainted by sexuality. It becomes difficult to connect sexuality with a Christian spirituality that has traditionally identified the body and sexuality with 'carnal Israel'.[10] Sexuality, identified with the 'sins of the flesh', is split from love. Young men, inheriting this split consciousness but unable to name it within a secular culture, find it difficult to acknowledge the source of their emotional conflicts. They often lock themselves into their own isolation, unable to reach out to others for support.

It is when men feel good about themselves that they reach out towards friends; when they feel down it can be harder to ask for support. Traditionally this is something women have done more easily, though within the new globalised economy women are also finding it difficult to express their emotional needs as they negotiate between work and home. Although they can offer emotional support to others, they often find it hard to ask for it themselves. Women have their own issues with intimacy and self-nourishment. So we need to rethink the sexual politics of the 1970s that left us with an inheritance that defined men's power alone as the problem, as if 'the trouble with love' is that men have not changed enough. We fail young men if we allow them to think that masculinity and male power are always the problem and never part of the solution. Young men need different models of diverse masculinities – straight, gay and bisexual – that can learn from each other, as they help create more equal gender and sexual relationships. This means listening to what young men say about their hopes, wishes and dreams.

Rather than men feeling bad about themselves because of their power within a patriarchal society, they should gain the sense that they can be tender and loving as much as clear and assertive. The concerns of young men need to be heard, and their need for support recognised as they engage in redefining their masculinities. Young men can be left feeling that the young women they know have found it easier to change, and they can feel envious. Rather than turn their feelings in and against themselves, which has produced high rates of male suicide, they can instead learn to draw the love and support they need from other men also involved in the processes of change.

As a split has opened up between different generations of women, with younger women feeling a certain distance from feminism while profiting from the sexual equality that an older generation fought for, so there is also apparent a split with men. A younger generation no longer feels so concerned with men's relationship to feminism, having grown up with more equal gender relations at school. If we want to speak to young men, we have to appreciate generational shifts in gender relations. We need to rethink the terms of gender equality, rather than view it as an ideal that requires no redefinition in light of the way power works both globally and locally to shape relationships.

If we are to engage with young men's concerns, it is necessary to think the experience of men and masculinities in ways that can give due attention to bodies, pleasures, sexualities and love. Young people often resist easy categorisation and do not want to be assigned to pre-existing categories. There is more fluidity in postmodern identities, as young people explore their embodied needs and desires. This involves also questioning psychoanalytic traditions that have assumed a particular responsibility for thinking subjectivities. There needs to be an awareness of the gendered and racialised assumptions that inform these traditions.

As we listen to young people, so we learn to respect what they have to say, aware of the need to question a rationalist modernity, including its theorisations of masculinities, if we are to validate emotions as sources of knowledge and of human dignity and self-worth.

8

authority, identities, bodies and intimacy

different worlds

As young people enter their teenage years they are clear that they do not want adults to treat them as children. They resent this treatment because they are no longer children, though they are still not adults. They want their parents to be there in the background for them, ready to support them in any way that is needed, but they do not want them interfering in their lives. As they come to define themselves in contrast to their parents, they construct lives of their own and affirm their separate identities by keeping secrets from the adult world. Young people feel that not only do their parents 'not understand' what they are going through, but that they should be excluded from their lives. With access to the Internet they can create virtual spaces of their own in which to conduct conversations with their friends. Their peers have become significant to them in new ways, and they are often more likely to rely upon their opinions.[1]

With access to new sources of information on the Internet young people are no longer so dependent upon their teachers and schools. Rather, school becomes a space in which they can continue their relationships with friends. They learn to discriminate between their teachers, appreciating those whom they can talk to and who would support them against the authority of the school. They want to be listened to and they distance themselves from teachers who, rather than listen, simply expect obedience from pupils. They might not challenge this authority directly, but they often take little notice of what is said by such teachers. A shift in relations with authority has been taking place since the early 1970s in the West, as well as elsewhere. In the Santiago conference on 'Adolescent Males: The Construction of Gender Identities in Latin America' (6–8 November 2002), there were shared concerns about radical shifts in authority relations between the generations. There was a widespread sense that young people would no longer submit to the traditional forms of authority and discipline. They could no longer be relied upon to respect the authority of their elders simply because of the position they held. Rather, respect was something that was due only if it was earned.[2]

Young people are growing up in a world in which they have access to a wide variety of sources of information that were unknown in their parents' youth. They are familiar with new technologies that their parents can barely use. Through music and popular culture they are influenced by sounds and voices unknown to the adult world. At the same time they have to deal with their own bodily changes and an intensity of emotions that can feel overwhelming. For example, experiencing an erection, a boy may feel no longer in control of his body, frightened that others might see his desire, making him vulnerable to the ridicule of other boys and so threatening his male identity. Within a Catholic culture boys might be left feeling shamed by the pleasures of masturbation and the fantasies about women's bodies that accompany heterosexual desire. They might feel scared of the desire they feel for contact with other boys, or perhaps of the intensity of feeling they have for a male teacher, knowing that these desires are prohibited within a homophobic culture. They might seek to conceal their desires from others, not wanting to acknowledge them.

Young men can also find themselves preoccupied with getting close to women's bodies. There might be a circulation in school of pornographic images that both excite and intimidate them. But they can also be haunted by their own ignorance about women's bodies, unsure whether to believe information disseminated among friends. Young men live in a world of emotions and desires that they cannot share with their parents. Seeking to define themselves in opposition to the adult world, they search for their identity through their own bodies. They might feel a need to get close to women's bodies as a way of establishing intimacy. With their girlfriends they can allow themselves to be vulnerable, and share more of their feelings than with their male peer group. In the company of other boys they might feel a need to prove their male identities through the consumption of alcohol, or through smoking dope. Needing money to buy music and drink, they show off to friends within the competitive relations of young male teenagers. Unsure of their ground, they feel the need to sustain a 'front' in the company of others, hiding their true feelings for fear of rejection.[3]

intimacy

In early heterosexual relationships young men can create a space of intimacy with their girlfriends, recognising that they can share more of their tenderness and love than with their male friends. This can be a significant discovery, as young men can learn to trust their partners in a search for intimacy. They do not want to appear 'soft' with their male friends, because this can be grounds for rejection. Often it is only in the intimate space created with their girlfriends that they can risk showing more of themselves. Sometimes this is a space that boys can create for themselves within gay relationships, but within homophobic cultures there is a fear of being 'found out' and exposed to the ridicule of others.

There is an intensity in teenage relationships that can be difficult to recall as an adult. There are desires which young people might find overwhelming and difficult to speak about. But sometimes these feelings can be shared within intimate relations in which young people negotiate their sexual contact. Often clear boundaries are set within particular cultures, especially those in which sexuality remains shamed. This makes it difficult for young people to affirm their own desires. It can be easier for young women to recognise themselves as objects of male desire than to acknowledge their own active sexual desires. This represents a significant shift in the sexual cultures that have emerged since the 1970s in the West, and subsequently more widely. Even in rural areas, young women are more aware of their own sexual needs than in previous generations. They are more likely to think about sexuality as an expression of love, even if in practice it can be difficult to escape from the uneasy feelings they have about bodily desires.[4]

Within the intimate space that young couples create, secrets can help bind each to the other. Where friends sometimes fail to understand, a lover can allow the vulnerability that young men cannot otherwise show. They might feel they are falling in love, possibly for the first time, as they struggle to find a language in which to express their feelings. These are experiences of which adults might be only dimly aware, as young people escape into their own worlds. Though adults might feel they have lost contact with their teenage children and that they are beyond their control, they must trust the relationship they established in earlier childhood years. This is why it is so important for parents to forge strong emotional connections with their young children. Only through learning to respect their emotions and feelings will the relationship survive the inevitable distance and difficulties of the teenage years.

In traditional patriarchal cultures it can be difficult for parents – especially fathers – to establish close and intimate relations with their children. Fathers can be locked into a view of themselves as the source of authority within the family. They might have learnt from their own fathers that involving themselves emotionally with their children can only compromise this authority, and that sustaining distance is something they owe to their children. This produces its own difficulties, as children resent their fathers' distance, wanting to be closer and more intimate but not knowing how to achieve this. Often fathers can feel betrayed by a culture that teaches them that it does not matter if they are absent through work when their children are young, since they can always take up the relationship later. But a distance that has been created cannot easily be undone, and older men often carry an unspoken sadness from the loss of contact with their children.

When young people's first love relationship breaks up, they might find it difficult to turn to their parents for support. They want their pain to be acknowledged and validated, not to be reassured that there will be other relationships. Fathers are often silent about their own difficulties when they were young. They often portray an image of themselves with their sons that leaves young men feeling that they alone have suffered from feeling lonely and vulnerable. Rather than supporting their sons, this can leave them feeling even more isolated. This serves to produce a further silence in the father–son relationship. A son often learns not to reach out again.[5]

recognition

Young people learn to define themselves as teenagers through the ownership they affirm over their bodies. Bodily changes transform the identities of young women and men. Such transformation is often more profound for young women, who might feel that with the onset of puberty they no longer exist as the person they used to be, but are not sure who they have become. This process receives cultural recognition in rituals, through which young women are able to accept that they have made the transition from childhood to being 'a young woman'. Bodily changes, then, make young women feel different, separated from the childhood they have left behind.[6]

Teenagers want their parents to recognise these changes so that they are no longer treated as children. They want greater responsibility, but can be so taken up with their own lives and experiences that as teenagers they allow themselves little space to think of others. In the affluent West, responsibility can often mean asking their parents to show trust in allowing them to stay out late. They do not want to be questioned; nor do they want to have to give an account of themselves. Rather, they want their parents to trust them to make their own decisions, though given the insecurities of modern urban life this can be difficult. Parents who want to set limits and boundaries for their teenage children my find it hard if they did not do this when their children were younger.

Many parents of present-day teenagers grew up in the 1960s and 1970s. As teenagers themselves, they challenged parental authority, growing up in the shadow of the social movements of the 1960s, where authority was identified with authoritarianism. As parents, they wanted a freedom for their children that they themselves had never experienced. Fathers especially wanted to be closer to their children than their fathers were with them.

Robert Bly described this father hunger in *Iron John* in mythical terms. Such new fathers often feared that setting limits, or saying no and sustaining it, would somehow damage their relationship with their children. In some ways they were more like brothers than fathers. Sometimes this meant that mothers became the figures of authority, and could feel unsupported by their partners. Fathers felt unable to be authorities without being authoritarian. They so wanted their children to enjoy a freedom they had not known in their own childhood that they found it difficult to set limits. But often this left children with a power that they did not really want. In some cases they abused their parents and even hit them. When they became teenagers, they found it difficult to set boundaries for themselves. They resented their parents, and were so used to 'acting out' with them that they would break whatever boundaries were set. It is often through risk behaviour that teenagers test themselves, as if exploring their own limits.

Tony Overman shared his experience as a US teenager in a poem that can hopefully speak across cultural differences:

It's Tough To Be a Teenager

It's tough to be a teenager, no one really knows
What the pressure is like in school, this is how it goes.

I wake up every morning, and into this face
I wanna be good lookin', but I feel like a disgrace.

My friends they seem to like me, if I follow through with their dare,
But when I try to be myself, they never seem to care.

My mom, well she keeps saying, I gotta make the grade
While both my parents love me, it slowly seems to fade.

It seems like everyone I know it trying to be so cool
And every time I try, I end up just a fool.

I've thought about taking drugs, I really don't want to you know
But I just don't fit in, and it's really startin to show.

Maybe if I could make the team, I'll stand out in the crowd
If they could see how hard I try, I know they would be proud.

You see I'm still a virgin, my friends they can't find out
'Cause if they really know the truth, I know they'd laugh and shout.

Sometimes I really get so low, I want to cash it in
My problems really aren't so bad, if I think of how life's been.

Sometimes I'm really lost, and wonder what to do
I wonder where to go, who can I talk to.

It's tough to be a teenager, sometimes life's not fair
I wish I had somewhere to go, and someone to CARE.[7]

The feeling that they should be able to deal with their problems on their own can lock young men into an isolation where they begin to turn their feelings against themselves. Often they do not want to acknowledge their own depression and will not be able to describe what they are going through. In front of others they often feel obliged to 'stay cool' and to give the impression that they are coping, even if they are not.

desires/intensities

A young man might desperately want to have a girlfriend with whom he can share his intimate thoughts and feelings. He wants someone to care in a way he can no longer accept from his parents. He longs to be able to communicate his love and friendship. He wishes to share his desires with a person he cares for. But it can be difficult to take the initiative. He won't risk rejection, so he seeks to find out indirectly through his friends whether his feelings are reciprocated. Complex networks exist within peer groups to transmit such information. Teenage cultures have their own subtle rules.

Sometimes scared of their own desires, teenage boys can 'act out' violently in their relationships with others. Wanting to hide their desires, which they assume are somehow visible to others, they distract attention through their behaviour. They can feel unsettled by the intensity of feelings they have for someone, especially if she is going out with someone else, hiding their emotions from themselves so that others will not read their minds. Young men can be concerned to prove themselves to their peers, engaging in risky behaviour as a way of affirming their masculinity. Searching for their own identities, they can feel disconnected from the public world of politics, which they feel belongs to the adult public sphere. They are more concerned with finding their own space in which they can be with their peers.

Experimenting with drink and drugs can be a way of exploring their inner selves, establishing what they want and need for themselves. Peer pressure can make it difficult to follow their desires.

As Carol Gilligan has shown in her work with adolescent girls, the lives of young girls change when they are 11 or 12, as they lose their own voice and learn to see themselves through the eyes of the dominant culture. This may result in a certain loss of confidence. Gilligan observes that older girls often refuse to give an opinion, concerned that it might not be acceptable to others.[8] Gilligan believes this process happens much earlier in the case of boys. My own view is that the process occurs at a similar age for boys, as they move from primary to secondary school, even though it does not take quite the same form. During the early teenage years there is a shift in boys' feelings about their sexual identities, in which they have to deal with the intensity of their feelings. This can be difficult to share with other boys. They are more concerned with body image than ever before, faced with the images of toned male bodies that have become a feature of postmodern consumer culture. Thus they learn to see themselves through the eyes of a dominant culture in ways unfamiliar to earlier generations of men, who might have been more concerned with proving their male identities in competitive relations with male peers.

How are young men to come to terms with their sexual desires? In traditional societies, such as rural Mexico, boys become men through their first experience of waged work, which gives them the money to pay for their first sexual experience with a prostitute. This waged work is very different from the unwaged labour they are expected to do on the family plot. It is through waged work and marriage that young men make the transition to adulthood. They can then set up house on their own as 'real men'. As Mathew Gutmann reports from his fieldwork in Mexico,[9] if men lack a regular partner then there is an expectation that they will gain their sexual pleasure through masturbation. Until they are married and have obtained regular work they are not considered 'equal' to other adults.

Young men from border regions may shift their understanding of gender relations through working in the United States. Their attitudes and behaviour might then have more in common with young men from urban areas, who are likely to have had their first sexual experience with a friend. But within Catholic cultures, which have for so long separated the figure of the virgin from the whore, there is an inherited ambivalence about desire. Traditionally there was a sharp distinction between a woman you would have sex with and a woman whom you would consider marrying. To an extent this separation still exists in urban areas, where young men might distinguish between relations with girls who are 'easier' and those with girls with whom they might want to have a steady relationship.

In both urban and, increasingly, rural areas, girls seem to be taking more of an initiative in sexual relations. As Benno De Keijzer reports in his fieldwork in rural Mexico, a girl might surprise a boy by saying 'I love you.' The boy's response is likely to be 'I am supposed to say that.' At first he may be speechless, but later he will affirm his male identity by insisting that they go through the usual rituals of courtship. If he has already become a man, through having sex, he might not feel so insistent that his partner is a virgin when they get married. Sexual cultures are changing even in rural areas: young people increasingly expect to have sexual relations before they get married. De Keijzer's fieldwork across three generations shows that young people are more likely to put off marriage, and so having children, so they can feel they have lived more. This is something older people have begun to accept.[10]

In a world dominated by mass-media images, and, in the case of Mexico, given the experiences of migration and having relatives across the border in the United States, a variety of new influences shape the expectations and desires of young people. Latin American countries have been witness to a widespread shift in relation to authority, desire and sexuality. Young people increasingly feel they own their bodies and should be free to express themselves as they wish. They separate themselves from adult generations as they learn to define their own values. If communication is to take place between the generations, then sex education must recognise the changed realities of sexual experience. Adults must learn how to listen to young people, and to respect their rights as sexual citizens.

bodies, ethics, fears and desires

desires

Why should young men risk sharing their emotions and desires if they already know that their desires are bad and their dreams ugly? Is it not wrong to assume that it is always a good thing for men to learn to express their emotions, if this means that they have to face bad feelings and desires that they would otherwise conceal from others? Does not such concealment at least allow men to behave properly towards others, and shape their emotions and desires so that they are culturally acceptable?

These questions show the continuing grip of Protestantism in the West, even within cultures that are largely secularised. There is often a prevailing sense of guilt and unease that people do not expect to share with others. Young people – for example within the post-feminist cultures of Scandinavia – still grow up fearful of their own desires and feeling the need to discipline themselves so they do not betray themselves in the eyes of others.[1]

Whereas in traditional Protestant cultures desires were private, even shameful, in our increasingly globalised consumer cultures young women and men find themselves surrounded by images of desire. Desires are constantly being named for them; the mass media and advertising even suggest they exist as desiring machines. Somehow they learn that their desires are very close to the surface of their experience, and that in a postmodern culture desires should define their identities. In a post-Cartesian culture desire has often taken the place of thinking in the affirming of identities. It is through shopping and consuming that people know they exist. The widespread and radical shift towards equality in gender relations has meant that both young women and young men learn to experience themselves as objects of desire. They feel that they ought to be thin; and that thinness depends on controlling their appetite for food. The notion of self-control traditionally identified with masculinity, requiring that young men assert control over emotions and desires, has become equally defining for post-feminist women's identities.

In a post-feminist culture we can no longer assume that young women are more 'in touch' with their emotions and feelings than young men. Young women have learnt that they need to be 'independent' and 'self-sufficient', and that they are entitled to their own desires. Feminism has left its mark in affirming women's sexualities, pleasures and desires. Willy Pedersen's research in contemporary Norway has shown that, in the post-war welfare state, there has developed a widespread assumption, partly inspired by Karl Evang's readings of Freud and Reich, that sex is 'good for you' and 'good for society'. This helped to produce a more open body culture in which the body was no longer shamed or identified with the 'sins of the flesh'.[2] Yet, given the concealed influence of Protestant religious traditions within a newly secularised post-war culture that has wanted to forget the past, and to teach the next generation to 'look to the future', this could produce its own tension between inner experience and people's perception of what they should be able to feel. Learning to fear their own inner experience, young women and men might feel obliged to regulate their behaviour according to these new ways of being. It remained a matter of adapting to prevailing cultural norms, which could sustain a fear of inner desires that might threaten 'how you are supposed to be'.

It was often a matter of adapting to new cultural values, with limited space to explore one's own desires. This was a tension that feminism could help expose, since it questioned the sexual objectification of women and explored, at least initially, the split between language and experience. Post-structuralist feminism tended to disavow this tension, as it was discourse that defined both prevailing femininities and masculinities. This was welcomed as a move beyond a discussion of gender based on power relations; but, while it was able to bring masculinities into the frame, it risked losing sight of the connection between power and emotional life. There was a fear that a stress on desires as 'inner' would sustain an essentialist discourse; by focusing on the externalities of discourse, a post-structuralist analysis helped unsettle given identities and allowed for a greater fluidity of fragmented identities, in contrast to Connell's notion of a hegemonic masculinity. But in both traditions there was an implicit disdain for emotions and an insistence on the fluidity of desires as shaped through prevailing discourses. It became difficult to understand the gendered processes of emotional development and growth.[3]

sexualities

In a post-feminist culture it has often been easier for young women to learn to talk about their sexual desires than it has for young men. Young men can grow up feeling that sexual desire should remain unspoken, and that their desires should be known without having been put into words. At the same time young men have learnt to accept their bodies as objects of desire, and, particularly within urban cultures, have learnt to present themselves through their thin and hard bodies.

Pedersen's research in Norway reveals that young girls are now sexually active younger – with the average age of first intercourse falling from 17.7 to 16.7 in a decade – and that they engage in more diverse sexual practices, including oral sex. He says that there is no gender difference in his data on the 'love norm' – that sex has to do with feelings of love and emotional intimacy. However, a problem can arise in survey-based research, inasmuch as people are concerned with conveying a certain image of themselves; they might speak quite differently in a more open qualitative interview.[4] It seems that young Norwegian women read much more in magazines about sexuality and desire than do boys. They have a greater awareness of the implications of divorce and separation and of the complexity of relationships, whereas boys seem reluctant to speak about these aspects of their lives.

Within the male cultures in which boys grow up, it is hard for them to seek support for difficulties or bereavements at home. Often they feel they ought to be able to deal with their feelings on their own. A strongly individualistic culture produces its own reticence. Boys often feel they need to deal with their emotions by themselves, and if they are feeling down they can feel this more acutely. Seeking help would be a threat to their male identity. Boys may find it easier to share their feelings with girls than to take the risk of being emotionally open with other boys. Others might take advantage of what they tell them, and they will 'lose face'.

Young people living in Western cities have become more tolerant of diverse sexualities, especially in their later teenage years. A more open culture of homosexuality has prepared the ground for the display of male bodies, and created images of the male body as an object of desire that have impacted upon heterosexual masculinities. There is tolerance of greater sexual ambivalence, and young people have learnt to experiment with sexual desire. Whereas girls may readily admit to kissing other girls, boys will often deny such same-sex acts, fearing a threat to their heterosexual identity. Yet such an issue can show the limits of survey-based research, wherein gender is established as a basis for the exploration of differences. While there might be little difference between the genders in the identifications people are ready to make as lesbian or gay, we might expect different responses from those young men who identify as heterosexual about their sexual contact with other boys, because of the ways heterosexual male identities are framed in contrast to homoerotic feelings. This might explain the more tolerant attitudes towards homosexualities to be found in the responses of young women. That is to say, although boundaries between sexualities are weakening, they are still more likely to be sustained by young men.

Pedersen's research tends to rely upon the difference in responses of young women and men to given questions. Girls may be more open to homosexualities than boys, but this difference can only be explained in the context of a particular understanding of masculinities and the ways heterosexual male identities are affirmed through a denial of emotions deemed to be 'feminine'. Boys tend to identify as either homosexual or not, thereby sustaining very clear boundaries. Young women see boundaries as more open and flexible, and tolerate greater ambivalence. But again this is something that research can find hard to illuminate without an engagement with critical work. For instance, Pedersen might suggest that his finding that girls do not like silicone implants while boys find them acceptable can be taken as reflecting 'different values', but this does not begin to recognise the ways that genders are positioned differently in relation to the issue.

Traditionally less attention has been given to young boys as they enter puberty. The intensity of the experience of their first ejaculations can frighten young men, as they no longer feel in control of their bodies. When they start to explore masturbation they will often be left feeling guilty about their desires if they are growing up in a culture in which the act is shamed. If masturbation is accepted, as with Evang in Norway, it is regarded as a temporary activity that will cease when men enter long-term sexual relationships.[5] Even relatively enlightened positions regard masturbation as pathological if it continues in relationships. This can make it difficult for young men to feel good about masturbation as a way of developing a relationship with their bodies and desires.

In assuming an instrumental relationship with their bodies young men can discover themselves as observers of their own experience, as if watching themselves perform. Unless they are aware of the Cartesian split between mind and body, with its ideal that the mind should always control the emotional life of the body, it becomes increasingly difficult for both men and women to develop a meaningful relationship with their embodied selves. Uneasy about touching themselves, they can be insensitive in the ways they touch others. Unsure of their own emotions, it can be difficult for them to listen to their partner's fears and anxieties. They may suddenly withdraw from relationships, blaming their partner because they are unable to take responsibility for their emotions. Young men may feel a duty to provide their partner with sexual satisfaction, and find that their attention is so focused upon performance that they have little connection with their own desire. This can produce an unequal relationship, lacking in mutality or communication. Unaware of their own desires, young men can find it difficult to explore their own sexuality and be responsive to both themselves and their partner.

ethics

Sexuality brings new energies and new pleasures that can be difficult to share with others. Some young men feel that they lack an adequate language in which to express what is happening to them. They may feel trapped in an ethics that says that men can only affirm their masculinities through being independent and self-sufficient. In Scandinavia, even to offer help to another man threatens to dishonour him, because it could suggest that he is somehow not capable of handling his own emotional life. In this way people often learnt to curb their impulse to help others. But rather than feeling supported this can leave them feeling isolated and alone.[6]

If a young man is overcome with grief, say because his father has just died, an older man might feel that it is his duty to tell him, 'Pull yourself together and stop crying.' He understands himself to be offering the younger man a form of protection from shame that, if he accepts, could prevent him from being severely damaged in his own eyes and in the eyes of other men. This resonates particularly in Norwegian culture, where there is still a strong sense of male honour. The younger man, as he later recounts such an episode, can still experience the feelings in his body, for it has proved to be a lesson for life. After the experience he will not cry in front of anyone else. Sometimes he reflects that this has created a distance between himself and his children, for he has never really been able to show his feelings to them. There were times when he wanted to reach out and hug them because he felt moved, only to pull himself back automatically. He recalls a moment when his son got bad news and cried, and he wanted to put his arm around his shoulders but felt that he could not. His own experience had inhibited him and made it difficult to reach out even when he wanted to.

There is an ethics of emotional life that allows men to express their emotions only when they are alone. They might not even share themselves with their long-term partner if they have been brought up to feel that they must be a 'rock' that others can rely upon.

Traditionally, women could show their emotions as 'the weaker sex' but men had to learn to keep their emotions to themselves. This often left an older generation of men feeling isolated, and they could be depressed without realising it. Sometimes they passed this depression on to their sons.

Men could feel worried about the threat of losing their job, but feel that it was a burden they had to carry on their own. Men also felt this about their experiences of war, which they would never share. They could not keep their tiredness or irritation to themselves, but they would not share the source of their feelings. A younger generation of men feel differently. If they have grown up in a culture of gender equality, they may want to share more of themselves with their partner and children. They want to be a good father and will accept that their partner will work and make a substantial contribution to the shared income.

Men nevertheless create boundaries, sharing themselves with their partner but still finding it difficult with male friends. Sometimes they wish it could be different, but they are wary of showing themselves as 'weak' in front of other men. Often they admit that they are able to talk more easily to women than to men because they assume that women are 'more understanding'. Even if they are suffering from stress or anxieties that keep them awake at night, they will tend to dismiss these symptoms and resist seeking medical help. Rather, they will opt to 'live with it' and will deny that anything is wrong. Men often need to feel that they are in control of their bodies and can 'sort things out' for themselves.

controlling bodies

A man from an older generation might feel that, even if his wife has died, he cannot expect the support of others. He is likely to behave as if nothing has happened, and consequently others might feel that they cannot say anything. This locks older men into a painful isolation; they will feel depressed without being able to identify why. They might feel that they need to make a joke of their feelings, since otherwise people might feel uneasy about what to say. Feeling that they do not want anything to change in their friendships, they behave as though they are not hurting or suffering from a sense of loss. Even if they do want to reach out, they can still feel locked into an ethics of self-sufficiency, as if, even in such an extreme situation of need, they have to show that they can cope on their own. Sometimes there is an unspoken fear that if they show themselves to be needy it will give their friends a reason to reject them, and they will be left even more alone.

If men have learnt a body ethics that demands that they build strong muscles and tight bodies, it can be difficult to develop flexibility in the ways they think and feel. Sometimes we find these strong boundaries in the different spheres of their experience. It can be difficult for men to tolerate ambivalence, so that the chaos and uncertainties of domestic life and childcare become intolerable. But this is something that women may also find difficult, and they can be equally concerned to flee to the regulated and disciplined spaces of the office.

Younger men involved in sports might feel that, as long as they can control their bodies, they can share more of their emotional lives with their partner. They might visit the gym as a way of 'letting off steam', and so taking pressure off their familial relationships. They want to keep themselves in shape, and fear 'letting themselves go', finding the thought of a flabby body 'disgusting'. But it can be difficult to sustain a routine at the gym if this means leaving their partner at home looking after the children, especially if they have been at work all day. If they believe in an ethics of gender equality they can feel unsure about whether they are doing enough and whether their partner's frustration might not 'boil over', since they know that they often do not pull their weight when it comes to taking responsibilities at home.[7]

It has been difficult for men to learn to take full emotional responsibility for themselves, rather than relying upon their partner to interpret their experiences for them. Yet as partners have refused to do this emotional labour, men have been forced to be clearer about their needs, so that they can communicate more directly in relationships. They might end up doing more than their share, through guilt.

Sometimes men will speak of feeling trapped between incompatible expectations at work and home. They might find it difficult to adjust to being a new father, expected to be 'soft' and 'caring' at home while needing to be 'hard' and 'unfeeling' in the competitive atmosphere of work. Often men feel desperate when there is a breakdown in the relationship and they have to face the fact that there is nothing they can do to change the situation. This goes against the ethical tradition men often grow up in. They want to believe there is always something they can do to make things better. When love has died, men are left without resources, because there is nothing they can do. Sometimes this feels unbearable, and men blame their partner for taking up what they assume is an unreasonable position. They can feel that she is saying this to hurt them, because there 'must be' something they can do.

As young women and men become more identified with their work, learning to think about themselves in more individualistic ways, they tend to think of relationships in contractual terms. Anxious to affirm control over their individual lives, they can assume a more instrumental attitude towards desire. Unsure of whether relationships can last, they might be wary of committing themselves, since 'something better' might be just around the corner. Even though women might traditionally be more focused upon the need for a loving and intimate relationship, they often deny their own fears of intimacy and commitment. They can find it easier to project their anxieties, sometimes blaming men as a way of not having to deal with their own emotions. This resonates with an earlier 1970s' feminism that assumed that if only men could change, more equal relationships would be possible.[8]

Whether we say that women have increasingly come to accept the disciplines of a masculine regime of independence and self-sufficiency at work, or that female identities have been transformed through women's increasing participation in the labour market, there is an ethics of self-control that works across the genders. This is part of a more general resistance to thinking in terms of gender, since these difficulties no longer relate to given gender differences. Young women have increasingly accepted the competitive cultures of work and have paid the price in terms of their intimate lives, even as they continue talking about the importance of an intimate relationship. Young women often do not want to give up the control they have managed to gain over their lives, and they have even started to fear their emotions as a sign of weakness. They have their own narratives of desire, but have little space in their lives for an ongoing relationship, assuming instead a more instrumental relationship to their desires. They are concerned with the image they portray to others and can be as much in love with their own image as young men are.

The present stress on intensity of desire can create its own impatience with long-term relationships. Young people can find themselves increasingly living single lives, in which they maintain control of their own space and have short-term relationships in which they do not have to share intimacy. Sexual desire comes to be separated from intimacy, which can be experienced as threatening. People can be so focused upon negotiating the fulfilment of their individual desires that they find it difficult to allow for the vulnerability that can create intimacy. If there is an ethics of desire it is often focused upon the self, and does not allow for a flow of feeling between bodies. Both women and men can feel they are living in a permanent state of readiness, anxious for opportunities to arise but unable to risk exposing themselves. They seek relationships and love without the threat of intimacy.

If masculinities have become eroticised within consumer culture, so that men have learnt to identify themselves as objects of desire, they can find it difficult to balance a traditional male 'activity' with the receptivity that goes with intimacy. When young women equally identify themselves with activity, it can be difficult to negotiate mutual intimacy and desire. Intensity becomes an indication of aliveness, and sexuality becomes an issue of performance where men are often focused upon 'giving an orgasm' to their partners. As desires are 'speeded up', so they require greater intensity. Supposedly endless, they can never be fulfilled or satisfied. Living in a state of constant sexual excitement, the body comes to be electrified as it turns in on itself, finding it hard to make contact with other bodies.

As relationships become more instrumental, each partner focused on their own desires, there is often less communication and depth of contact between people. Moving into different psychic spaces that deny the easy distinctions of gender, we need a body/ethics that can illuminate the complex identities people live with.

10

friends, risks and transgressions

spaces

Young men gather together in gangs in order to defend particular spaces or territories. Often it is through the control of these spaces that they affirm their dominant masculinities. As a group takes control of a space it polices the borders against the intrusion of others. Sometimes these gangs take shape in school playgrounds, while at other times they control large territories within the local community. Spaces are divided between different groups, and it is dangerous to transgress the borders that have been set. The message goes out: 'This is our space and you are not welcome here.' The world is sharply divided between friends who are allowed to enter, and enemies who have to be taught to keep their distance or else risk punishment.[1]

Teenagers test themselves against their limits as a way of establishing identities independent of their parents. They transgress the accepted rules of social life in ways that expose these rules to inspection. Sometimes the rules have been taken for granted, but in the face of teenage transgression they need to be articulated and defended, explaining a rationality adults might never have needed to articulate. Young people often insist on adults becoming much clearer about these rules. They are not ready to accept this rationality at face value, questioning the notion that because 'we have always done things in this way' it follows that we should continue to do so. Young women might question why they are expected to help with housework, while their brothers are allowed to play outside. The fact that this is 'tradition' is not a good enough explanation for many young women who are seeking more equal relations at home, possibly because of more equal relations at school. They will be aware whether their brothers have spoken up in their defence or passively taken their parents' side, thus consolidating traditional male superiority.[2]

As young people question the norms and values so often taken for granted in adult life, they are making space for reflection in which they can explore their own values. They create their own spaces away from the adult gaze where they can smoke and drink, or else engage in sexual contact. They can arrange meetings with other teenagers who know that these ritualised spaces are not to be spoken about. It is only much later that an adult might be aware that their teenager is 'going steady' with someone. They have been kept out of the picture. There is a magical quality to the relationship because it seems to have emerged from nowhere, so far as adults are concerned. It can feel threatening to parents because they are forced to recognise that they no longer have control over their teenager's life.

Boys often affirm their male identities through fighting. Traditionally this has been a mark of virility in relation to women, who supposedly need to be protected and defended. Across a wide range of cultures the willingness to fight still proves manhood. From an early age boys learn that their masculinity cannot be taken for granted, but must be constantly defended. As a young man one has to be on one's guard, willing to defend one's honour as a man. This need to defend masculinity takes a range of forms, which define the shaming and dishonouring of masculinities in different ways. But this is not proof that a 'hegemonic masculinity' is to be found in different cultural settings; rather, it shows the pervasiveness of male supremacy in relation to women and the diverse ways in which this is established.

transgressions

By getting drunk or taking drugs young people symbolically break the rules that represent their parents' and the larger culture. They can feel the need constantly to transgress, recognising that adults often do not abide by the rules themselves. They can experience themselves in a borderline state, sensing at some level that they have to push themselves through a kind of symbolic death to be reborn as adults. As Norma Fuller details in her work on the sexual initiation of young men by prostitutes in Peru, it is still through a visit to the whorehouse that young men become sexually active, so marking the 'end of childhood'. In an inversion of the domestic world the prostitute as the experienced older woman takes charge.[3] Within the masculine cultures that Fuller describes, virility remains a central value for affirming male identity. Often it is the peer group that encourages a young man into a brothel, even if he does not feel ready for the experience. The shock experienced when a young man is encouraged to engage in sexual activity for which he does not feel prepared can shape sexuality as performance, rather than as an expression of love and intimacy. This is not a matter of the 'meanings' young people assign to their first sexual experiences, but is rather an embodied experience that can be difficult to remake. It can produce its own anxieties about sexual experience that cannot be spoken about within the masculine culture of the gang. Sex becomes a statement, a demonstration of virility and an assertion of male identity.

Young men will tend to resist using condoms if they believe it can negatively affect their virility. This may be connected to the fear of losing an erection when putting on the condom or to a cultural feeling that sexuality should be spontaneous and not interrupted. Similarly, some people have difficulty in talking about their sexual relations, as if speech will somehow distract from the pleasure. There is rarely recognition that speech can add to the intensity of the experience. Since young men affirm their masculinities through taking risks, they often do not wear condoms, as this adds to the excitement. Fuller's interviews show that virility is more important to young men than the risks involved. But one could also say that such behaviour is not really experienced by them as a risk, since the future is a different world that barely connects to pleasures they seek in the present.

In considering the experience of young women in various urban and rural settings in Peru, Fuller observes that maternity is often postponed. Young women are beginning to value their own sexual pleasures and intimacies, and resent the double standards that allow young men to have other relationships. Traditionally young men were supposed to be experienced, while young women were expected to be 'pure', when they got married. Young women in urban Lima desire their own erotic moments, having become more independent and autonomous. Rather than just existing as the objects of male desire, they are more aware of their own active desires as young women. Like young men, they are experimenting with drinks and drugs, and declaring their own autonomy. But this does not have to mean, as Fuller suggests, that this is to assume a masculine code, even if there might be moments of direct imitation. It would be wrong to perceive these 'negative' behaviours as masculine, rather than recognising them as assertions of young women's developing autonomy and independence. There is a danger, within certain discourses of hegemonic masculinity, of suggesting that because these are assertions of power they should be identified as 'masculine' in some way. If we are not to pathologise these behaviours, we should recognise their meaning as resistance.

As young women learn to value their own sexual pleasures and take the initiative in relation to young men, refusing to accept macho behaviour, they are defining their own independent experiences as women. We should avoid the notion that when young girls transgress expected behaviours they are acting like boys, whereas when boys transgress it is because they cannot be expected to do otherwise. This perpetuates the traditional ethical position that boys are bad. Young boys are taken to be unruly, barbaric and uncivilised, which is why they need to be disciplined and their wills broken. As Alice Miller explains it, they have to be forced to submit because they cannot be reasoned with; the 'animal nature' of the child has to be disciplined through punishment. It is as though the disciplines of childhood break down in the teenage years, particularly with adolescent males but also increasingly in the West with young women, who thus are perceived to need a second civilising process. If they now exist beyond the authority of the traditional father, then the state must intervene to control their behaviour.[4]

This view of boys remains unquestioned within Connell's conception of hegemonic masculinity, in which they remain 'bad' because of the power they can take for granted. The sensibility of a traditional anti-sexist men's politics requires boys to be made aware of the suffering they cause within a patriarchal culture. This can leave boys feeling guilty and shamed. It may bring a commitment to challenge structures of patriarchal power, but it can leave men without a sense of how they can change. Connell rejects the notion that men have also been hurt and their emotional lives constrained within patriarchy. Even though this position draws upon a socialist framework, it tends to take up a familiar radical feminist disdain for men's efforts to change. More recently there has been a shift in Connell's work, where he is more open to a recognition of diverse masculinities – say in schools – but this remains at odds with the theoretical framework he uses.

Young men often learn to use violence to defend themselves – for instance, against other gangs who have 'invaded' their territory. They use violence to decide who is important and who can claim power over a particular territory. They know that they will gain respect from others through their willingness to use violence. They learn to use violence to protect their partner, whom they will often treat as a prized possession: 'She is my woman and I will protect her against the demands of other men.' Identifying as warriors, they have a stoical attitude regarding the future, in which they must be ready to defend themselves through physical strength. Identified with their own active masculinities, they will tend to represent their rivals symbolically as 'passive'. Life is a jungle in which only the strongest survive. They have to defend their territory against the encroachment of others. It is here that we can discern most readily a hierarchy of masculinities.

This sense of being 'on your guard' can range across diverse masculinities. One must be constantly ready to defend oneself against possible attack. Middle-class men tend to feel that they will never be called upon to defend themselves, and so can never feel secure in their male identity. This gives a particular edge to time. The fear of passivity echoes the rules of masculine gang culture, in which the enemy is cast as passive and in need of domination. The victorious warrior is at the top, while the defeated and passive enemy is at the bottom asking for forgiveness and ready to comply with the demands of the powerful. Yet within the group young men are constantly tested, to establish their position within the hierarchy of the gang. They have to show themselves ready to risk themselves, willing to take on dangerous tasks to defend the gang. They cannot show the smallest sign of vulnerability, but have to police their masculinities and sustain a hard body which has been transformed into an instrument of power. This is a pattern that men from diverse backgrounds can also recognise, even if they cannot identify with them. They know the hidden costs.

dangers

Why do we consider young men to be a danger to society? Is it because they constantly challenge traditional forms of authority? Do we constantly view 'adolescents' from the point of view of adult society, and so regard them as incomplete adults? Why is there such a prevailing feeling across diverse cultures that, as Gloria Careaga puts it, 'to be young is to be guilty'?[5] Is this a new feeling that adults have: that young people are 'dangerous' to themselves, if not to civil society more generally? These feelings can encourage young people to withdraw from the adult world. They do not expect to be listened to, let alone understood. They withhold their trust.

As long as adults insist that adolescence is a problem that needs to be solved, they will not listen to what young people have to say. For adults it can be a matter of overcoming the obstacles they encountered on the way to adulthood. Since adults have 'been there' themselves – even though they might have no connection with the feelings of their own teenage years – they can assume they have everything to teach and nothing to learn. This attitude can put young people off, as they further withdraw from communication with adults. They might still want to be listened to, but they do not want to be told what to do from an assumed position of adult superiority. Often they can feel adrift, knowing that they do not want to be like their mothers and fathers, but realising that they have no models of how they want to be.

If we insist upon defining men as the problem, which in some ways was a shared assumption of 1970s' feminism, then we tend to think that if only men could be made to surrender their power and change – a process which Connell's vision tends to identify – then gender equality could be restored. For years we have recognised that this view allows no space for children. Yet in other ways it does not give space to young people either, for if men are considered the problem, then young men are a 'double' problem. The issue for much social work in the 1980s and 1990s was making young men aware of their sexism, and so of the power that they wielded in relation to young women. This fostered a moralism which makes it difficult for young men to value their relationships with each other, and so to learn how to be supportive, open and loving in their peer relationships.

There are negative aspects of men's relationships with each other, especially in urban gangs, but solidarity and support also need to be acknowledged and valued. These can become spaces of resistance, and – as the work done on urban gangs in the suburbs of Gothenburg shows – they can also be resources of emotional support and recognition. But this involves breaking with a moralism that too easily demonises the bodies and pleasures of young men. If 'boys are bad' and young men's sexuality somehow affirmed as beyond their rational control, then at that very moment it is rejected in language. This makes it more difficult to recognise the difficult processes through which young men establish contact with their bodies and sexualities.[6]

friendships

If young men constantly feel that they have to prove their male identity then it is difficult for them to trust their friends enough to share their vulnerabilities. If they fear that whatever weakness they show will be ruthlessly exposed and used against them in the hierarchy that is being confirmed, they learn to police their words and regulate their bodies. Young men will thus find it difficult to reach out for support. We know that when there is a separation or divorce at home, young girls will more easily talk about it with their friends at school, while young men keep their silence. They might even refuse to talk about the matter if questioned, preferring a stoical silence which at least seems to affirm their masculinity at a moment it can feel so easily threatened.[7]

Women might attempt to deflect attention away from themselves and their own emotional difficulties by casting men as the problem: if only men would change, then women's lives would be fine. This remained a largely unspoken inheritance of second-wave feminism until women began to explore difficulties in their own relationships with women, with the awareness that this could not be understood as the fault of men. Some also began to explore women's violence in relationships, recognising that this could not always be explained as a consequence of their treatment by men. A more complex narrative often began to emerge, one which questioned the rationalism and moralism of much 1970s' feminism. Power remained a central concern, but it could no longer be theorised so crudely, as something that women always lacked. This was part of a developing recognition of women as active subjects, rather than as objects of male power. If power helped frame the analysis, it was not an end in itself.

This also relates to ways we conceive power in the relation between adults and young people. Too often we assume that if only young people would change, then adults could live an easier life. This can be to accept, as Gloria Careaga observes, adulthood as some kind of stable ideal that exists beyond question. But what is this stability and does it not often reflect a withdrawing from the idealism and questioning of youth? Adults may feel disturbed by the questions of youth, because it reminds us of our own aspirations and dreams, some of which we have given up with the passage of time. There is an intensity in the emotional relationships of young people that can recall the intensities of our own teenage love. This opens up the possibility of learning from young people, as we engage in more open dialogue in which we recognise that, as adults, we do not have the answers. We might, for example, have our own questions about substance abuse, but we feel uneasy when young people challenge our use of alcohol, saying that it is a drug like any other. This is a questioning that can disturb adult equilibrium, but one that we can learn from. We can be led to question the direction that our own lives have taken. Many teenagers feel they have little to learn when they see their parents slumped in front of the television, living 'dead lives' as they see it.

As we slowly learn not to think of homosexualities in terms of a dominant heterosexual culture, so we must be careful not to think adolescence from the point of view of adulthood. In considering it as a phase of life that young people will eventually 'get over', we reveal the moralistic and patronising framework that informs so many of our conceptions. Adolescence is a period in which options remains open and life is explored. This can provoke risky behaviour, especially as a means of proving male identities, but it can also affirm the independence of young women. It is a time when young people explore what they desire and need for themselves, and this can only be discovered through experience. They might listen to what their parents have to say, but need to discover in their own bodies what they desire.

As young people explore their own bodies, they do so in a climate of risk, partly produced by AIDS. This is a difficult sexual world in which to explore bodily desire. Increasingly in Latin America, for example, young people are turning towards their friends for first sexual experiences, rather than going to prostitutes as was the tradition. They still have to deal with the unspoken tensions between more liberal urban cultures that are still decidedly homophobic and the shamed bodies and sexualities they inherit unconsciously within Catholic culture. This is why it is so important to be able to rethink bodies, pleasure and desires within cultures where these have been traditionally identified with the 'sins of the flesh'. Such tensions also need to be illuminated within the discourse of power.

Given the social distance that exists between classes, especially in Latin America, it can be difficult to question a discourse of political radicalism that thinks of power in relation to gender without having to rethink the rationalism that has informed so much Marxist thinking. Rather than engage critically with a Marxist tradition that has tended to deny the personal and the emotional, there is an obvious appeal in a structural analysis of genders in relation to power and its vision of hegemonic masculinities. Though Connell's work has helped us reflect upon relationships of power between diverse masculinities, it lacks the means to think productively about bodies, pleasures and emotional life beyond simply positioning them within a larger structural framework. It does not help us think the processes through which men can learn to establish more meaningful connection with their bodies, so breaking with the disciplines of docile bodies that cannot feel pleasure, contact and love.

I I

risk, fears, race and belonging

risks

Young men can feel that they have little to learn from the experience of adults; instead, they define themselves in opposition to the adult world. Needing to prove they are no longer children, they can feel hostile to the world that adults have created. They can feel they have to show their independence by taking risks that affirm their masculinity, constantly testing themselves against their environment. They need to prove themselves both in their own eyes and in the eyes of their peer group. In Britain this can be a matter of proving that you 'aren't chicken', that you can endure risks and that you will not concede in the face of danger. So young men are often no strangers to risk. They might subsequently look back to their teenage years and wonder how they could have taken such risks with themselves, but conclude that this is part of a process of 'growing up'.

In communities that are racially divided this can involve, in post-9/11 Britain, taking action against those who have suddenly become suspect as Muslims because of the way they look. The attacks on the Twin Towers in New York have somehow rendered invisible the suffering of so many in the world. It is the fear and suffering of those in New York that have to be revenged. In Britain – a target because of the close relationship between Bush and Blair in the declared 'war on terror' – the fear is often projected onto others. Young racist white men may feel that they have to defend 'their communities' against the imagined threats of others who have been newly 'racialised' as Muslims. These threats intensified in the wake of the London bombings of 7 July 2005.[1]

Young men were involved on both sides in the racial disturbances that took place in Oldham, Bradford and Burnley. Young people who had known each other in school found themselves on different sides of the racialised dividing line. If there is a danger that younger generations are growing up in more segregated communities in which they are increasingly being schooled separately, this did not apply to those who took part in the urban disturbances of the summer of 2000. After 9/11 there were new sources of conflict, as young Muslims became positioned differently within racialised discourses as potentially linked to terrorism. They became suspects because of the way they looked, whatever their beliefs happened to be. If they dressed more traditionally then they could more easily be identified.[2]

Young people could find themselves marked, even if they objected that they were falsely identified as Muslims. Yet this is not the main issue, as an older generation learnt in the 1970s when they were called 'Pakis'. When a young Sikh man declared 'I am not a Paki', this was largely beside the point within these racialised designations. All were equally implicated and disdained, whatever they might seek to disavow. In the eyes of the young racist, these differences did not exist. In the brutal world of the post-9/11 'war against terror', people are suspect because of the way they look. Sometimes it barely matters whether someone is a Muslim or not, as this has ceased to exist as a purely religious designation. The fact that you look different means that you can have 'dangerous ideas'. You become defined as a potential threat, and the social world is full of new risks and dangers that were not there before.

As young people who might previously have identified themselves as Pakistanis increasingly identify themselves as 'Muslims', a transnational identity, we are forced to recognise the fluidity of postmodern identities. A younger generation born in Britain might think of Pakistan as the country their parents came from. Although they have many relations still living there, they do not feel they belong there. Having grown up in London or in Birmingham, they feel little connection with their parents' home country. This might make it easier for them to identify themselves as Muslims, even though they are well aware this can cover a range of identities and beliefs. It does not help to think of this as a religious, as opposed to a racial or ethnic, identification, since these distinctions are not easily made. If we find ourselves thinking more generally about 'racialisations', this is partly because this term has been used to designate how people can be treated as 'less than human', and so their experience devalued, because of their 'racial' or 'ethnic' differences.

identities

Within the militarised definitions of the post-9/11 world, there are new risks and uncertainties that shape young lives. This can affect the ways young people think and feel about themselves. They might sense that identities they could have assumed with ease have now become threatening. The boundaries of identity have changed, and young people can feel a need to identify themselves in new ways.

This marks a generational shift, in that an older generation was more able to identify itself through a collective racial consciousness. The notion that 'Black is beautiful', which had such a powerful influence on a particular generation, no longer has the same currency, at least in Britain. 'Black' was defined politically in the 1970s in ways that crossed the boundaries between Afro-Caribbean and Asian identities. A generation learnt to revalue identities that for long had been shamed. They learnt to feel pride in histories and identities that had been denigrated. But as mass-media images and new technologies became more powerful instruments in shaping identities this became more difficult to sustain. Asian communities felt a need to identify themselves separately, in order to be able to name their own histories, cultures and traditions. Young people whose families had migrated to Britain felt a need to define themselves in contrast to their parents. Sometimes they identified themselves with the British cultures they discovered in school. If they lived relatively isolated from Asian or Afro-Caribbean communities, it was easier for them to define themselves in relation to prevailing white cultures. Sometimes this shifted, if their families moved closer to ethnic communities where they were exposed to new musical influences, for instance. Young people might develop multiple identities, defining themselves differently according to whom they were with.

In Britain a much more complex ethnic picture has emerged in the wake of globalisation, with mass economic migration resulting in the movement of large numbers of people across national borders. Rather than being linked together by the old histories of empire, many are fleeing war and ethnic conflict in order to find places of refuge where they can support their families. Children arrive in the country with very little preparation. If they have not been put in detention centres they find themselves in schools where they get on as best they can with the other children, often learning English without knowing how long they will be in the country. Although they are aware of the costs and risks their families have taken in reaching Britain, and know that things were much worse where they came from, they often feel unwelcome, and have to deal with their feelings of cultural isolation and loneliness very much on their own. It can be difficult to have a sense of belonging, and to relate to the complex race relations in Britain.[3]

When young teenagers ask their teacher, 'what is the colour of God?', they are showing a willingness to ask questions for themselves. They want to make sure that this is a world they want to belong to. They demand that adults come clean about their own conceptions, and so also make spaces for difference. The new Home Office citizenship rules – according to which immigrants can 'belong' only if they are prepared to learn the prevailing rules of a white dominant culture, speak English and 'learn the manners' which would allow them to 'fit in' – are speaking the language of integration. But it is a mistake to think that this marks a return to the politics of assimilation that defined race relations in the 1950s. If things are bad for migrants and asylum seekers under New Labour, they are not the same as they used to be. The terms of belonging have shifted within a vision of multicultural Britain.

If New Labour felt threatened by the Parekh report, sponsored by the Runnymede Trust, it was because it could not deal with its questioning of Britishness, which highlighted the historical connection, through traditions of empire, between being British and being white. The report sought to disarticulate the connection between race and nation, so that people could begin to explore different relations between states and nations. But at some level this was at odds with the ways that Britishness was already being redefined, especially in relation to an Afro-Caribbean community that felt a connection between Englishness and whiteness. They sought to image 'British' as a more complex identity that was open to invention by diverse ethnic and religious groups. But this definition also tended to exclude refugees and asylum seekers.[4]

belonging

Reflecting back to my own teenage years in London in the 1950s, we very much wanted to belong, to become English even if this meant rendering our Jewishness invisible. We were ready to be Jewish at home and within the religious community, whilst being English or British – these terms had not separated so clearly then – at school and within the wider community. You felt uneasy about being too visible, and learned to hold back any reference to Jewishness, especially if you were with new people. This 'passing' produced its own anxieties, but it was an option that people of colour do not have. They cannot attempt to pass, only to make their racial or ethnic background incidental. They do their best to present an image of themselves in public, even if in their private emotional lives they might feel quite different.

A young woman with a mixed-race background might have grown up to identify with her white mother and not really see herself as black, especially if her father has not been around. She might feel 'different', but not really be able to name its source. But in her teenage years she might need to define herself differently, and blame her mother for not encouraging her to recognise her black heritage. She might wish to explore her Afro-Caribbean background and seek out her father, not because she wants a relationship with him but because she wants to have more of a sense of her own background.

Sometimes a young woman or man might need to explore the local black club scene, in order to immerse themselves within a culture from which they would otherwise feel estranged. This can be a self-exploration that is at the same time a cultural exploration, in which a young person tests their limits. In this context they might explore their identity through drugs or alcohol, but these need to be understood as expressions of different needs. Rather than focus upon the substance use, as if the issue were how to curb and control these 'acting out' behaviours, we need to recognise how the existential questions of love, death and identity are central to teenage experience. Since adults often remain unresolved about these issues, they hesitate to remember how much of their own teenage years were taken up with them. Adults' refusal to listen to their teenage children about these concerns helps to produce its own separations and distance. Rather than listen to what young people have to say, adults can dismiss questions about life and death, pain and sexuality. The result is that young people refuse to risk themselves with their parents and seek refuge in their peer relations.

Increasingly young people refuse the attempts at racial monitoring that an older generation valued as a necessary step on the way to racial equality. Often they do not want to give the single account of themselves that seems to be demanded. They can resent being asked to give this account, and feel wary about how it might be used, often experiencing it as an infringement of their privacy and personal liberty. Aware of their complex identities, they want to be able to choose when and how they give an account of themselves, reserving the right to give a different narrative depending on whom they are talking to.

Young people do not want to be fixed by the classification, and feel they are being controlled in some way through exercises in disciplinary rule. They sense an authoritarian streak in New Labour's assurance that the classification is 'for their own good', so that services can be more equitably distributed. They can feel as if they are not being listened to, and their freedom not respected. We find a similar unease with young people when they are asked to classify themselves in relation to sexualities. They might feel their freedom threatened by attempts to pin down their identities, knowing that on different days they might give a different response to questions on their sexual orientation. They insist upon the freedom to explore, and do not want to be patronised by being told that experimentation is only a temporary position before adult rational choices are made. They can insist that their sexuality is for them to explore themselves, and of no concern to government.

Ulrich Beck has attempted to define this new individualism, which is different from a liberal individualism focused on the satisfaction of individual desires. Young people are often very much concerned about the sufferings in the world around them, but do not trust traditional politics either to define these issues or to do much about them.[5]

individualisms

Young people explore different ways of thinking their relation between individual and collective identities. These explorations are facilitated by new technologies which allow for new forms of contact and communication. The virtual space of the Internet enables young people to explore their identities in a way that their parents were unable to do. They are able to 'try out' different identities on others, and to recognise aspects of themselves they might otherwise have hidden. The Internet is a space in which young people experience their independence from parental traditions and cultures, and in which they more easily 'pass' in relation to their own racial and ethnic identities. It can afford a sense of freedom from the everyday tensions of being different within a dominant white British culture.

As a virtual space that allows for the exploration of new identities, the Internet can give people the strength and sense of self-worth to relate to others in 'real time' more easily. Particularly in urban cultures, young people are facing new everyday challenges in a changing world. Unlike their parents, they cannot take for granted the continuity of work, aware that they might take on many different kinds of job over their lifetime. This makes it harder for men to shape their identities in relation to work, and so requires a revisioning of masculinities so that men are not so exclusively identified as the breadwinner.

Richard Sennett and Jonathan Cobb looked at this identification within working-class communities in *The Hidden Injuries of Class*, an exploration of how self-worth and self-respect are sustained through work and trade unions. Sennett's more recent *The Corrosion of Character*, inspired by meeting the son of one of his earlier interviewees at Boston airport, looks at the breakdown of these collective identifications. Twenty-five years after the first interview the son was working for a computer company. Sennett wants to understand not only the differences between the worlds of work they inhabit, but also different identities and 'characters' that are fostered within these environments. There are losses but also gains that people might not be aware of themselves.[6] As Sennett reflects upon the son's experience within the changed work environment of the computer company, he realises that it embodies a different, more individualistic sense of self. There is no longer the sense of future that an older working-class generation could take for granted. A younger generation can only take their present for granted, uncertain as to what the future will bring. Often they work in small groups that come together for particular projects and last only as long as the project. This puts a premium on people being able to get on with others quickly, so that they form good working relations. In this context it can be a disadvantage to have strong beliefs and values, which might get in the way of the necessary compromises demanded by work. This involves a loss of character, in the sense that people have to be adaptable, holding their beliefs provisionally, always ready to satisfy the demands of the organisation. People must be able to deal with the break-up of the project group; it does not do to create lasting friendships. People must be able to move on to the next project without carrying a sense of loss for the people they used to work with.

In some ways, as Beck explores, these new individualisms reflect wider social processes. Within the universities one can sense a more instrumental attitude towards academic work. An academic degree becomes a means towards an end, a passport into the world of work. Compared to the 1970s, far fewer students have strongly held political and intellectual beliefs. Within a postmodern culture they seem to hold their beliefs in a more provisional way, learning to assume different positions rather than feeling committed to any particular view. This does not mean they are not committed to notions of gender and racial equality or not concerned with questions of ecology and animal rights. But they know that, even if they do their best to realise their beliefs in their everyday lives, they also have to be ready to compromise in order to 'get on' and 'make it' in the world.

Teenage boys often voice very radical beliefs or identify with extreme styles as ways of differentiating themselves from others, but do not want their beliefs and lifestyle to get in the way of their chosen career. Young people learn to present themselves, just as they do on the Internet. Differences can be valued in a way that contrasts with past generations, so that in later teenage years there is often a greater ease in relation to issues of race and sexuality. Especially within urban cultures there is more fluidity across boundaries of difference, with greater tolerance for different lifestyles. But at the same time class relations can find themselves inscribed differently, say in relation to 'townies', deemed threatening to middle-class youth styles. These patterns are shaped differently in different urban settings, especially in a global city such as London. Each neighbourhood has its own pattern of relationships and forms of territorialisation.

As young men and women move across cities to work or socialise, they will be very aware of the different spaces they move through. Sometimes they seek refuge in the sound worlds they create for themselves with their iPods, so that they feel supported by the familiarity of particular tracks as they move through space. This is an issue Michael Bull explores in *Sounds of the City*, though he is less sensitive to issues of race and gender than he could be, in the sense that they create particular insecurities and dangers that need to be addressed. But he illuminates well the ways young people withdraw into their own sound worlds to ward off the threats of the city. Young black women and men might still have one eye on possible dangers, since racism remains a present issue for them, even if it does not seem to show in the everyday ways they use their iPods.[7] As young people prepare particular sounds for themselves they are expressing themselves individually through the tracks they have selected. Sometimes, as Michael Bull shows, they choose to listen to the same tracks as they pass certain places. By identifying particular spaces with particular sounds they can take the 'sting' out of potentially hostile spaces. This does not mean that they are not aware of dangers, but that they have developed their own ways of 'moving through' spaces they cannot really identify with until they reach familiar parts of towns where they can relax. Once again, young people are shaping their relations with themselves, as well as with the social world, through new technologies. This is not a matter of withdrawal, as adults might describe it, but of learning to relate to the world in their own ways, knowing they will inherit a very different world and different opportunities and dangers to their parents.

I2

risk, self-harm, abuse and control

the first sex?

How are boys brought up to expect to be treated as the first sex? This question is framed differently within different cultures, and we have to learn how to trace the reproduction of practices of superiority whereby boys are left feeling that they should occupy the centre and that their sisters somehow come second. In some cultures this is marked through watching their mother walk several paces behind their father, or through seeing their father always being served first at the table and the family organised around his needs. Sometimes children recall the shift of atmosphere in the family when their father returns from work; it can be like walking on eggshells, the children fearful lest he take his frustrations out on them. They know his anger but have little sense of where it comes from. Some boys have had to watch their mothers being beaten up, fearful of intervening and guilty that they could not defend her against their father's wrath. Emotionally tied to their mother, they can feel anger towards their father but are powerless to express it.

Some boys grow up distant from their fathers and unaware of how they have absorbed into their selves their father's depression. Men may feel depressed but unable to locate the source of their emotions.

They may feel powerless to change, which produces its own feelings of self-rejection. Rejecting the path that was set out by their father and refusing to express their anger at their partner, they can turn this anger against themselves. In this way, depression can often be unknowingly passed down from father to son.[1]

Every year across the UK, 142,000 cases of self-harm are treated by accident and emergency departments. Reports suggest that the majority of self-harmers are adolescent, typically female. Films such as *Thirteen* and *Girl, Interrupted* reinforce the notion that self-harm is a rite of passage, like experimenting with drugs. But it is a problem that many adults also wrestle with. According to the National Self-Harm Nework, 'There is no evidence to show people "grow out of it".'

As Nick Johnstone has written,

> If you know the most common tell-tale signs of self-harm – lots of angry little red cuts, burn marks or healed white scars on arms and legs – then you realise just how prevalent it is.... I know this secret skin code because I went through it myself. Like most self-harmers, for me it was a typical morbid behavioural symptom of depression. It was never a failed attempt at suicide. I didn't want to die. I just wanted relief from depression and self-harm does exactly that: after cutting or burning, endorphins rush to the source of the pain, the accompanying euphoria yanks the self-harmer from the numb, alienating, catatonia of depression, instils a blissful disassociation.[2]

Johnstone recognised that self-harm was part of his everyday life from 18 to 22. He didn't grow out of self-harm but found less self-destructive ways to cope. He recognises that self-harm was essentially a coping mechanism. As he says,

> For five minutes, you feel OK again. Bizarre as it sounds, for that five-minute high, it's worth hurting yourself. As a self-harm expert told me: 'Depression is a downer, self harm is an upper. If you're battling depression, it's easy to get hooked on something that picks you up.'

Part of what Johnstone was dealing with was his experience as a man in a changing world where feminisms had challenged the supremacy of the first sex, so encouraging men to ask questions their fathers often refused to ask: 'Who am I?' 'What does it mean to be a man and have more equal gender relations?' 'If I am no longer first then who can I be?' Many young men absorb a fear of failure: 'If I am second, does this mean that I am a loser?' The fear of being a loser has wide currency within contemporary Western cultures.

voicing experience

As I read Johnstone's article I was struck by his advice to others: 'Find out *why* you're doing it.' Is the implicit suggestion that then you will be 'on the way' to finding your own voice? And that it would help to talk to others you feel you can trust, rather than silently remain with your shame? There can be a sense that this is what women might do, but men as the 'first sex' have the control to resist such temptations. As we explore new orders of gender relations we have to question the top-down terms of Connell's vision of hegemonic masculinities, which makes it difficult to explore the changing realities of men's lives, brought up within different regimes of gender power. It becomes difficult to listen to men and so appreciate that drug abuse, self-harm and eating disorders have gripped so many young men's lives.[3]

Within the dominant medical cultures, and often reflected in social research and policy, we tend to see the problem as the drug abuse or the self-harm, thinking that if these activities can be stopped, and methadone substituted for heroin, then a solution has been found. Social research does not easily listen to what men themselves have to say, or help to understand why it is that men are engaged in these practices. As Johnstone writes,

> You learn that self-harm is a short-term solution, a quick fix. You learn that there will always be days when the swipe of the razor blade across depressed flesh will seem like the easiest way out of an unbearable mood. But you don't give in. You sit it out and it passes. And, most important and difficult of all, you learn to like yourself.

We need to take seriously the notion of learning to like yourself. This is a difficulty that Connell's vision in *Masculinities* does not allow us to understand. Where his rationalism is concerned, as long as men are the first sex they have all the opportunities to live a good and fulfilled life. Even though it is not intentional, the theoretical framework works to silence the contradictions in the lived experience of men within diverse cultural settings. This is apparent in the ethnography of bikers we find in *Masculinities*, where there is a sense of horror at what these men believe and how they behave, but little sense of the genealogies that have shaped their experience and identities. We are left lacking the intellectual means through which to think relations between the psyche and the social in gendered terms. We need to learn *how* to listen to the voices of men caught within diverse cultural relations of power and dominance, and reflect upon the influences that have shaped them.

In Dean Whittington's work with heroin users at the Orexis project in Deptford, Southeast London, he recalls how therapy was deemed to be a no-go area for working-class men. They were interested not in the therapy but in getting hold of the drugs. As a counsellor he had to rethink his person-oriented psychotherapy, finding that it was important to speak as well as listen to these men, who often found silence difficult. He was constantly 'tested' by the men, who were initially wary and distrustful, since he was inevitably identified with the police and the probation service.[4]

The clinical literature was mainly concerned with harm reduction, and there was little work exploring why these people were using drugs, nor any sense that it might be helpful to 'find out why you're doing it, how you can stop, learn new ways to cope'. Nobody before had listened to what these men had to say about their own drug use and how it fitted into their lives. It took time for them to believe that anyone could be interested in what they had to say because nobody else had been, with the possible exception of their mothers. It seems to be a feature of white working-class culture in Deptford that men have a close and enduring relationship with their mothers. Some of these men were still living with their mother in their thirties, while they often had a distant relationship with their father. A surprisingly high proportion of users had experienced violence and humiliation at the hands of their fathers, and had witnessed their mothers being beaten up. They had also experienced humiliation at the hands of institutions such as schools and juvenile prisons.

These men's stories showed the centrality of the psychic pain they suffered, both in their families and at the hands of institutions that constantly misrecognised the traumatic histories they were living with. They often suffer from powerlessness in relation to their parents or institutions. They carry their psychic pain in silence, unable to show their vulnerability without threatening their male identities. Institutional power, rather than listening to boys, is used to humiliate them as it works its disciplines on their bodies and closes off their minds. Often refusing the alcohol that they witnessed causing havoc in their families, they turn to drugs. Drugs become a coping mechanism of choice as they learn to self-medicate themselves when unwelcome emotions and memories begin to emerge. Drugs allow a strategy of forgetting.

Listening can work as a form of validation, especially if young men feel that no one has ever really listened to them, or been interested in what they have to say about their lives. People have always told them what to do and how to think, but rarely listen to what they have to say. Often they suffered from scenarios of humiliation in their families and also at school, where they were left sitting with their emotional pain, unable to share fears and anxieties about what was going on at home. They would often be punished for showing a lack of attention or for acting out in class, with teachers having little interest in why they might be behaving in these ways. It was because they were 'bad' boys: what they needed was discipline and a firm hand. Often male teachers had learnt this discipline from military experience. They could be harsh and uncaring, and boys would grow up fearful of showing any signs of weakness that might be used to humiliate them.

There is a temptation to subsume under different theoretical categories the diverse voices we hear when interviewing men, so that the experiences of different men are read as instances of particular masculinities. This tendency is reinforced within research methodologies that assume theoretical frameworks need to be developed before they can be applied to data. This can make it difficult for researchers to think masculinities, because it is difficult to ask respondents what they feel about themselves, or how they relate to their masculinities, if researchers have not really explored these questions for themselves. This can help to explain some of the resistance that social researchers can feel when working with small groups of men in qualitative research, assuming that 'patterns' can only reveal themselves with large data sets. Researchers prefer to think of people as rational subjects who control their experience and have reasons for their actions.

Voice-related methodologies, as developed by Carol Gilligan and others, have sought to voice different levels of experience, so hoping to reveal what might otherwise remain silenced.[5] As researchers explore their own inherited masculinities and so acknowledge aspects of their experience they might otherwise take for granted, so respondents can also feel acknowledged. This involves ethnography as validation, which allows experiences that might otherwise be shamed to be brought to the surface and spoken. Research is a process that involves researchers exploring their own emotional investments in issues, before they can feel ready to interview others. Rather than treating the interview text as a conversation that needs to be analysed according to the protocols of conversation analysis, where the text provides the 'reality' that needs to be analysed, an ethnography as validation needs to listen for what is not spoken as much as for what is said. This shows the importance of establishing trust, especially when one is interviewing men who are uneasy about sharing themselves emotionally.

This shows research as a process that involves the researcher doing their own inner emotional work as they explore the genealogies of their own masculinities. Only when the researcher is clear about, for instance, how the alcohol abuse of a grandfather influenced his parents' relationship and echoed as an unspoken issue across generations, might he be ready to recognise the family dynamics of fear and humiliation at work. As you learn to listen to yourself you become more aware of different cultural histories.[6]

fear and control

Even though you are guided by a theoretical structure when interviewing, you can be surprised by the voices you hear, which can bring your ideas into question. As you probe and feel your way in interviews you can be surprised by the directions they take. At some moments you sense avoidance, but at others the interview can give permission to explore new areas that have long remained silenced. Sometimes it is only with hindsight, as you listen to the tape, that you develop a notion of what someone is trying to say. Often there is a tension between available language and what they are trying to express through it. They might be reaching for memories that have long been suppressed and that can feel difficult to voice, especially if they seem shaming. As a psychoanalytic practitioner prepares a space in which to explore emotions that might be culturally or morally unacceptable, so a social researcher might be suspending judgement in order to explain masculine behaviours. Though a man might reject any identification with a father they have rejected, you might detect certain similarities in relation to their masculinities. The effects of a father's violence might be lived out quite differently, but we might see certain patterns emerging across generations and within particular communities that share histories.

Where a father is somewhat distant from the family and a mother's attention switches to the newborn child, he might feel jealous of the flow of love and attention that is being directed towards the child. He might find it hard to accept that he is no longer at the centre of his partner's love and attention. He feels displaced, especially if she feels withdrawn sexually. This can be a difficult time for a father, who can become angry and abusive, feeling competitive with the new child and wanting revenge. These emotions can haunt the relationship between the father and his son, especially if he feels his son has replaced him in the mother's love. This is the inverse of Freud's Oedipal story, for it is about a father's jealousy of the son and his wish to destroy him. Men might also turn their anger against their wives, unable to control their emotions. A young man who has grown up in a family with these dynamics might carry unconscious fears about his own partner's pregnancy. He might want a child, but at the same time feel fearful of rejection and full of self-blame.[7]

Though some men might learn to turn their anger against themselves, through self-harming, it is often by controlling their partner that men affirm their position as 'the first sex'. As the 'man of the house' they feel entitled to be hard, and this means that their word should be obeyed. Often children learn that to question is already a sign of disobedience. Children who grow up in the kind of family that Dean Whittington was working with in Deptford do not expect to be listened to. Often they have little sense of what this could mean, which is partly why it can take them so long to believe that a counsellor is really interested in what they have to say about their lives. This is often a new experience for them, and they can grow to appreciate how they can use their time in counselling for themselves. For the first time they might allow their 'front' to slip, as they begin to share what it has been like for them growing up in their family. In interviews respondents are often anxious to provide the kind of script the researcher is looking for. They answer the questions that have been asked, but often researchers engaged with quality-of-life measures indicate how the most interesting conversations seem to fall outside the interview schedule. Often they are commented on separately and do not find their way into the findings.[8]

Social researchers often assume that it is only by working with large numbers of people that we can discern patterns in behaviour. This gives them the confidence to make judgements, which they cannot do when working with smaller numbers in a qualitative study. Yet this can create a false opposition. A researcher might want to draw upon intensive work in a qualitative study for a larger study. For example, the recognition that the heroin use of a particular group of white working-class men in Southeast London can be connected to a rejection of their alcoholic fathers' violence towards their mothers can lead to an exploration of this finding in other areas, where men do not have such a close relationships with their mothers. We might connect this to the fathers' feeling that their position is threatened by the arrival of children. Unconsciously they might carry memories from their own childhoods, recognising how their own fathers were displaced and fearing that the same might happen to them, and so might seek to affirm their control through violence.

threats and violence

Lisa Johnson of the Women's Aid helpline insists that 'It's a myth that domestic violence only happens on council estates, or among the unemployed, or that it's connected with alcohol. It happens in every class, every culture.'[9] She recognises that abusing men often tend to be suspicious of professionals caring for their partner while she is pregnant. 'They like to keep their partners isolated so they can keep the violence secret.' As she says, 'They feel threatened by her contact with midwives – its not uncommon for them to stop the woman from having any antenatal care at all, which puts her at risk of physical pregnancy complications as well as from the risk of his violence.'

Pregnancy is often a difficult time for men, but for some men it can be intolerable, especially if they feel that their status is about to change and their control is slipping away. As Joanna Moorhead writes,

> This man is angered by his partner's rounded, blooming state. He hates the way people ask her about her health all the time, loathes people telling her to take it easy, feels furious when he is questioned about how she is feeling. In public, of course, he is solicitous: in private, he is brutal. Instead of taking on extra burdens to spare her, he increases the pressure, ups the stress, insists she does more work, not less. And sometimes the abuse is not just psychological, it is physical, too. At a time when she most needs his protection, he turns on her, beats her up, kicks her swollen belly, punches her tender breasts.

She writes about Mary, whose partner would sit on her belly, saying he was trying to squeeze the baby out, after he had hit her.

> The violence got worse as the pregnancy wore on. He hated me being fat and, of course, I got fatter and fatter. ... I think it was worse when I was pregnant because he knew there was nowhere to go when I was eight months pregnant. He had me where he wanted me.

A survey carried out by the Royal College of Midwives among 700 of its members across the USA reinforces a study in the *British Journal of Obstetrics and Gynaecology* in March 2003 that found that one in six women, in a study of 500, had experienced domestic violence while they were pregnant. Some men can feel particularly threatened by the realisation that their partner is no longer going to be there exclusively for them. Often unable to express their own needs and vulnerability, men will focus their unconscious anger on their partner.

Moorhead recounts how Mel, whose ex-husband was eventually convicted of domestic violence, says that he could not stand the thought that she needed looking after.

I never remember him saying, 'Sit down and take the weight off your feet.' It was always, 'Get off your fucking fat arse.' He was always controlling, but he was much worse when I was pregnant – he couldn't bear the focus being on me. I was in the hospital at one stage, because I needed a blood transfusion, and said he had to sit down because he felt ill. He had all the nurses running around after him, he couldn't stand the idea that I was the centre of attention.

Given the disciplines he might have had to adapt to at work, his relationship becomes central in affirming his status as 'the first sex'. It is as if Adam could only exist as 'the first sex' if he knew that he had control over Eve because she was born of his flesh. He had 'given birth' to her and so could affirm a myth of masculine self-sufficiency that has haunted Western culture.

The fact that men are born of women is threatening to the vision of a singular patriarchal authority. Luce Irigaray explores how men, fearful that pregnancy is a threat to their power, refuse to acknowledge that they are also 'of woman born'.

Sex can also become an exercise of power during pregnancy, a way of securing a woman's body when this control is threatened. As Sandra Horley, chief executive of Refuge, recognises, when it comes to violence against pregnant women 'It's often the breasts and the abdominal area that the men go for when women are pregnant – they're the focus of their anger.'[10]

Over the last thirty years in the UK men have been encouraged to attend antenatal clinics with their partners, but this can make disclosure difficult, as it is harder for a woman to speak out. As Sue Macdonald of the Royal College of Midwives admits,

> Getting a woman on her own can be difficult. Abusing men try to control their partners even during antenatal appointments – we ask a question, they answer for them. But we do have strategies – we put notices about domestic violence in the women's toilets, for example – and we try to signal to a woman if we suspect they're at risk.[11]

This can involve asking every time a woman is seen whether she is being abused. Astrid Osborne, consultant midwife, says: 'In my experience, they don't tell you until the last trimester, by which time the violence has escalated. Typically, women don't disclose what's going on until they feel their life or the life of their baby is in danger."[12] As GP Dawn Harper has said, many doctors

> erroneously believed pregnancy might be some kind of respite for victims of domestic violence. What's becoming clear now is that injuries caused by this kind of violence could be one of the commonest complications of pregnancy, up there with pre-eclampsia and diabetes. We're obsessed with testing their wee and checking their blood, but we're blind to the biggest threat of all, which in many cases could be the man sitting right next to them.[13]

A problem with wide ramifications for the restructuring of health services – especially under a neoliberal ideology of service provision that sees professionals as essentially interchangeable – is that women tend only to open up to people they've grown to trust. Staff shortages mean that women often do not get the continuity of care provided by a one-to-one relationship with a trusted midwife. This might seem an impossible aspiration unless we think imaginatively about different forms of community health care in which pregnant women can feel supported. But it is vital for men to establish relationships of trust.

There is a danger of creating a fixed category of 'abusing men', rather than learning how pregnancy invokes unresolved emotional feelings in men. If we are to find new ways of conceptualising male violence we need to go beyond the assertion that violence is exclusively an expression of power. We need to understand the complex interrelations between power and emotions, social and psyche, 'embodied memories and life politics'.

If the first priority is the protection and safety of the woman, we also have to engage with men and their complex relationships with their masculinity and family history. We have to 'find out why they are doing it', and understand the difficulties they face in establishing a more open and self-accepting relationship with themselves. We have to understand the power of the myth of 'the first sex' and the way it continues to shape dominant masculinities, and to open up spaces in which men can learn to curb their violence and focus their energies in more positive ways. As Nick Johnstone recognises, 'most important and difficult of all, you learn to like yourself.'

13

young men, bodies, sexualities and health

gender equality

Gary Barker reminds us, in his introduction to a Population Council publication, that

> The population and family planning field began paying attention to 'male involvement' in the 1980s, primarily because men were often the decisionmakers regarding family size and contraception use. An inescapable lesson learned from two decades of fighting sexual violence and HIV, however, was that men are also frequently the decisionmakers about whether – and under what conditions – women and girls have sex.[1]

This shows how the lessons learned in one field can affect others. But we might feel suspicious of the rationalist language of 'decision-makers', since this shows the difficulties of integrating understandings to do with the relationships between power, desire, bodies and sexualities.

Barker goes on to remind us that, 'Gradually, program planners, international development organisations, and researchers came to understand that gender inequalities – in sexual relationships, domestic life, and in society more broadly – are a root cause of poor sexual and reproductive health outcomes among men and women.'

A concern with gender equality showed itself in Cairo in 1994 at the International Conference on Population and Development, which affirmed that men must be included in efforts to improve not only the reproductive health of women but also their social and legal status worldwide.[2] But questions remained about how men were to be included, especially as it remained unclear how we can also talk about the sexual and reproductive health of men, and whether it is helpful to think in terms of a discourse of rights. In different ways this reflected uncertainties about how we should think gender equality. Since it is women who suffer institutional and personal violence, and men so often feel entitled in their sense of male superiority, it seems right that the focus should be upon making men aware of their responsibilities for the oppression and subordination of women. Young men should commit themselves to gender equality.[3]

In September 1994, Eddie Madunagu, a nationally known and respected Nigerian journalist, scholar and political activist returned home to Calibar, in the south-eastern region of Nigeria. As Françoise Girard reports,[4] he had decided that it was time to 'get back to basics' in his progressive activism: educating, developing critical thinking and raising the consciousness of young people. Eddie had been greatly influenced by Ingrid Essien-Obot, a German feminist and Marxist who had taught at the University of Calibar until she was murdered in 1981. Eddie recalls that he walked in as his wife and fellow activist Bene was talking to Andrea Irvin of the International Women's Health Coalition (IWHC) about the Girls Power Initiative (GPI), which Bene had just set up. Eddie said, in a light-hearted manner: 'Don't you know that boys also need this kind of programme? Boys are not educated.' Thinking back on that comment. Madunagu explains that he felt concern for the GPI girls, who, with all their newly acquired knowledge, would still have to face 'uneducated' boys and their patriarchal families.[5]

Madunagu was also thinking of the boys' own development and growth. He explains:

> It is also necessary to let boys know that ultimately, men cannot win and cannot be truly happy and liberated as long as they hold down a section of the society in bondage.... They have to understand that their superiority and advantage are, ultimately, illusory.[6]

This does not mean that their superiority as boys does not rest upon power, but it a matter of how this power is perceived and understood. For there are certain visions of male power that somehow remain focused upon the sufferings and indignities suffered by women, as in traditional anti-sexist discourses. Learning to think of masculinities exclusively as relationships of power, we would see the task as deconstructing masculinities seen as the problem but no part of the solution. This is a 'gender perspective', but it tends to render invisible issues around men and masculinities. Young men are rarely encouraged to reflect upon their own experiences, since it is assumed that as the bearers of male power they cannot themselves have suffered.

This anti-sexist vision of a 'gender perspective' tends to be focused upon the experience of women in ways that can make it difficult to work with boys. Traditionally this has meant that 'anti-sexist' work with boys has been about making boys sensitive to the oppression and subordination of women within patriarchal cultures. This vision is reflected in an early document of the project initiated by Madunagu, Conscientizing Male Adolescents (CMA), in which he explains that

> Educating men on issues of specific concern and interest to women is an important, even critical, contribution to the universal struggle against the discrimination and injustices suffered by women and perpetrated mainly be men (or in the interest of men) both in private and public life.[7]

A number of programmes aimed at males focus most intensely on adolescent boys, rather than adult men. This is partly because across the globe there has been a radical break between generations, with young men growing up in a very different world to that of their fathers. As well as the new forms of communication engendered by the globalised media, they also face new risks, with the spread of HIV and sexually transmitted diseases. But it is also because boys are learning to be men during their teenage years, absorbing styles of interaction in intimate relationships that they are like to carry through their adult lives. In diverse cultural settings many boys learn to view girls and women as objects of their sexual pleasure, to use force to obtain sex, and to view sex as performance.

Where there is a strong gender demarcation – as for example in Thailand, where traditionally there is greater focus upon gender differences than upon sexualities – young men are most anxious to affirm their masculinity. Young gay men in Thailand might be told that they are feminine (*kathoie*), and even that they have 'a woman's mind' in a male body. In a culture like this, which emphasises 'appropriate' behaviours regardless of what people might be feeling, and which frames the distinction between public and private spheres in a quite different way to the West, it can be difficult to break boys' reticence when talking about sexuality.[8]

working with young men

In a 1999 review conducted for the World Health Organisation (WHO) of programmes that had been designed to engage young men, Barker described a wide range of activities, including, for example, offering boys-only hours at health centres, connecting boys with mentors who are positive role models, providing vocational training and conducting sexual health outreach. As Barker describes it,

> Broadly speaking, programmatic experiences are generating a series of priorities: identifying boy's own rationale for change; engaging relatively few young men intensively in small groups over an extended period; tapping into the positive power of male peer groups to encourage gender equity; addressing homophobia; planning high-energy activities that involve multiple themes; working with boys on self-care and prevention; and creating settings where young men can talk openly about their doubts and question issues that are often seen as unquestionable (such as what it means to be a man).[9]

These lessons are helpful because they show how programmes have been encouraged to go beyond the traditional anti-sexist framing of gender equality to explore with young men their tensions and inner feelings in relation to the patriarchal masculinities they might have witnessed in their fathers. They might feel uneasy about the ways their father consistently puts their mother down, but unable to verbalise their frustration and unease. They might see their father constantly giving instructions in the family on the assumption that he knows what is best for them, without having to listen to what they have to say themselves. They might have learnt that this is what is expected of them as men, having learnt that girls and women cannot be reasoned with. In Thailand this is reflected in the image of woman as the hind legs of an elephant, who can only follow the lead that is provided them. Another metaphor has it is that men are rice that can grow anywhere, but women are rice that can only grow where they are placed.

As Madunagu understood it, the principal objective of the CMA programme would be to engage adolescent males in ongoing discussion groups to increase their awareness of gender-based oppression. A second and equally important objective would be to foster participants' skills in critical thinking and analysis, teaching them, in Madunagu's words, 'to question information and reality before bowing before them'. But, as Girard reported it,

> early experience, however, showed that the boys were also concerned about subjects that touched them personally, such as inequality in the family, violence against women and girls, and relationships between boys and girls. Madunagu concluded that boys could be reached more effectively by integrating psychosocial approaches into the material, as Irvin had suggested in their initial discussions.[10]

What is at issue here is not well framed in terms of 'integrating psychosocial approaches', since what is being hinted at is a different vision of gender equality and a different practice of working with young men. This involves another way of questioning the framework provided by Connell, in *Gender and Power* and in *Masculinities*, which tends to present masculinities exclusively as relationships of power. This does not mean that Connell makes no space for exploring men's emotions and feelings, but the space that he allows is within his general distinction between the 'therapeutic' and the 'political'. In some ways it echoes the framework of an anti-sexist politics that allows space for emotions only within a process of 'consciousness-raising' intended to bring people to an awareness of structural relations of power.

In Connell's work there is an implicit movement from emotions to power in which we are still trapped within a zero-sum conception of power. At least this view of gender and power allows Connell to sustain a grasp of the institutional power that men take for granted, and so resist Foucault's move towards discourse, in which 'femininity' and 'masculinity' are recognised as the effects of particular discourses.[11] Within a Foucauldian tradition it has been difficult to engage with the relations between gender and power, since power itself becomes an effect of discourse. If this has helped question notions of power as exclusively repressive, thus helping us to appreciate the ways in which power is also productive and even inescapable within social life, it has produced dualities that simplify the complexities of gender relations. But with Connell's structural analysis, which remains so appealing because of its important attention to institutional and structural violence, there is little understanding of the dynamics of emotion, communication and power, and so of the need for young people to learn to communicate more equally in their relationships, as part of a process of transforming structural relations of power and institutional violence.

We need to understand why a programme like the CMA – which understandably gives much attention to violence because it is pervasive in Nigerian society – still finds it difficult to give full emphasis to 'traditional' sexual-health topics like condoms, contraception and STDs/HIV. Girard reports that boys in the programme 'were not shy about using accurate terminology, for example, penis, erection, sexual desire, and sexual relations. The language of moralising and shame were absent.... The atmosphere and tone were positive and respectful, and the majority of boys participated.' She also witnessed a discussion that focused on defining rape. As she recalls,

> A debate ensued about whether it is better to rape than to masturbate. The group concluded that juxtaposing masturbation and rape in this way is inappropriate, and that rape is always unacceptable. Some boys said they needed more information about masturbation. The next topic was whether a woman can rape a man – a subject of evident fascination! The boys agreed ultimately that rape of men by women is not a significant social problem in Nigeria.
>   The boys then discussed why rape occurs by exploring the power relations between men and women and the belief that men should be dominant and in control. The session ended with boys brainstorm-

ing about what they can do as activists to address rape. They decided they can inform other men and boys about what rape is; create awareness that rape is violence; counsel women and girls on rape prevention and how to deal with it; escort a girl or women who is raped to the police or the hospital; intervene in cases of violence; speak up against harassment of girls; and change Nigerian laws to recognise marital rape as rape.[12]

Girard realised that not all the boys were at the same level of awareness, but 'nonetheless, the climate of dialogue allowed for frank expression'. Soon after the programme was established, Madunagu and his staff became aware that some boys needed in-depth counselling. Some had personal problems, whereas others wanted to discuss their goals and aspirations, or to ask more questions about issues generated in group meetings.

Staff members told Girard that many boys still blame rape victims, or think that girls and women, in most circumstances, are just 'there for the taking'. Therefore they have problems understanding and condemning marital rape and even incest: 'The underlying assumption is that women are somehow to be blamed for uncontrolled male sexual desire and that "women force men to have sex."'[13] Girard also recognised that topics such as sexually transmitted infections, sexual experiences and negotiation of contraception still carry a measure of taboo among some of the field officers, who hesitate to discuss sexuality and sexual health in depth. She became aware that speaking out against such commonly accepted behaviours as female genital cutting or domestic violence has placed some boys and CMA staff in complicated and conflictual situations. The project hopes to strengthen the counselling service better to support boys who face repercussions for their outspokenness.

The boys that Girard interviewed had not reflected explicitly on their own masculinity and its pitfalls from a personal or societal point of view. In some way this might link to difficulties in opening up issues around bodies, sex and sexuality. She reports that

> They were not able to say much about what pressures they experience as boys per se, what they didn't like about being boys, or how they might suffer at the hands of other boys and men. Paul Away reported that, in some discussions he had led, boys have remarked

upon some of the ways in which the norms of masculinity affect them adversely. They mention, for example, that men have to go to war and men suffer political assassinations. But he admits their analysis is not fully developed, because 'boys are not ready to state that being boys causes them problems.'[14]

Possibly this would be to expose a vulnerability that could be threatening to their male identity.

Staff also reported that boys from devout families often have problems reconciling what they have been told in their religious practice with the idea of gender equality. Religious teachings that assert that the man is the head of the family because this is what the Bible says support prevailing social norms, and therefore seem incontrovertibly 'true' to many of the boys. Many of the boys' initial views on sexuality, masturbation, abstinence and abortion are heavily influenced by religious teachings. But CMA insists on pluralism as the guiding principle, and the programme content is entirely secular. Arguments based on religious texts are not admissible in discussions. Some students who stay on the programme are left struggling with the dissonance. Igwe Dermot explained that some boys wish they could discuss with their parents what they learn at CMA, but feel they cannot raise certain issues, notably sexuality, because of their parents' religious beliefs. In one of the counselling case studies presented,

> Benjamin wants to remain totally abstinent until marriage because of his religious beliefs, but is not sure he can manage it. The counsellor probes to find out what Benjamin means by total abstinence. They discuss various ways of expressing love and sexual feeling without full intercourse. Although Benjamin says he cannot consider masturbation because of his religion, he feels that he can consider other methods for 'outercourse'.

bodies and sexual desire

During Françoise Girard's visit to the CMA project, several boys she interviewed said they had changed a great deal. They explained that before their participation in CMA they would have been too shy to talk to her. As she explains, 'Their ability to challenge adults or speak up in their presence goes against deeply held social norms

– even if the young people speaking are male.' Since there is also reverence for knowledge in Nigeria boys are often admired and tend to become popular. The boys understand that their past behaviour of harassing and touching girls was a violation of a girl's rights. As Kingsley, 18, explains:

> My friends who are not in CMA ... they see a girl passing, they'll whisper embarrassing things, touching the girl, saying some things that are not pleasant to the girl. Already some of us that have been in CMA have been told not to do this, because it will make girls embarrassed.... I've stopped all this whispering, standing on the road, touching girls anyhow.... I abstain from those things now.

Felix explains that,

> Before I did not know that women have a right to express their opinion in the family. Now I know it. I thought that only women should wake up early in the morning to work, and that men can sleep. Now, I wake up early before my sister, sweep the floor and help out. Sweeping the floor is not just the work of women.... My mother tried to stop it, but I explained to her. Now she is proud of it.

Moses explains the traditional situation in families in relation to gender relations of authority, recognising its wider implications:

> The fact that Nigeria is patriarchal is not helping the development of the country. Parents tell a girl to get married; they think she is not worth educating. They spend a lot of money educating a boy, but not every boy becomes something. Women are not supposed to be heard. If a woman talks she is told to sit down.[15]

A few boys in the programme still had mixed feelings about women, violence and sex. They still tended to think of women and girls as 'temptresses', showing the influence of religious language in shaping cultural expectations. This means we need an awareness of religious traditions in order to understand where the boys are coming from, and the influences they have to deal with. Rather than seeing these religious conceptions are 'irrational', as bound to give way to the progress of reason, science and modernity, we need to rethink the Enlightenment distinction between the religious and the secular, faith and reason. This can be particularly relevant when it comes to education around reproductive and sexual health. It might be part of breaking the silence around the issues of bodies, sex and desire that young men often feel a need to know more about. Often they cannot express what they are feeling so they search for sources of knowledge that they can trust.

All the boys talked to Françoise Girard about unwanted pregnancy and the need to refrain from sex if they were not ready for it. As Emeka explains, the fact that it is possible to have friendships with girls without necessarily being sexual is not a widely held belief among young men in Nigeria: 'We discuss these issues in CMA, about girlfriends and boyfriends. Many have sex, but since they don't know anything, the girls get pregnant.... They can't be friends with a girl without sex. Don't have sex if you're not ready.' At the same time most of the respondents reflected a great deal on love and marriage. Several said they wanted a very different relationship from that of their father and mother. They expressed particular concern about early marriage and polygamy. Felix commented: 'I would not have more than one wife, because of the problems my dad is facing now. He is regretting he married more than one wife. Children of different marriages are not treated equally.'

Some of the boys seem to recognise the importance of feeling and understanding within a relationship, something they might feel is absent in their parents' relationship but they are seeking for themselves. This can mark a significant shift across generations. As Victor, a Special Group member, says:

> I'll be a different husband [from what my father is]. I won't just pick any woman! There must be courtship. We must reach certain agreements, must understand each other and agree on how our lives will. I must understand my wife, know her feelings, and we must agree on almost everything. I'll be by my wife. I'll share domestic chores, support her outside the house, give her freedom, I won't tie her down, I'll allow her to explore her own world. I'm not everything that matters.

Even if not many of the boys share this view, at least these ideals are circulating within the community.

Some boys feel clearly that they would want a relationship with their children that is different to the one they have with their father. This attitude, if it became widespread, could make a difference to young men taking more responsibility over contraception. It could indicate a shift in their relationship with their desires, bodies and sexualities. As Harry, a member of the CMA vanguard, explains:

> For example, now if one day I marry a woman and decide to divorce that woman, and this woman has a child from me. What'll I do? I'll make sure that I'll take care of that baby and provide a comfortable life for the mother also.... I'll make sure that I'll end the relationship in a way that even the woman would not be hurt.
>
> My father did not think this way. He would send the woman and the baby away and would not want to know anything about it. That's basically what he did with his first wife and children [Harry's stepbrothers and stepsisters]. The reason I'll be different is because of CMA.[16]

That some of the changes have been sustained and that it is not a matter of telling researchers what the boys think they would want to hear is supported by Grace, a university student. She says:

> I know several CMA boys, including one of my neighbours. Before, they used to have many girlfriends, say that you can use the weaker sex ... make bad comments when a girl passed by. Now they stick to one girlfriend and don't bring her down. They don't harass girls anymore.

Veronica, a secondary-school student, confirms this through her own experience:

> I know a boy from CMA in school. He is not behaving as the other boys do. He can speak in public. He can tell boys how to avoid sexually transmitted diseases, HIV and AIDS.... I've seen him do that. Before CMA, he behaved as someone ignorant.... He could not talk in public, was very shy, but he harassed girls.

This also reflects wider changes, as one teacher at the Christian Commerial Secondary School in Uyo confirmed. Before the CMA programme, she said, boys harassed girls so much that girls would refuse to sit in the school library. Now he sees boys and girls sitting quietly together, and he shakes his head in amazement. When asked how working with only thirty boys a year could make such a difference in a large school, he replied that the CMA boys are the brightest, and that many of them are leaders. They set the tone. The impact of CMA teachers as role models in school is also mentioned. Harassment of female students by male teachers is common in Nigerian schools. As Girard reports it, 'Boys (and girls) are intrigued by these teachers who practise what they preach. Many boys seek them out as mentors and advisers.'

It appears that the influence of the CMA boys on their peers is gradually changing prevailing norms of social behaviour at some schools. One teacher in Calibar reported that a small group of bullies in his school had harassed girls and other boys constantly. One of them, a natural leader, joined CMA, and has since stopped harassing others. His fellow bullies, who are not in CMA, do not seem to understand his new ideas, but they can see that he and a few others are changing their behaviour and taking their studies more seriously. As Girard reports it, 'Peer pressure has gradually encouraged them to stop harassing others, even if they do not necessarily understand why.'

Madunagu is aware that educating boys and young men about sexism and fostering critical thinking skills can appear threatening to some, but he recognises the value of what CMA has been doing within the larger Nigerian community. As he explains it,

> Obviously, oppression and power are very central to what we are talking about in CMA. In this country, many believe that you are either oppressed or oppressor.... You are standing on that person, or that person stands on you.... But to stand side by side, we don't know that.[17]

young men's sexual and reproductive health

research

Talking to Jaray, a young Thai student engaged in a research project on Thai gay identities, I asked him about men's sexual and reproductive rights. He looked puzzled for a moment and said that he thought that sexual and reproductive rights were to do with women. Contraception, like pregnancy and birth, was generally left to women. Then he thought for a moment and said he could recognise the importance of talking about young men's sexual and reproductive rights, especially if it meant that young men could assert a right to their own sexualities and pleasures. Initially he had thought the language of rights might not be necessary, because – possibly because of the more tolerant attitudes of Buddhism – there were no legal restrictions on homosexuality. But he realised that there was a silence, and that this was part of a more general cultural silence around sex and sexuality. These were not issues that people could speak about, at least not from Jaray's class background. We discussed the fact that there was no word for 'gender' in Thai, and that a term for 'gay' had only recently been introduced.[1] We talked about different attitudes to masturbation, which is taboo in China for instance, because of the loss of vital male energy supposedly involved. He said that Thai culture was different, and that he had been encouraged by his sex education to talk positively about masturbation. He observed that the culture was changing rapidly, and that his 15-year-old younger brother could talk openly about sexuality at the dinner table in a way that would have embarrassed his own peers.

Research has to be grounded in an awareness of changing sexual cultures and of the difficulty of generalising across cultures with diverse religious and spiritual traditions. What might work in rural Mexico needs to be tested in pilot projects in India with an awareness of the diversity of cultures of masculinity. We have to know the pressures on particular groups of young men, and appreciate how young men can experience themselves as relatively powerless, rather than as the bearers of power in relation to women and gay men. Their feeling that emotions are a sign of weakness can lock them into an isolation that makes it difficult for them to own up to the ignorance they can feel in relation to their own bodies. Having learnt to treat their bodies as instruments of power, they can take out their frustrations on young women whom they might otherwise want to feel close to. As a young girl in a Xalapa high-school workshop organised by Salud y Genero commented, 'We know boys want to get near to us, but why should they do it by kicking?' A young man in Queretaro said: 'We hit as a way of not caressing. How should we get close to each other?' It is because young men often feel they 'should know' how 'to get close' that they cannot admit otherwise without 'losing face' in front of their peers.[2] They want to talk about their emotions, and research shows that young men will often speak freely if they are feel they are being listened to without judgement. As soon as they feel their male identity is being threatened they withdraw.

Young men often look to their intimate relations to speak more openly about themselves. But if within a globalised economy they are without the job that has traditionally been able to sustain notions of maculinity, they are left with their body as the site within which to affirm their male identity. This can sometimes make it harder to reach young men, at least initially. However, they want to know more about their own bodies, and about the bodies of men and women, because they want relationships. They know that young women are no longer prepared to live with the double standards of their parents' generation. Girls know better: they do not want to be ordered around. If they are going to be faithful, research in rural Mexico shows they demand fidelity of their partners.[3]

Boys can feel threatened by the relative autonomy of young women. They live with the question: 'How should we get close to each other?' They want to caress but they find themselves hitting. They know that this is wrong, and often they feel frustrated with themselves. Living in a world of globalised media and mass economic migration they are aware of new sources of knowledge and new kinds of relationship. A radical break exists between generations as the young reject their parents' emotional world, and there is often a thirst for knowledge.

action

Women frequently complain that their men refuse to listen to them. A young man might see his father regarding 'his' women – wife, mother, sister – as inferior because they are female, and may have experienced violence at his hands. If such young men want something different for themselves, they are open to change. If they are able to feel a need to be caressed, they might learn that hitting will only lead to rejection. They want to learn different ways of being, but they also do not want to 'lose face' with their peers. This has implications for the spaces in which young men can be reached. It is a matter not simply of getting a health message across, if the concern is with effective changes in behaviour, but of developing appropriate forms of sex education that also relate to emotions, desires and relationships.

Interventions can be developed through community projects, such as Coriac in Mexico City, where the work related to violence can be a useful background to work more specifically addressing young men's sexual and reproductive rights.[4] We should not assume that activists are best able to research their own projects. However, researchers who specialise in evaluation are often trapped within quantitative methodologies. If projects are to be effectively generalised, or are to serve as a basis for materials that can be used within school settings, it is essential that qualitative data are not marginalized. Often the skilled trainers in community projects are the best people to train sympathetic teachers, who can then pilot the projects within the school system, working alongside researchers who recognise the value of the practice-related theoretical work often developed in close relationship with NGOs. A cohort of such researchers who could communicate across diverse national and cultural settings would be a valuable development.

Sometimes high-profile figures, such as sporting icons, can help open up available masculinities. For instance, David Beckham has been a crucial role model for young men in challenging stereotypes of sexuality and fathering. We need to examine the images circulating in the mass media and appreciate the ways new technologies are shaping young male identities and expecations of intimate relationships, as well as creating new spaces of communication.

Although it is important to create connections with research institutions, in order to encourage work in national settings, it is necessary to interrogate prevailing research cultures. Even though they might recognise theoretically the importance of practice, and working with NGOs, they are often locked into searching for a theory of masculinities. A weakness in Connell's theory that conceives of masculinity exclusively as a relationship of power is its blindness to issues of cultural difference and the emotional lives of young men. Its very universalism has made it appealing to international organisations, which seek to apply it across diverse cultures with only regional adjustments. This makes it difficult to listen to the voices of young men themselves. When men are told they are the bearers of gender power they can turn off, feeling their experience is quite different. While it is crucial for young men to learn about gender relations of power, this can only be the beginning in the context of sexual and reproductive health and rights.

Connell's dismissal of the 'therapeutic', contrasted with the 'political', leaves little room to engage with the emotional and sexual lives of young men. It is only as young men learn to take greater responsibility for their emotional lives that they can recognise the harm they do to themselves when they affirm their male identities through having as many heterosexual relationships as possible. If we are to change the feelings young men have about condoms, for instance, we have to appreciate the insecurities concealed by their complaints. Young men have to appreciate the risks they take with unprotected sex, both of pregnancy and of STDs, and that they have to learn to take responsibility for themselves (although warnings can add to the appeal of risk-taking). Sometimes it is by relating to fears of rejection that one is able to reach young men who have learnt to distrust adults. It can be through tapping into their relationship with their father that some young men may come to realise that they should use contraception, feeling they only want to have children they can love and relate to.

As we envision programmes in which young men can trust enough to make themselves vulnerable, we can move from small projects concerned with health matters towards health centres where their anxieties and fears can be addressed, along with their hopes and dreams for more equal relationships. It is important to recognise the uneasy feelings of guilt and shame produced within specific religious cultures, which are so often ignored within social and medical research. We need to be able to engage seriously with young men's moral concerns as they reach towards more equal gender and sexual relationships.

As young people learn to respect diverse sexualities, so they recognise how respecting their own emotions and desires can involve respecting the feelings of others. For young people a sense of respect, so often denied them, is vital if sex education is to work for them, within both health clinics and schools. In moving from the personal to the institutional, and from the local to the level of government agencies, it is vital that we train teachers and health workers who believe in what they are doing with young people.

defining issues

The point is not to think in terms of 'including' young men in sexual and reproductive health, but to understand why it has taken us so long to recognise that they are already there, influencing and shaping what goes on in relationships. For such thinking has tended to reinforce the assumption that contraception and pregnancy are the concern of young women alone, and that the responsibility is solely theirs.

Traditionally research into adolescence has not been gendered, and has viewed young people from the perspective of adults. Programmes tended to blame young men for their reckless behaviour, and as long as the dominant discourse was centred on 'male responsibility' the narrow objective tended to be to convince men to adopt, or at least support, contraception. Unbalanced gender relations were rarely questioned, and sometimes they were even reinforced – for instance, when vasectomies were promoted as enabling men to have sex free from responsibility. MacArthur helped pioneer work in helping men to develop egalitarian relationships and foster new masculinities, and in working with young people to change their sexual and fertility behaviours. Devoting attention to young men is a vital commitment, central to being able to do effective work in lowering the age of first conception and the rate of teenage pregnancy.[5]

Recent research in Brazil into condom promotion, informed by a sense of the emotional life of young men, found that their complaints about reduced sexual pleasure to a large degree provided socially acceptable cover for a deeper preoccupation with sexual performance – the quite reasonable fear of losing one's erection while putting on a condom. Tens of millions of dollars had been spent on condom promotion which completely overlooked this phenomenon. Randomised control trials – designed as a way of testing the efficacy of medical procedures – should not be uncritically adapted and applied to research on social change.

As Richard Parker has argued, whereas individuals should not be seen as the only unit of analysis, we have to appreciate the presence of emotional and power dynamics within young peoples' sexual relationships. Research on sexual identities and relationships that does not focus solely upon reproductive sexuality allows us to understand power as socially produced, reproduced and constructed. Unless we incorporate insights from the social sciences we will be destined to repeat much of the work already done.[6] As Margaret Neuse recognised, the historical reliance within the family-planning field on contraceptive methods that involved little or no involvement of partners means that few programmes involve discussion of use in the context of young peoples' sexual relations.[7] Although research shows that young men are often eager to learn about their bodies and sexualities, this knowledge is unavailable to them within families and often in school. Evidence shows that it is not a matter of simply delivering health messages or teaching young men a particular role, but of opening up spaces for reflection and communication.

Rather than think dualistically in terms of 'women's empowerment' and 'male involvement' in a way that can too readily assume masculinity as a relationship of power, we need to listen to young men as they question the myth that 'all men are powerful'. Young men can deny their lack of knowledge of their own bodies, let alone women's bodies, because they feel they have to show they are in control of their lives and relationships. Young men need to learn skills of communication, negotiation, self-confidence and awareness in health environments where they can acknowledge their own fears and vulnerability.

The MacArthur Foundation has supported groups, such as Salud y Genero in Mexico, that have developed innovative methodologies to engage young people in broad discussions related to pleasurable and responsible sex. Trained researchers who are sensitive to issues of practice are needed to assist in the long-term evaluation of these projects in ways that can provide generalisations while being aware of the specific cultural contexts of young masculinities in countries such as Mexico, Nigeria and India. For example, where there are cultural taboos against masturbation, such as on the Indian subcontinent, young men can feel they literally have no acceptable outlet for sexual expression other than intercourse, even if this means risking HIV/AIDS with a commercial sex worker.[8]

interventions

If we are concerned with change not only in attitudes but also in behaviours, we must develop appropriate evaluations that involve an appreciation of the best moments for intervention. First-time fatherhood can be a critical period in getting young men to reflect on their own fathers, as a basis to start planning what they will want to be like as fathers and men. As a prison inmate and promoter working with Salud y Genero said so beautifully, 'Not to be so lonely in my fatherhood ... to have my wife to share living. I think we win life. We win freedom.'

The demand for young men to be involved has often come from women at the grassroots, who have also known that young men have often felt marginalized and excluded by the focus upon young women's reproductive health. Family-planning clinics have been an important space for young women, in which they have autonomy, information and education that may be lacking in other areas of their lives. But the context in which young women live has often been ignored. We need to engage with the pressures young women face in their relationships with young men when they leave the clinic. We have to understand the dynamics of power within intimate and sexual relationships, so that methodologies are framed relationally. Young men who have failed within a globalised economy to find traditional work to sustain their male identities have felt disempowered. Their bodies and intimate relationships become the exclusive spaces in which to affirm themselves. This can make it vital to engage with young men directly. Evidence from Belize shows that male-only groups were particularly valuable in eliciting concerns about unemployment and male powerlessness, feelings of disrespect from women, issues of control and dominance, and erectile dysfunction. In other contexts men have trained male promoters from villages. A case study assessment of RepoSalud by Rogow and Diaz in several Andean villages found that changes had been sustained over time, with drastic reductions in alcohol consumption and domestic violence, and marked increases in contraception use.[9]

Even though risk behaviour is associated with young men across diverse cultures, it is important to recognise the different pressures that young men grow up with. In earlier generations in Mexico, as we have seen, young men's first sexual experiences were in brothels, because of pressure from peers and family members. The shock to the body could shape subsequent sexual experiences. Even in rural areas this has begun to change. Young women have begun to question double standards and expect more from their relationships. This creates hope for the future, but it depends upon young men in their turn being more open and responsive in negotiating sexual needs and desires.

Traditional sexual moralities are changing, but this can create new conflicts. Programmes need to be aware of conflicting religious pressures in making their interventions. Sometimes, as in Calibar Nigeria, a programme finds it easier to deal with issues of gender equality and male identities than with questions of bodies and sexualities. But by working with trainers on issues of sexual and reproductive health it is possible to develop materials that can be used both in schools as well as at state and national level. Where there are already national commitments in place, it can be easier to generalise from particular projects and build upon their experience.

As young men learn to draw support from others and no longer feel trapped into thinking they have to be self-sufficient, they often seek to share themselves in their intimate relationships. It does not help to say that young men must confront the consequences of unwanted pregnancy, including early parenthood or abortion, since this reproduces the kind of moralism they often seek to escape. This prevailing discourse has failed to engage with the lived experience of young men, so has yielded programmes of limited success. Researchers have recognised this as a leading-edge issue that has only grown in significance in the post-9/11 world. Young men who are frustrated in their intimate relationships can find themselves attracted to fundamentalist religions that legitimate patriarchal control. Feeling that they have no role in a changing world, they can turn to violence and terror. Masculinity is not homogenous and there are different ways in which young men can relate to their risk behaviours without withdrawing into depression and practising self-harm.

A focus on young people's sexual health and rights must include working with young men if they are to learn to relate more equally. Sometimes a focus on young men and masculinities is a necessary starting point for work in relation to reproductive and sexual health, since the health literature often treats gender as a discrete variable and has limited experience of qualitative methodologies that can deal with relational issues. At a national level we should support clinics that have shifted from one-directional didactic monologues to a frank two-way exchange that allows young men to express their fears and hopes for intimate relationships. These could serve as the model for a health system in its treatment of young men. They would encourage young people to reflect upon the consequences of their own actions, so helping them explore contraception in the context of pleasure and emotional intimacy.

Materials that have been pioneered in projects and proved useful in specific communities can be adapted and scaled up for more general educational use in schools. However, it is important to give attention to training teachers, especially male teachers, who have often not confronted these issues themselves. The development of sex education materials that treat sex not simply biologically but also in terms of emotional relationships – what people might expect to feel and the dilemmas they face at different stages of a relationship – could make a real difference to the ways young people relate to each other. It is crucial to develop trained workers aware of the best practice in working with young people on sexual and reproductive health issues, especially where a government agency is involved.

There have been challenges to traditional sexual norms and behaviours across the globe. Young people, influenced by the global media and by their peers, have often been the leading force in the sexual revolution, while the older generation, unable to engage in open dialogue, try to contain change by withdrawing into conventional positions. Established churches have traditionally resisted greater sexual freedom, and the Catholic Church continues to oppose strongly the use of condoms. Rather than avoiding questions of ethics we need to engage young people in ethically revisioning more equal genders and sexualities in ways that avoid a traditional moralism but can provide a new sense of self-worth and equal respect.

men's involvement

As Judith Helzner wrote in 1996:

> For at least 20 years, the idea of increasing men's participation in family planning has received periodic attention. However, there is as yet no generally accepted understanding of what men's involvement actually means. Often, it has been defined as the importance of increasing the popularity and prevalence of vasectomy or condoms. However, the seemingly simply phrase 'male involvement' still hides a variety of different meanings and philosophies.[10]

Though in theory we have moved on, our global practices are still often undermined by the difficulties we inherit, in diverse cultural settings, in discerning these 'different meanings and philosophies'.

In order to reach men it is necessary to listen to what they have to say about their own lives and relationships. Many people have been engaging creatively with men in different projects around the world. But if our understandings of gender power are to be developed from the 'bottom up', we have to recognise that in different cultural and religious traditions we are dealing with very different issues. Too often academic researchers have assumed that if they developed the right theoretical approaches these could be applied to different projects. This arrogance has been sustained unwittingly through Connell's distinction between the 'therapeutic' and the 'political', which has served to silence men's experience. Theory as politics remains split from the everyday experience of men, and the link between researchers and activists is broken. If we are to renew these connections and learn to listen we need to keep a number of issues in mind.

1. Men need to be made aware of their institutional power and violence in relation to women, where the primary focus is on making men taking responsibility for what they have made women suffer. This has been a crucial strategy in working with male violence, but it has tended to be most effective when it is not purely a strategy of guilt and shame. Projects have been able to reach men when they have connected with their own experience of violence, say as boys who had been beaten by their fathers. This in no way excuses their own violent behaviour, but can help them learn to take more emotional responsibility for themselves and their behaviour towards their partners.

2. We need to reach men not just in ways that psychological training tends to foster, but through their relationship with their masculinities. We have to engage with how boys are brought up to be men in different class, race and ethnic settings, so that boys can learn to name their own experience as masculine and recognise new possibilities for themselves. This involves communicating appropriately with different generations of men and asking whether projects are more effective with younger men, who are dealing with prevailing cultural masculinities. But we also have to recognise that tensions exist between generations, and between fathers and sons, in worlds where younger people often feel their elders have no grasp of the new technologies that are helping define their realities. In Nigeria, young men often use the Internet as a source

of sexual knowledge, often through accessing pornography. They might feel these are the only sources of knowledge available to them, within a culture that finds it difficult to speak about bodies, sex and desires. If young men feel a need to speak what is deemed unspeakable within their traditions, they need to feel that others are there to listen.

3. Young men must appreciate how certain dominant masculinities – ways of being and of affirming male identities – can be harmful to health. Young men often learn to defend themselves against painful childhood experiences through 'cutting off' from their emotional selves and presenting themselves rationally towards others. They can be left disconnected from themselves. Unable to reach out towards others, they learn to give orders rather than open up communication. They often seek intimacy but feel unable to ask for it. Learning to identify emotions as 'feminine', they can grow up fearful of their own tenderness, particularly within homophobic cultures. They can often transmute these feelings into anger and violence that do not threaten their male identities.

4. We need to recognize the diversity of masculinities in different cultures. For example, in India – where young men do not see themselves as macho, but perceive such an attitude as belonging to Latin American 'others' – it can be difficult to discern the workings of male power and the ways in which young men remain trapped within prevailing masculinities. In Nicaragua CANTERA has been able to organise a campaign that recognises that 'real men' do not hit their partners – possibly because the war allowed men to recognise that their behaviour at home had been shaped by their experience as soldiers. They would lose their temper and resort to violence more easily. They expected their partner to obey.[11] In other cultures, husbands who pay a bride price might expect obedience – though this is also true in India, where wives provide a dowry. If we are to learn through these differences we must discard the idea that 'men are all the same', recognising instead that the world is changing rapidly, and that young men are often growing up with different expectations to their fathers.

5. Sometimes it is when young men are preparing to be fathers that we can reach them more easily. They might feel they want to have

a new kind of relationship with their children. The feeling that they only want to have children they can love can help them to accept greater responsibility for contraception. However, young men might have knowledge about contraception but nevertheless resist using it.

6. Qualitative research methodologies can all too easily reflect masculinist assumptions. Respondents often say what they think the researcher wants to hear, and we have to recognise the importance of trust in the process of generating more reliable data. Sometimes it is through peer education that also supports peer involvement in the research process that we can begin to understand what makes particular projects effective. Experience in Nigeria shows both the importance of gaining support from traditional leaderships and the cultural sensitivities needed to work in different regions – for example in the north, where Muslim traditions are strong. They needed to work both within and outside school projects, as well as place adolescent sexual and reproductive health within their vision of an Expanded Life Planning Education (ELPE), taught in public secondary schools in Oyo State, south-west Nigeria. Sometimes people will accept a focus upon health when they would be likely to resist the conception of sex education.

learnings

It is clear that young men can easily lose respect for their teachers. Professionals tend to be trained, in both health and education, to consider themselves the source of knowledge. They do not expect to have to listen to young people, and often have little awareness of what they are living through. This is what makes it difficult to develop friendly clinics, where young people feel they will be treated with respect. It follows that young people are often best reached in out-of-school projects, or in street projects where peers are able to relate to their emotional needs. If young men, who are often without jobs that could provide them with a sense of male esteem, feel they might lose face before their peers, they will avoid these spaces. In a globalised economy in which traditional employment opportunities have radically declined, young men may feel that their bodies are the only means by which they can affirm their male identitiy.

The widespread 'crisis of masculinity' that has taken shape in the South in the absence of work that can sustain traditional masculinities has tempted some to indentify with religious fundamentalisms that reinforce traditional patriarchal assumptions. We need to examine the ways in which Western Enlightenment rationalism treats spiritual faith as a form of 'backwardness' that will inevitably give way to reason. If we do not question this arrogance, there is a danger that universalist theories that fail to appreciate the interconnections between power and emotion, love and fear, will make it harder to reach men. Traditional male power will be sustained unless we learn to reach men, by encouraging them to question their taken-for-granted masculinities. As men learn that their lives can also be enriched through a vision of gender equality that includes them, they will recognise the importance of improving the reproductive health of all. As women are empowered to make decisions for themselves, men will lose power and control but gain through the love and intimacy that will flow. No longer so isolated, they will recognise their partners as equally deserving of love and respect.

Helzer is helpful when she says that 'If a gender perspective is not used to review possible work on male involvement, the results could vary widely – from challenging patriarchy to ignoring its existence, or even worse, to increasing its dominance.'[12] But we have learnt that there are very different kinds of 'gender perspective', and different ways that men can be included. Rather than thinking that these theoretical issues have been settled and can be 'applied', it is through learning from projects in diverse global and cultural settings that we give shape to the complex relationships between male power and different 'cultural masculinities'. Rather than simply seeking 'good practice' that can be applied universally, we need to learn from diverse practices how to respect, and at the same time critically engage with, traditional masculinities and cultural traditions.

young men, heroes, violence and conflict

excitements

Chris Hedges in his illuminating book *War is a Force that Gives Us Meaning* draws upon his extensive experience as a war correspondent when he observes that

> The prospect of war is exciting. Many young men schooled in the notion that war is the ultimate definition of manhood, that only in war will they be tested and proven, that they can discover their worth as human beings in battle, willingly join the great enterprise. The admiration of the crowd, the high-blown rhetoric, the chance to achieve the glory of the previous generation, the ideal of nobility beckon us forward. And people, ironically, enjoy righteous indignation and an object upon which to unleash their anger. War usually starts with collective euphoria.[1]

Discussing young men in their relationship with masculinities, he comes to include himself in the recognition that 'The myth of war entices us with the allure of heroism.' At the same time he realises that the images of war handed to us, even when they are graphic, 'leave out the one essential element of war – fear. There is, until the actual moment of confrontation, no cost to imagining glory.' Even if representations in books and films make the experience appear real, as

Hedges recognises, 'In fact the experience is sterile. We are safe. We do not smell the rotting flesh, hear the cries of agony, or see before us blood and entrails seeping out of bodies.' If young men still grow up with these dreams of glory, he realises, 'It is all the more startling that such fantasy is believed, given the impersonal slaughter of modern industrial warfare.' The technological and depersonalised organised killing first seen in World War I has defined warfare ever since.

Although we live in a new age of technological warfare, we still cling to the outdated notion of the single hero able to carry out daring feats of courage. Somehow these myths have become more rather than less significant in enticing soldiers into war. Many soldiers never actually see the people they are firing at, nor those firing at them. This produces its own anxieties, which need to be assuaged in the ecstatic high of violence. Erich Maria Remarque, a German veteran of World War I, knew that it takes little in wartime to turn ordinary men into killers. He wrote in *All Quiet on the Western Front* of the narcotic of war that quickly transformed men: 'We run on, overwhelmed by this wave that bears us along, that fills us with ferocity ... that multiplies our strength with fear and madness and greed of life, seeking and fighting for nothing but our deliverance.'[2]

The historian Christopher Browning noted the willingness to kill in *Ordinary Men*, a study of Reserve Police Battalion 101 in Poland during World War II. The battalion was ordered to shoot 1,800 Jews in the Polish village of Josefow. The victims, including women, children and the elderly, were shot at close range. The soldiers were given the option to refuse, an option that only about a dozen men took, although more asked to be relieved once the killing began on 12 July 1942. Those who did not want to continue, Browning says, were disgusted rather than plagued by conscience. When the men returned to the barracks they 'were depressed, angered, embittered and shaken'. They drank heavily. They were told not to talk about the event, 'but they needed no encouragement in that direction'.[3]

In the massacres that followed, the killings became less personal. The executioners drank now before their work – as they did in Bosnia and Kosovo sixty years later. Having killed once, Browning wrote, the men 'did not experience such a traumatic shock the second time'. It no longer became hard to find volunteers, and the killings escalated.

In a massacre that became known as the 'Harvest Festival' some 500 men killed 50,000 Jewish inhabitants of the work camps Trawniki, Poniatowa and Majdanek in a matter of days. As Browning reports, the men in the battalion, aged between 37 and 42, were not elite troops. They had not been highly trained or specially picked for the task. They were 'ordinary men' of middle- or lower-class origins. As Hedges observes,

> their behaviour, given the savagery of modern warfare, has been widely replicated. There are no shortage of former soldiers and militiamen in Algeria, Argentina, Rwanda, El Salvador, Iraq, or Bosnia who have done the same. There are always people willing to commit unspeakable human atrocity in exchange for a little power and privilege.... The task of carrying out violence, of killing, leads to perversion. The seductiveness of violence, the fascination with the grotesque – the Bible calls it 'the lust of the eye' – the god-like empowerment over other human lives and the drug of war combine, like the ecstasy of erotic love.[4]

perversion

One of the most widely read works of Holocaust literature in Israel is Ka'Tzetnik's sextet *House of Dolls*, in which the main character is a young woman forced into becoming a prostitute for German soldiers. This book was recommended reading for high schools studying the Holocaust. What troubles Israeli historian Omer Bartov is that what makes the books so gripping is 'their obsession with violence and perversity':

> Nothing could be a greater taboo than deriving sexual pleasure from the fact that the central sites for these actions were the concentration camps. Nothing could be a greater taboo than deriving sexual pleasure from pornography in the context of the Holocaust; hence nothing could be more exciting. That Israeli youth learned about sex and perversity, and derived sexual gratification, from books describing the manner in which Nazis tortured Jews, is all the more disturbing considering that we are speaking about a society whose population consisted of a large proportion of Holocaust survivors and their offspring.[5]

The effects of the books on the larger society can only be guessed at, Bartov argues, but there is little doubt that those subsequent generations 'have not been wholly liberated from this pernicious trap, whereby they must have more of the violent and ruthless attributes associated with the perpetrators so as not to become their victims (whom on some level of consciousness they are still defending).'

The violent break-up of Yugoslavia, which was preceded by economic collapse, began in 1991. In the same year the Yugoslav government decided to allow hardcore sex movies to be broadcast on public television stations, and the first locally produced pornographic film was produced. As Hedges recalls, 'The first graphic pictures of mutilated and dead from the war, along with the racial diatribes against Muslims and Croats, hit the airwaves at the same time Yugoslavs were allowed to watch porno films.' Distraught teachers said they struggled to cope with children as young as 11 who had been exposed to scenes of graphic sadomasochism on television. Hedges comments:

> There is in wartime a nearly universal preoccupation with sexual liaisons.... Men, and especially soldiers, are preoccupied with little else. With power reduced to such a raw level and the currency of life and death cheap, eroticism races through all relationships. There is in these encounters a frenetic lust that seeks, on some level, to replicate or augment the drug of war. It is certainly not about love, indeed love in wartime is hard to sustain or establish.... Casual encounters are charged with raw, high-voltage sexual energy that smacks of the self-destructive lust of war itself.... The fleeting sexual encounters, intense, overpowering, and largely anonymous, deflate with tremendous speed and leave behind guilt, even disgust, and a void that expands into a swamp of loneliness.[6]

The war in the Balkans saw the rise of rape camps, where women were kept under guard and repeatedly abused by Serbian paramilitary forces. Hedges recalls from his time as a correspondent in Bosnia,

> When this became boring – for perverse sex, like killing, must constantly entail the new and the bizarre – the women were mutilated and killed, reportedly on video. Women were also held in very similar conditions, and later murdered, in Argentina during the Dirty War. Sexual slaves in Argentina were used and then discarded like waste, their drugged bodies at times dumped from helicopters into the sea.[7]

'No one ever forgets a sudden depreciation of himself/herself, for it is too painful,' Elias Canetti writes in *Crowds and Power*.

And the crowd as such never forgets its depreciation. The natural tendency afterwards is to find something which is worth even less than oneself, which one can despise as one was despised oneself. It is not enough to take over an old contempt and to maintain it at the same level. What is wanted is a dynamic process of humiliation. Something must be treated in such a way that it becomes worth less and less, as the unit of money did during the inflation. And this process must be continued until its object is reduced to a state of utter worthlessness. Then one can throw it away like paper, or repulp it.[8]

The fear of 'losing face' resonates for men across diverse cultures. In the West it goes along with a sense that masculinities can never be taken for granted, but must be affirmed even at the cost of putting others down. The way dominant masculinities are constructed often means that men can only feel good about themselves at the expense of others. Canetti helps us to recognise how this can produce and sustain 'a dynamic process of humiliation' that within patriarchal cultures often involves the exercise of violence against women. 'If we are honest', J. Glenn Gray wrote in *The Warriors: Reflections on Men in Battle*, 'most of us who were civilian soldiers in recent wars will confess that we spent incomparably more time in the service of Eros during our military careers than ever before or again in our lives. When we were in uniform almost any girl who was faintly attractive had an erotic appeal for us.' He also writes that 'an essential difference between comradeship and friendship consists, it seems to me, in a heightened awareness of the self in friendship and in the suppression of self-awareness in comradeship.'[9]

dislocations

It is generally the victims who survive that suffer the most guilt and remorse. They can feel in debt to those who have died, and they know that it is not the best who survive war but often the selfish, the brutal and the violent. The world, as it is in war, had been turned upside down. Those who worked hard all their lives and struggled to live on pensions and savings lost everything in inflation-hit former Yugoslavia. The unscrupulous, who had massive debts, never had to repay them. Often they lived off the black market or crime, using force to get what they wanted as they became rich and powerful. The moral universe disintegrated. Drugs, protection rackets, prostitution, not to mention smuggled duty-free cigarettes, became major businesses as state-run factories folded.

As Hedges recalls,

> Hedonism and perversion spiralled out of control as inflation ate away at the local currency. Those who had worked hard all their lives were now reviled as dupes and fools. They haunted the soup kitchens.... Their children, no matter how well educated, worked in menial jobs abroad so they could mail back enough for their parents to buy food.

As the domination and brutality of the battlefield is carried into personal life,

> Rape, mutilation, abuse and theft are the natural outcome of a world in which force rules, in which human beings are objects.... The infection is pervasive. Society in wartime becomes atomised. It rewards personal survival skills and very often leaves those with decency and compassion trampled under the rush.

Hedges knows that

> Those who abandoned their humanity, betrayed their neighbours and friends, turned their backs on the weak and infirm were often those who made it out alive. Many victims grasp, in a way that the perpetrators again do not, the inverted moral hierarchy.[10]

In wartime nearly everyone becomes an accomplice. The huge dislocations in which people lose their homes and properties are often compensated for by the properties of those who were forced out of other areas. Those who had their homes taken from them in Srebrenica by the Bosnian Serbs were later given the homes of Serbs who had fled the suburbs of Sarajevo.

The moral destructiveness of ethnic cleansing, like the psychic wounds of war, reverberates throughout society. Families who are stripped of all they own, and then handed by the state apartments that were seized from others are complicitous, whether they like it or not. These dislocations destroy communal structures and weaken ties beyond the immediate ethnic group. As Hannah Arendt observed, they create a population of stateless individuals, refugees with their own countries, who to survive must share in the loot of war.[11] As Hedges learnt, 'Political or moral dissent is silenced, since nearly all are forced to become accomplices. It is hard to condemn ethnic cleansing when you live in someone else's home.' The Croat and Serb and Muslim leaders in Bosnia often made secret deals to 'trade' minorities, whether these families wanted to leave their homes or not.

For many people the war never ends; their lives can never return to how they were before. Beneath the physical rehabilitation of Sarajevo, there is another reality. Men, out of work and often wounded physically or emotionally, waste hours in dingy coffee shops. Peace has not returned for them, for they know their lives have been scarred for ever. They have lost hope that the city could regain its old identity. Many of the young gather in the lines for visas outside foreign embassies. In the evening they meet in smoky clubs where they can buy marijuana, Ecstasy and heroin. An army of war invalids lies trapped indoors. 'My son is inside', said an angry 70-year-old man, who would not give his name, to Chris Hedges, as he stood outside his small house fitting new aluminium drainpipes to the roof. 'He can't get up. Every night my wife has to go in and turn him over so he can go to the bathroom.'

notes

preface

1. For some helpful discussions around developments within the sociology of family and intimate relations, see David Morgan, *Family Connections* (1996); P.M. Nardi, *Gay Men's Friendships* (1999); C. Ramazanoglu, *Feminism and the Contradictions of Oppression* (1989); b. hooks, *Salvation: Black People and Love* (2001). See in particular Judith Stacey, *Brave New Families: Stories of Domestic Upheaval in Late Twentieth Century America* (1990), and her *In the Name of the Family: Rethinking Family Values in the Postmodern Age* (1996). See also Arlie Hochschild and Anne Machung, *The Second Shift: Working Parents and the Revolution at Home* (1989); Lillian Rubin, *Families on the Faultline: America's Working Class Speaks about the Family, the Economy, Race and Ethnicity* (1994); Neil Miller, *Out in the World: Gay and Lesbian Life from Buenos Aires to Bangkok* (1992); Suzanne Sherman (ed.), *Lesbian and Gay Marriage: Private Commitments, Public Ceremonies* (1992); Michael Warner (ed.), *Fear of a Queer Planet: Queer Politics and Social Theory* (1993).
2. For some helpful reflections upon the experience of young Asian girls in Britain, see Amrit Wilson, *Finding a Voice* (1976); N. Puwar and P. Raghuram (eds), *South Asian Women in the Diaspora* (2003).
3. By recalling our own teenage years and their intensity of emotions we may relate honestly to young men in the present. I have shared some of the complexities of growing up in a refugee family in London in Victor J. Seidler, *Shadows of the Shoah: Jewish Identity and Belonging* (2001).
4. For some illuminating discussions that recall the excitements and new thinking in relation to sexual politics in the 1970s, see Sheila Rowbotham, *Woman's Consciousness, Man's World* (1972), and *Dreams and Dilemmas* (1983);

Jeffrey Weeks, *Coming Out: Homosexual Politics in Britain* (1977), and *Sex, Politics and Society* (1989); and Victor J. Seidler, *Rediscovering Masculinity: Reason, Language and Sexuality* (1987).

5. For a sense of the development of Bob Connell's important work, see R.W. Connell, *Gender and Power: Society, the Person and Sexual Politics* (1987), and the new edition of *Masculinities* (2005). We have been involved in an ongoing creative dialogue over many years. For a more sustained engagement with Connell's work, see Victor J. Seidler, *Transforming Masculinities: Men, Cultures, Bodies, Power, Sex and Love* (2005; originally published in 1995).

one

1. For a useful account of different generations of men and masculinities in Britain that goes back to the 1950s, see Lynne Segal, *Slow Motion: Changing Masculinities, Changing Men* (1990). For the ways these backgrounds influenced the emergence of discussions of men and masculinities in the 1970s in Britain, see my *Rediscovering Masculinity*.

2. For helpful discussions about ways masculinities are shaped within schooling, see M. Mac an Ghail, *The Making of Men: Masculinities, Sexualities and Schooling* (1994); A. Nayak and M. Kehily, 'Playing it Straight: Masculinities, Homophobias and Schooling', *Journal of Gender Studies* 5(2), pp. 211–30. There is also useful research on the ways boys learn their masculinities in school in Britain in S. Frosh, A. Phoenix and R. Pattman, *Young Masculinities: Understanding Boys in Contemporary Society* (2002).

3. The distinction that Connell makes between the 'therapeutic' and the 'political' serves to discount the ways that men's sexual politics in the 1980s sought to explore the connection between the personal and the political. Rather than learning from these diverse experiences, Connell tends to discount them as 'therapeutic', and so develops a vision of hegemonic masculinities that embodies a structural universalism in its vision of politics that is unable to make connection with the contradictions of men's lived experience. This is a theme that first appears in Connell, *Gender and Power*, and is continued in his influential *Masculinities*.

4. The crisis of authority in late capitalism and the ways this impacts upon fathering relations is explored in 'Fathering, Authority and Masculinity' in R. Chapman and J. Rutherford (eds), *Male Order: Unwrapping Masculinity* (1988).

5. Some interesting interviews with men around issues of negotiation in relation to contraception and sexuality are presented in J. Holland, C. Ramazanoglu, S. Sharpe and R. Thompson, *The Male in the Head: Young People, Heterosexuality and Power* (1998). This followed an earlier monograph, *Wimp Or Gladiator: Contradictions in Aquiring Male Sexuality* (1993).

6. Issues in relation to diverse male sexualities were initially explored in Victor J. Seidler (ed.), *Men, Sex and Relationships* (1992). See also J. Wood,

'Groping Towards Sexism: Boy's Sex Talk', in A. McRobbie and M. Nava (eds), *Gender and Generation* (1984); K. Mercer and I. Julien, 'Race, Sexual Politics and Black Masculinity – A Dossier', in Chapman and Rutherford (eds), *Male Order*. For a discussion in relation to Latin American masculinities and the continuing influence of the Catholic Church in the shaping of gender and sexual relationships, see the papers gathered in Jose Olavarria, *Varones Adolescentes: Genero, identidades y sexualidades en America Latina* (2003).

two

1. How Western modernities were established in largely secularised Protestant terms is a theme that is explored in Zygmunt Bauman's *Modernity and Ambivalence*. The ways in which others were defined as lacking is a theme that is explored in Paul Gilroy's *Black Atlantic: Modernity and Double Consciousness* (1993) and implications in relation to bodies and sexualities in Victor J. Seidler, *The Moral Limits of Modernity* (1991).

2. Gramsci explores the evolutionary assumptions implicit in guiding social theories in the *Prison Notebooks* (1971). He was interrogating Marxist traditions he had inherited, particularly the influence of Lenin and tendencies within orthodox Marxist traditions to construe Marx in positivist terms. Drawing on the influence of Croce's readings of Hegel, Gramsci questions the universalism of scientific Marxism, which made it difficult to engage critically with traditions of Italian Catholicism, too easily dismissed within rationalist traditions as 'backward' and 'irrational'. Gramsci's *Letters from Prison* (1975) show the efforts he was making to engage with particular histories, cultures and religious traditions, rather than treat them as 'lacking' in contrast to a secular modernity.

3. For an exploration of some of the Christian notions that framed the Conquest of Central and Latin America, see Eduardo Subirats, *El Continente Vacio* (1996), a text to which I was introduced in discussions with Teresa Ordorika. This is also a theme that is explored in Roger Batra, *The Cage of Melancholy: Identity and Metamorphosis in the Mexican Character* (1992). Carlos Fuentes claims that one of the implications of Conquest in Mexico has meant that people have lived with issues of identity ever since. In *Los Cinco Soles de Mexico* (2000: 17) he writes: 'Mexicans are the oldest citizens of the twenty-first century ... captured between traditional identity and modern otherness, between the local village and the global village, between economic interdependence and political balkanization. Mexico has been living with this, our radical present modernity, since five hundred years ago.'

4. Simone Weil explores how Roman notions of power and greatness have helped to frame Western cultural traditions and conceptions of 'civilization' in *The Need for Roots* (1972). She was reflecting upon the importance of

rethinking inherited traditions in the wake of the liberation of France from Nazi rule. She was seeking to identify alternative values within French historical traditions that could sustain a notion of the life of the nation that was not framed within Roman terms of power and greatness, which she recognised as also sustaining Europe's imperial and colonial relationships. This theme is explored in Lawrence A. Blum and Victor J. Seidler, *A Truer Liberty: Simone Weil and Marxism* (1991).

5. Walter Benjamin in his seminal late essay 'Theses on the Philosophy of History', in *Illuminations* (1973), was questioning the evolutionary assumptions that so often shaped traditions of orthodox Marxism and the conceptions of history and progress that they fostered.

6. For an exploration of the place of *mestizaje* in Mexico it is still helpful to recall the insights of Octavio Paz: 'The Mexican does not want to be either an Indian or a Spaniard. Nor does he want to be descended from them. He denies them. And he does not affirm them as a mixture, but rather as an abstraction: he is a man. He becomes the son of nothingness. His beginnings are his own self.' *The Labyrinth of Solitude* (1961), p. 87. For an interesting discussion, see Monica Moreno, 'On the Mexican Mestizo: or About How to Survive between Affirmation and Denial', MA dissertation, Department of Sociology, Goldsmiths, 2000.

7. For some interesting discussion on the history of 'race' in relation to *mestizaje* in Mexico, see Magnus Morner (ed.), *Race and Class in Latin America* (1997); Graham Richard (ed.), *The Idea of Race in Latin America 1870–1940* (1990); Peter Wade, *Race and Ethnicity in Latin America* (1997).

8. Universalist theories of masculinities that can be applied to particular societies, cultures and traditions tend to be blind to the anglophone traditions that shape them. Even though there is a general acknowledgement that these theories have to be 'reworked' within particular cultures in the South, many believe that theoretical frameworks can be established that can then be applied to particular settings. This may reflect the different status given to theoretical work and its distance from projects actually working with young men and masculinities. It therefore becomes difficult to engage theoretically with the practices being developed.

9. For some useful historical background to the Inquisition in Spain and the ways it prepared the legitimations for Conquest, see H. Kamen, *The Spanish Inquisition* (1965); the classic study by H.C. Lea, *A History of the Inquisition in Spain*, 4 vols (1906). See also the interesting Ph.D. thesis of Teresa Ordorika, 'Heresy and Madness in the Spanish Inquisition', University of London (2003).

10. The social and historical background of revolutionary Mexico against which Frida Kahlo was working is explored in Paz, *The Labyrinth of Solitude* (1961) and in Claudio Lomnitz-Adler, *Exits from the Labyrinth: Culture and Ideology in the Mexican National Space* (1992).

11. For a sense of the ways in which the personal was related to the political in men's lives and relationships in *Achilles Heel*, a journal that brought together

writings on men and masculinities in Britain, see Victor J. Seidler (ed.), *The Achilles Heel Reader* (1991), and *Men, Sex and Relationships: Writings from Achilles Heel* (1992).

three

1. The ways in which young men learn to relate to language as an instrument of self-control within a secularized Protestant modernity is a theme explored in Seidler, *Rediscovering Masculinity*. I draw upon Wittgenstein's later philosophical writings in *Philosophical Investigations* (1958) and *On Certainty* (1967), which break with a Cartesian rationalist tradition that tends to sustain an autonomy of language as a system of signs. Wittgenstein explores the ways language can be understood in the context of use, and appreciates how often it can be used to distance and defend against shaping a connection with lived experience.

2. Protestant moral culture works to establish the autonomy of morality and law by framing human nature as flawed and radically evil, so that people silence the impulses of their own natures and learn to obey the dictates of the moral law. This was a vital theme for Luther and Calvin. This vision that had shaped the 'common sense' of a Protestant moral culture was challenged by Erich Fromm in *The Fear of Freedom* (1963). Fromm was developing a theme drawing upon psychoanalysis, which had already shaped Max Weber's *The Protestant Ethic and the Spirit of Capitalism* (1970).

3. For a sense of how discussions around gender equality have taken shape within the Protestant modernities of diverse Scandinavian cultures, see the helpful collection edited by S. Ervo and T. Johansson, *Among Men: Moulding Masculinities*, vols 1 and 2 (2002). In recent years discussions have also focused upon the discrete cultures, histories and traditions of specific countries, as well as what they share through a secularised Protestant inheritance. Through sustained intergovernmental support, Nordic research networks have established significant discussions across gender, sex and generational boundaries.

4. For a sense of the development of Connell's important work, see the shifts between *Gender and Power* and the later edition of *Masculinities*. There seems to be a connection between his adoption of the distinction between the 'therapeutic' and the 'political' as a framework within which to understand a genealogy of the critical study of men and masculinities, from its early responses to feminism in the 1970s, and the misleading claim that sexual politics was concerned to reduce the political to the personal. If this helped to establish the viability of a notion of 'hegemonic masculinities', it made it more difficult to validate diverse histories, cultures and traditions, as well as the emotional lives of young men struggling to define new masculinities for themselves against prevailing expectations.

5. The relationship within a Protestant modernity between masculinity, work and self-denial is a theme within Weber, *The Protestant Ethic and the Spirit*

of Capitalism. It is also a theme that was explored in relation to changing post-war class relations in the United States and the ways working-class men sustained a moral sense of self-respect and self-worth in Richard Sennett and Jonathan Cobb, *The Hidden Injuries of Class* (1970). These themes were explored more explicitly in relation to men and masculinities in Victor J. Seidler, *Recreating Sexual Politics: Men, Feminism and Politics* (1991) and David Morgan, *Discovering Men* (1992). For a study that is more directly focused upon Max Weber and his relationship with issues of gender, see R.W. Bologh, *Love or Greatness: Max Weber and Masculine Thinking* (1990).

6. It can be helpful to identify transformations across generations in gender and sexual relations within specific cultures, in order to appreciate the diversity of possibilities. If there is a danger in comparative work of seeming to establish norms against which other cultures and traditions can be judged as lacking, there is also the possibility of recognising how different cultures have their own emotional and embodied histories, and that young men and women in both straight and gay relationships need to be listened to if we are to grasp the difficulties they face. This is not to sustain a vision of cultural relativism, but rather to recognise the ethical terms being shaped within diverse cultures to contest patriarchal and homophobic assumptions.

7. Though there were issues that needed to be contested in Robert Bly's *Iron John* (1990), particularly in relation to feminism and gay identities, there were also very important and vital insights into the emotional lives of men, particularly in relation to their fathers. Similarly with the mythopoetic movements Bly inspired; even if he did not support many of the activities they fostered, there were important insights. In different ways the book divided the anti-sexist men's movement. Many were dismissive, including Connell, who could not recognise what was of value. An early critical response was offered in H. Brod and M. Kaufman (eds), *Theorising Masculinities* (1990). Michael Kimmel shifted his position as he worked with Bly, and brought together an important collection on the different responses; see his *The Politics of Manhood* (1995). The various responses to Bly reflected on whether masculinities had to be deconstructed as relationships of power because they were the problem, so transforming masculinities could be no part of a solution. In *Man Enough: Embodying Masculinities* I attempted to mediate a way between an anti-sexist men's politics that still echoed, within a vision of hegemonic masculinities, the tradition of self-denial and moralism, and an appreciation of Bly's contribution, which had often been too readily dismissed. This called for a more complex genealogy that could also engage with the embodied emotional lives of men.

8. In researching young men and masculinities we must be ready to develop methodologies that are appropriate to the research we do, and not just assume that feminist research methods can simply be applied to a new research object. Aware of the ways positivist research methodologies within the social sciences have traditionally echoed masculinist assumptions in

their suspicion of the 'subjective' and the 'personal' as 'anecdotal', we also need to recognise specific difficulties of working with young men who will often have an investment in maintaining a public front. Unless interviewers have asked themselves the questions they want to ask others, it is difficult to establish the necessary trust. This raises both ethical and political issues to do with research practice.

four

1. El Primo Sexo? was the first international conference held in Mexico specifically on the theme of men and masculinities. It took place in Puebla, 23–25 June 2004, in the restored Edificio Carolino, a room with its own histories and memories of torture dating back to when the Inquisition came to Mexico. It created a particular atmosphere that recalled the violence and murderous brutality of colonial masculinities and the centrality of the Catholic Church in preparing the legitimations for Conquest. The memories are still very much alive and they resonate in diverse ways within contemporary Mexico.

2. For an interesting discussion of Walter Benjamin's writings on Mexico and his recognition of how different layers from the past continue to resonate in the present, see the essays collected in Andrew Benjamin and Peter Osborne (eds), *Walter Benjamin's Philosophy: The Destruction of Experience* (1994). For a sense of the early development in Benjamin's writing, see Howard Caygill, *Walter Benjamin: The Colour of Experience* (1998); Richard Wolin, *Walter Benjamin: An Aesthetic of Redemption* (1994).

3. Simone Weil appreciated that those who had conquered inherited the power to write history and so could shape it in their own terms. In *The Need for Roots* (1972) she explores the injuries created within the self-understandings of the West through the identification of power and ethics. It is often the defeated and the conquered who have values that we need to recognise and cherish.

4. In their respective conceptions of different traditions, Weil and Benjamin questioned the ways in which history is taught in the West, and how narratives of progress have ordered the ways we think the relationship between Europe and the continents it colonised and sought to remake in its own image. As we become aware of diverse histories, so we refuse the notion of a singular narrative of nation that legitimates existing rulers, while working to silence those whose cultures and traditions were framed as 'uncivilised', and so who had everything to learn and nothing to teach. If young men are to shape alternative masculinities for themselves, they will also need to discover different versions of history.

5. Though feminisms in the West tended to develop as secular discourses that have often treated religion as patriarchal traditions that women must break with to seek liberation, there have also been developments within the diverse Abrahamic traditions of Judaism, Christianity and Islam, as well as

in Eastern traditions, to reclaim womens' voices and experiences, even if they have been largely silenced within malestream interpretations. Women have their own histories to tell. In the crisis that has emerged in the West's relationship with Islam post-9/11, there has been a developing recognition of the need to rethink distinctions between the 'secular' and the 'religious' if we are to engage with young men and the appeals of a radical Islam.

6. For a sense of how the figure of the Jew was shaped through a dominant Christian iconography, see Joshua Trachtenberg, *The Devil and the Jews* (1995); Leon Poliakov, *The Aryan Myth* (1974), and *The History of Anti-Semitism* (1990). For some helpful discussion relating to the possibilities of conversion in the early modern period, see Karl F. Morrison, *Understanding Conversion* (1992).

7. For a consideration of different readings of Genesis within Jewish, Christian and Islamic traditions, see Elaine Pagels, *Adam, Eve and the Serpent* (1998), and her *The Origin of Satan* (1995). See also Avivah Gottleib Zornberg, *The Beginnings of Desire: Reflections on Genesis*, (1995); and Karen Armstrong, *Daughters of Abraham: Feminist Thought in Judaism, Christianity and Islam* (2002).

8. Julia Kristeva, *New Maladies of the Soul* (1995), p. 118.

9. Julia Kristeva, *Powers of Horror: An Essay on Abjection* (1982), p. 94; 'Opening: Cracking the Binding', in Timothy K. Beal and David M. Gunn (eds), *Reading Bibles, Writing Bodies: Identity and the Book* (1997), p. 4. For a sense of the development of Kristeva's work, see Kerry Oliver, *Reading Kristeva: Unravelling the Double-Bind* (1993).

10. Danna Nolan Fewell and David M. Gunn, 'Shifting the Blame: God in the Garden', in Beal and Gunn (eds), *Reading Bibles, Writing Bodies*, p. 16.

11. Genesis 1:27–28, 31; Fewell and Gunn, 'Shifting the Blame', p. 18.

12. Fewell and Gunn, 'Shifting the Blame', p. 21.

13. Ibid., p. 22.

14. For a helpful introduction to the writings of Irigaray, see Margaret Whitford, *Luce Irigarary: Philosophy in the Feminine* (1991). See also Tina Chanter, *Ethics of Eros: Irigaray's Rewriting of the Philosophers* (1995).

15. Fewell and Gunn, 'Shifting the Blame', p. 23.

16. In *Unreasonable Men* I explored implications of the idea that a dominant white European masculinity can alone take its reason for granted, and the consequences that this has had for Europe's relations with its colonised others, as well as the forms of rationalist social theory that have often worked to render colonial relationships of power invisible. This is a theme reflected in Signe Howell and Marit Melhus, 'The Study of Kinship; the Study of the Person; a Study of Gender?', in Teresa Del Valle (ed.), *Gendered Anthropology* (1993): 'Unreflectively, Western philosophers have pursued truth about human nature from the point of view of the aristocratic (reasoning) male. Unreflectingly, this exclusive bias has, by and large, continued when Western anthropologists have sought comparative conceptions. We are here confronted with a blindness to empirical realities, surprising in

a discipline (anthropology) which prides itself on working within native categories. Non-Western ideologies may operate with several conceptions of human nature, not just one. Not only are there gender differences in concepts and attributes of personhood, there are also age and class differences' (p. 48).

17. In *The Moral Limits of Modernity* I explored different conceptions of Christian equality, and the ways they have helped to shape different visions of modernity. Through Kant and Kierkegaard I explored Protestant traditions, while with Simone Weil I explored aspects of the Catholic tradition with which she was engaging. In this way I began to understand implications of cultural and religious differences for different conceptions of men and masculinities, and the blindness created through generalising from anglophone Protestant notions of universality.

18. To explore histories of sexuality within a Christian tradition, particularly in relation to issues of bodies, sexualities and emotions, see Peter Brown, *The Body and Society: Men, Women and Sexual Renunciation in Early Christianity* (1990). Brown's writings influenced Foucault as he was writing the first volume of the *History of Sexuality* (1976).

19. The ways in which a Platonic tradition that recognises death as a moment of liberation, wherein the soul can eventually find freedom from a body conceived of as a prison, has helped shape powerful traditions within Western culture is a theme explored by Val Plumwood, *Feminism and the Mastery Of Nature* (1993) She argues that a disconnection from the body reflects the denigration of material and earthly life that has to be transcended if people are to realise their spiritual identities within dominant Christian traditions.

five

1. For some helpful reflections upon the different Abrahamic traditions and the ways they frame conceptions of authority that still shape secular cultures, see Karen Armstrong, *The Battle for God: Fundamentalism in Judaism, Christianity and Islam* (2001), and her *A History of God* (1999). To explore some Eastern traditions and the different ways they imagine relationships between divine and secular authority, see Karen Armstrong, *The Great Transformation: The World in the Time of Buddha, Socrates, Confucius and Jeremiah* (2004).

2. Daniel Boyarin's *Carnal Israel: Reading Sex in Talmudic Judaism* (1993) and *A Radical Jew: Paul and the Politics of Identity* (1994) have helped to rethink the historical relationship between Judaism and Christianity, and so to reveal tensions in relation to bodies, sexualities and pleasures within different Catholic and Protestant modernities. Not only has it helped to deconstruct notions of a 'Judeo-Christian tradition' that has tended to silence vital differences in the hope of fending off Christian anti-Semitism, but it also opens up the possibility of different kinds of dialogue with Islamic traditions.

So often prevailing secular masculinities, even within globalised cultures, tacitly reflect the secularisation of particular religious traditions.

3. For helpful reflections upon the ways different religious traditions have interpreted Genesis and the implications this has had for the ways gender and sexed relations have been moralised through the different readings of the figure of Eve, see Elaine Pagels, *Adam, Eve and the Serpent* (1988), and *The Origins of Satan* (1996).

4. Simone Weil's seminal essay 'Human Personality', in *Selected Essays 1934–43* (1962), explores this vision of suffering that goes beyond an infringement of rights. Weil shows the inadequacy of a language of rights to illuminate the 'moral realities' of humiliation and violation. In this way she resonates with later feminist critiques that argue that rape and bodily violation involve forms of injustice that cannot simply be understood in terms of 'psychological damage', but require a new form of ethical language that goes beyond an Enlightenment rationalism. This is an issue explored further in the later chapters of Blum and Seidler, *A Truer Liberty*.

5. Kant's radical distinction between reason and nature and the implications this had for inherited conceptions of morality within a Protestant modernity is explored in Victor J. Seidler, *Kant, Respect and Injustice: The Limits of Liberal Moral Theory* (1986).

6. Alice Miller has explored in different works the implications of certain authoritarian pedagogies and the abuse of power that fathers could so easily legitimate within patriarchal cultures that allowed them to take out their anger and frustration on the bodies of their children. Since obedience was required, children were often powerless to speak back without being further accused of disobedience and a lack of respect, so proving themselves deserving of further punishment. See, for example, *For Your Own Good: Hidden Cruelty in Child-Rearing and the Roots of Violence* (1983) and *Thou Shalt Not Be Aware: Society's Betrayal of the Child* (1984).

7. Leonore Davidoff explores some of the implications of the split between love and work on the ordering of gender relations in L. Davidoff and C. Hall, *Family Fortunes: Men and Women of the English Middle Class, 1780–1850* (1987). See also the essays collected in L. Davidoff, *Worlds Between: Historical Perspectives on Gender and Class* (1995).

8. Tabitha Freeman, 'Conceptualising Fatherhood: Gender, Discourse and the Paradoxes of Patriachy', Ph.D. thesis, Department of Sociology, University of Essex, 2004, p. 56.

9. John Gillis, *A World of Their Own Making: Myth, Ritual and the Quest for Family Values* (1996), p. 181; Alexander Mitscherlich, *Society without a Father* (1993), p. 147.

10. For a discussion of changed conceptions of childhood, see Philippe Aries, *Centuries of Childhood: A Social History of Family Life* (1962).

11. D. Blankenhorn, *Fatherless America: Confronting Our Most Urgent Social Problem* (1995), p. 13.

12. Stacey has written well about the predicaments of fatherhood and the ways

it has emerged as a central cultural issue in the United States in *Brave New Families*, and more generally in *Family Values* (1996).

13. Freeman, 'Conceptualising Fatherhood', p. 64.
14. B.E. Carroll, '"I Must Have My House in Order": The Victorian Fatherhood of John Shoebridge Williams', *Journal of Family History* 24(3), pp. 278–9.
15. John Tosh, *A Man's Place: Masculinity and the Middle-Class Home in Victorian England* (1999), p. 71.
16. Davidoff and Hall, *Family Fortunes*, p. 329.
17. Freeman, 'Conceptualising Fatherhood', p. 70.
18. Griswold, Introduction to special issue on fatherhood, *Journal of Family History* 24(3), p. 252.
19. Freeman, 'Conceptualising Fatherhood', p. 70.
20. Ruth Hill, 'How New Man Turned into Distant, Confused New Dad', *Observer*, 20 June 2004, p. 9.
21. Ibid.
22. Ibid., p. 25.

six

1. Connell, *Gender and Power*.
2. Connell, *Masculinities*.
3. Seidler (ed.), *The Achilles Heel Reader* and *Men, Sex and Relationships*.
4. Seidler, *Recovering the Self: Morality and Social Theory*.
5. Seidler, *Recreating Sexual Politics: Men, Feminism and Politics*.
6. Seidler, *Man Enough: Embodying Masculinities*.
7. *Guardian* Review, 11 October 2003, p. 37.
8. Ibid.
9. *Guardian* G2, 16 October 2003, p. 8.
10. Emmanuel Levinas, *Alterity and Transcendence* (1999), p. 98.
11. Boyarin, *Carnal Israel*.
12. Later published as 'Masculinity and Violence' in the *Achilles Heel Reader*.
13. Jane Gardam, *Old Filth* (2004); Stevie Davis, 'Pearls beyond Price', *Guardian* Review, 20 November 2004, p. 26.

seven

I would like to thank Teresa Valdes and Jose Olavarria for the warm hospitality during the conference and the interesting discussions. This chapter was originally paired with a paper delivered by Mara Viveros; the rewriting has been enriched by the discussions that followed our session and the intense conversations that followed.

1. The relationship between Kantian moral theories and a vision of modernity that has largely been set within the terms of a dominant European masculinity is a theme I initially explored in *Kant, Respect and Injustice*.
2. The relationship between the seventeenth-century scientific revolutions and the reordering of gender relations of power set crucial terms for an

Enlightenment vision of modernity. This was a central theme in Carolyn Merchant's *The Death of Nature* (1982). The implications for traditions of social theory are explored in my *Unreasonable Men: Masculinity and Social Theory*.

3. The framework for Carol Gilligan's later work with adolescent girls was originally set in her work that established a critical distance from Kohlberg's more universalist work on moral development, implicitly based upon the experience of adolescent boys; see *In a Different Voice* (1982).

4. The insistence that women's oppression is structural, and therefore has to be related to questions of history and power, while men's experience can only be understood in more personal terms, is an issue that already emerged in the sexual politics of the 1970s. It made it difficult to theorise issues of structural violence in ways that could also illuminate the destruction of emotional and personal lives. This was a theme that I originally explored in *Recreating Sexual Politics*.

5. For some helpful discussions in relation to the schooling of young masculinities in Britain, see Frosh, Phoenix and Pattman, *Young Masculinities*; Mac an Ghail, *The Making of Men: Masculinities, Sexualities and Schooling*.

6. These are assumptions that help to shape Connell's arguments in *Gender and Power* and *Masculinities*.

7. For an understanding of how Foucault came to think about the development of his own work, see his 'Technologies of the Self', the opening essay in *Technologies of the Self*, ed. Martin et al. (1996).

8. It can be useful to read Foucault's later work on the *Care of the Self: The History of Sexuality, Volume 3* (1994) in relation to the more general text by Hubert Dreyfus and Paul Rabinow, *Michel Foucault: Beyond Structuralism and Hermeneutics* (1982).

9. In *Rediscovering Masculinities* I share a particular history of the way in which men responded to the challenges of feminism and the ways it helped to imagine a new form of politics. In the later work *Man Enough* I develop a position that learns from the strengths and weaknesses of an anti-sexist men's politics as well as the influence of mythopoetic work in the United States and Britain.

10. Daniel Boyarin has done significant work exploring how the different visions of Judaism and Christianity in relation to the body and sexuality help to explain some of the sources of Christian anti-Semitism. See, in particular, *Carnal Israel*. Within the dominant secular traditions of social science it is often difficult to explore the cultural influence of particular Christian traditions in the shaping of gender relations. This explains the temptation of particular universalist theories, which in their own ways sustain, rather then critique, prevailing dominant masculinities. People can disavow their lived experiences as 'personal' and 'subjective', and so of little relevance to positivist traditions of social research. It has been the strength of feminist research methodologies to frame more complex methodologies between experience and power.

eight

1. The importance of the Internet in reshaping peer relations and allowing for different forms of contact across space that redefine relationships both inside and outside of work is a theme that is suggested in Jeremy Rifkin, *The Age of Access* (2000) and *The End of Work: The Decline of the Global Work-Force and the Dawn of the Post-Market Era* (1996). For a warning against the implications of these new technologies, see Jonathan Kozol, *Illiterate America* (1985).

2. Changing conceptions of authority and respect within postmodern cultures have been explored partly through the influence of the Frankfurt School. For a helpful introduction to the Frankfurt School, see Martin Jay, *The Dialectical Imagination* (1973); Susan Buck-Morss, *The Origin of Negative Dialectics* (1977). See also Zygmunt Bauman, *Liquid Modernity* (2000) and *The Individualised Society* (2001); Richard Sennett, *The Uses of Disorder: Personal Identity and City Life* (1996).

3. For a study that helps illuminate how young people work to sustain a 'front' with others, see Frosh, Phoenix and Pattman, *Young Masculinities*, based on interviews with young men in secondary schools in Britain. But there can be methodological issues in researching experiences of young men using discourse methods since the fronts young men so often sustain can make it difficult to know how to interpret what they say in interviews, unless time has been taken to establish relationships of trust, which can involve a series of interviews in different settings. Interviewing young men with their peers may involve the issue of 'losing face' in front of others.

4. For an interesting study that explores how young people in rural Mexico learn to negotiate their desires, intimacies and sexual relationships, see Ana Amuchastegui, *Virginidad e iniciacion sexual en Mexico: Experencias y significados* (2001); Mathew C. Gutman, *The Meanings of Macho: Being a Man in Mexico City* (1996); and the work around young men, bodies and health in Sandy Ruxton (ed.), *Gender Equality and Men: Learning from Practice* (2004).

5. For some helpful historical reflections on the relations between fathers and sons that can help illuminate predicaments in the present, see Edward Goss, *Father and Son*; Turgenyev, *Fathers and Sons*. There have also been some useful collections, though often drawing exclusively on experience from the West. See, for example, David Seybold (ed.), *Fathers and Sons: An Anthology* (1995); John Lewis-Stempel (ed.), *Fatherhood: An Anthology* (2003).

6. The ways that young women's identities are tied up with their embodied experience so that with changes in their bodies they can find themselves experiencing a crisis of identity is explored in Carol Gilligan (ed.), *Women, Girls and Psychotherapy: Reframing Resistance* (1992); Lyn Mikel Brown and Carol Gilligan, *Women's Psychology and Girls' Development* (1992). These themes are also developed in Carol Gilligan et al., *Making Connections: Relational Worlds of Adolescent Girls at Emma Willard School* (1990); Jill

McLean Taylor et al., *Between Voice and Silence: Women and Girls, Race and Relationship* (1997).

7. Tony Overman, 'It's Tough To Be a Teenager', in Jack Canfield et al., *Chicken Soup Teenage Soul 2* (1998), pp. 141–2.

8. For a sense of Carol Gilligan's work with adolescent girls, see C. Gilligan, J.V. Ward and J.M. Taylor (eds), *Mapping the Moral Domain* (1988). Gilligan recognises the significance for adolescent girls of the moment when they come to see themselves through the eyes of the dominant culture and the crisis in self-confidence and self-worth that this can produce. This can be acutely felt by young women of colour, who can feel that they have to deal with issues of race as well as gender and sexuality. It is a moment when they can be thrown off-balance in ways that can affect their achievements at school.

9. For a sense of the richness of the ethnographic work that Matthew Gutman has done in urban Mexico, see *The Meaning of Macho* (1996).

10. For a sense of the significance of the work that Benno de Keijzer has been doing with Salud y Genero, see Gabriela Rodriguez and Benno de Keijzer, *La Noche Se Hizo Para Las Hombres: Sexualidad en los procesos de cortejo entre jovenes campesinas y campesinos Edamex Libros para Todos* (2002).

nine

1. Within secularized cultures where religious traditions have generally been disavowed it can be difficult for young men and women who regard themselves as largely secular to recognise the source of some of their own fears, anxieties and bad feelings. It can be more difficult for people to explain their uneasy feelings and desires and to grasp why they so easily blame themselves. They are likely to fall for forms of misrecognition within individualistic cultures that have insisted upon denying the significance of religious and cultural histories in the ways they read a postmodern present.

2. For a sense of Willy Pedersen's work, see his 'Parental Relations, Mental Health, and Delinquency in Adolescents', *Adolescence*, Winter, 1994.

3. For helpful introductions to post-structuralist feminisms, see J. Butler and J.W. Scott (eds), *Feminists Theorise the Political* (1992). See also the different views explored in Nancy Fraser et al., *Feminist Contentions: A Philosophical Exchange* (1995); Judith Butler, *Undoing Gender* (2004).

4. For an evaluation of some of the difficulties of survey research, particularly in relation to the images young people often want to sustain in front of others, see J. Holland and C. Ramazanoglu, *Feminist Methodologies* (2004).

5. For discussion in relation to sexed bodies and issues around masturbation in different body cultures, see Tom Lacquer, *Making Sex: Body and Gender from the Greeks to Freud* (1990). See also Jean Stengers and Anne Van Neck, *Masturbation: A History of a Great Terror* (2001), in which the authors recall Rousseau's personal experience with masturbation recounted in his

Confessions. He was initiated into the vice, he said bluntly, by a Moorish bandit he met in Turin and succumbed: 'I learnt this dangerous supplement which deceives nature and leads young men of my disposition to many excesses at the expense of their health, their vigor and sometimes even of their lives. This vice which shame and timidity find so convenient is, moreover, particularly attractive to active imaginations.' See also Claude Quetel, *The History of Syphilis* (1992).

6. For some interesting work exploring the diversity of Scandinavian masculinities, see S. Ervo and T. Johannsson (eds) *Among Men: Moulding Masculinities*, (2002).

7. For useful explorations that draw materials across diverse cultures concerning relationships between men, masculinities and sport, see M.A. Messner. *Power at Play: Sports and the Problem of Masculinity* (1992); R.W Connell, *The Men and the Boys* (2000).

8. For some reflections upon the fluidity of relationships within postmodern cultures and the conditional character of intimacy, see Anthony Giddens, *The Transformation of Intimacy: Sexuality, Love and Eroticism in Modern Societies* (1992); Zygmunt Bauman, *Liquid Love* (2003). For a sense of how these relationships are gendered, see Seidler (ed.), *Men, Sex and Relationships* (1992) and *Man Enough: Embodying Masculinities* (2000); L. Jamieson, *Intimacy: Personal Relationships in Modern Societies* (1998).

ten

1. For some influential background research initially done by the Chicago School in relation to gangs, see William Foote Whyte, *Street Corner Society: Social Structure of an Italian Slum* (1993).

2. For a sense of how traditional gendered relations are being negotiated within diverse cultural settings, see Sandy Ruxton (ed.), *Gender Equality And Men: Learning from Practice* (2004). See also the collection, Frances Cleaver (ed.), *Masculinities Matter! Men, Gender and Development* (2003); and examples provided in S. Chant and M. Gutmann in *Mainstreaming Gender and Development* (2000).

3. Norma Fuller, *Masculinidades: Cambios y permanencies* (2001). To place the work on men and masculinities in Peru in the context of research on Central and Latin America, see M. Viveros, J. Olavarria and N. Fuller (eds), *Hombres e Idendides de Genero: Investigaciones desde American Latina*, (2001); Teresa Valdes y Jose Olavarria (eds), *Masculinidades y Equidad de Genero en America Latina* (1998).

4. Miller in *For Your Own Good* opens up an important discussion on how young men, in particular, have been disciplined by their fathers. Since they could not be reasoned with, the argument went, they had to be disciplined through violence. Victorian pedagogies served to train later colonial rulers, particularly in relation to public schools, where hierarchies were established with younger boys being forced to 'fag' for older boys, in the knowledge

that they would later be served in their turn. This is a theme explored in relation to Arnold's Rugby in Thomas Hughes, *Tom Brown's School Days* (1999).

5. Gloria Careago, PUEG Mexico, at conference 'Adolescent Males: The Construction of Gender Identities in Latin America', Santiago, 4–6 November 2002.

6. Though Connell's work on 'hegemonic masculinities' has been enormously helpful and influential, it often sustains a universal rationalism that fosters its own moralism, against which men are so easily found lacking. The tensions between his empirical studies and theoretical framework can make it difficult to appreciate how, for instance, pervasive cultural notions that 'boys are bad' can shape a particular ethic of masculinity that is inseparable from the workings of gender relations of power. Though reinforcing a misleading distinction between the 'therapeutic' and the 'political' and an anxiety that other theoretical positions are somehow reducing the political to the personal, it becomes difficult to relate structural relations of patriarchal power and violence to the lived experiences of young men in ways that can validate their aspirations to change. For a more sustained exploration of Connell's work, see Seidler, *Transforming Masculinities*.

7. For some interesting research and reflection on men's friendships, some of which reaches across diverse cultures and traditions, see Stuart Miller, *Men and Friendship* (1983); P.M. Nardi (ed.), *Men's Friendships* (1992), and *Gay Men's Friendship: Invisible Communities* (1999). See also interesting discussions in Ken Plummer, *Telling Sexual Stories: Power, Change and Social Worlds* (1995).

eleven

1. Islamic communities in the West have been refigured as they face new dangers in the wake of 9/11, and more recently in relation to the London bombings of 7/7, with the rise of Islamophobia and threats to mosques and communities. Many young men and women talk about the effect of 9/11 and the wars that followed in Afghanistan and Iraq, and the ways they impacted upon their identities as young Muslims. It marked a shift towards the increasing significance of religious identifications for young people. For reflections that provide a global context for some of these shifts, see Benjamin Barber, *Jihad vs McWorld* (2001); Zygmunt Bauman, *Globalisation: The Human Consequences* (1998); Giovanna Borradori, *Philosophy in a Time of Terror: Dialogues with Jürgen Habermas and Jacques Derrida* (2003).

2. For some reflections on the riots in some of Britain's northern towns in the summer of 2003, see Paul Gilroy, *After Empire: Melancholia or Convivial Culture?* (2004); Michael Keith, *After the Cosmopolitan? Multicultural Cities and the Future of Racism* (2005); Achille Mbembe, *On the Postcolony* (2001); D. Ritchie (2001) Oldham Independent Review Panel Report.

3. For a discussion of changing patterns of migration in Britain and the ways

these have been refigured within the discourse of multiculturalism, see Bhikhu Parekh, *Rethinking Multiculturalism: Cultural Diversity and Political Theory* (2002); J. Rex, *Ethnic Minorities in the Modern Nation-State* (1996); A. Phillips, *The Politics of Presence: Issues in Democracy and Group Representation* (1995); D. Morley and K. Chen, *Stuart Hall: Critical Dialogues in Cultural Studies* (1996); T. Modood, *Not Easy Being British: Colour, Culture and Citizenship* (1992).

4. For attempts to revision Britain as a multicultural society, see Parekh, *Rethinking Multiculturalism*; T. Modood and P. Werbner (eds), *The Politics of Multiculturalism in the New Europe: Racism, Indentity and Community* (1997).

5. Ulrich Beck explores the implications of new individuals within what he calls the second modernity of risk societies in *The Risk Society: Towards a New Modernity* (1992), and in the essays collected as *Ecological Enlightenment: Essays on the Politics of Risk Society* (1995). Some of the implications for intimate relations are explored in U. Beck and E. Beck-Geresheim, *The Normal Chaos of Love* (1995). To relate these issues of questions of gender, particularly masculinities, see Seidler, *Recreating Sexual Politics*, where entanglements between the Protestant ethic of self-denial and dominant masculinities are explored.

6. For a sense of how Sennett's work has sought to illuminate changes in the organisation of global capitalism and the ways they shape distinct forms of identity, see the shifts from *The Hidden Injuries of Class* (1972) to *The Corrosion of Character: The Personal Consequences of Work in the New Capitalism* (1998), which show how a relationship between 'inner' and 'outer' is shaped differently at different times through cultural notions of self-worth, dignity and respect. These notions are not simply defined differently within alternative discourses but are formed differently through the ways shifting social relationships help shape identities.

7. Michael Bull's interesting study *Sounds of the City* (2003) explores how personal stereos help to shape the ways that people can move through urban spaces, and how they can mark both familiar and threatening spaces through different tracks they might be listening to. Sometimes they organise their listening in ways that recognise particular threats, say in relation to the possibilities of racial or homophobic violence. Though issues of 'race', gender and sexuality are hinted at, their implications for the use of new technologies, including the currently all-pervasive iPods, are still to be fully explored.

twelve

1. For a rich and personally engaged exploration of how depression can often be unknowingly passed on from father to son, see Terrence Real, *I Don't Want to Talk About It: Overcoming The Secret Legacy of Male Depression* (1997). For classic statements on depression as a kind of mourning, see Sigmund Freud, 'Mourning and Melancholia', in *Collected Works of Sigmund Freud*, vol.

14 (1917) pp 243–58; J. Bowlby, *Loss: Sadness and Depression*, volume 3 of *At-tachment and Loss* (1980); Melanie Klein, *Envy and Gratitude and Other Works* (1957); and H. Kohut, *The Analysis of the Self* (1971), and *The Restoration of Self* (1977). The ways in which emotions can be passed on is a theme also explored in Seidler, *Man Enough*, which engages with relationships between fathers and sons as they were explored in Robert Bly's *Iron John*.

2. Nick Johnstone, 'Blue Notes', *Guardian* G2, 8 June 2004, p. 9.

3. For discussion of the relationships between men's bodies and men's health and illness, see D. Sabo and D.F. Gordon (eds), *Men's Health And Illness: Gender, Power and the Body* (1995). See also P. Atkinson, *Medical Talk, Medical Work* (1995); N. Bradford, *Men's Health Matters* (1995); E. Cameron and J. Bernades 'Gender and Disadvantage in Health: Men's Health for a Change', *Sociology of Health and Illness* 26 (1998), pp. 675–93; T. Csordas, *Embodiment and Experience: The Existential Ground of Culture and Self* (1994); C. Ellis, *Final Negotiations: A Story of Love, Loss and Chronic Illness* (1995); M. Korda, *Man to Man: Surviving Prostate Cancer* (1996); J. Stacey, *Teratologies: A Cultural Study of Cancer* (1997). See also the interesting Ph.D. thesis by Daniel Kelly, 'In the Company of Men: Embodiment and Prostate Cancer', Department of Sociology, Goldsmiths, University of London, 2002.

4. Dean Whittington's work was completed while he was director of Orexis, a drug centre in Southeast London and was done in the context of a Ph.D. where he interviewed men about their drug use. It includes rich ethno-graphic work that seeks to develop methods for revealing different levels of men's emotional lives that are often concealed through a 'front'. By establishing trust over a period of time, Dean was able to explore territory that is often generalized about. The Ph.D. thesis was submitted as 'Men, Violence and Substance Misuse: A Study of White Working Class Mascu-linities in Deptford', Department of Sociology, Goldsmiths, University of London (2004).

5. For a sense of the development of voice-relational methodologies as they were developed by Carol Gilligan and partners to understand the develop-ment of adolescent girls, see C. Gilligan, J. Ward and J. Taylor, *Mapping the Moral Domain* (1988); C. Gilligan, P. Lyons and T. Hanmer, *Making Connections* (1990).

6. For discussion about the relationships of masculinity to research methodolo-gies, see Seidler, *Unreasonable Men*. It is important for men to explore their own investments in particular research projects, since it is only when they have asked themselves questions they wish to ask others that they can establish a more equal research relationship. Rather than treating men and masculinities as new research objects, where researchers might learn to apply feminist research methods, we need to explore the particular issues that emerge when researching men. Sometimes they might be more open to talking to women, whom they deem to be less threatening because less tied into competitive relations. Sometimes interviews need to be repeated and trust established over time.

7. For reflections on the impact of witnessing and experiencing violence on young men and how this can continue to echo through their lives, see Jim Gilligan, *Violence: Reflections on our Deadliest Epidemic* (2000); Bill Buford, *Among the Thugs* (1991); Anthony Clare, *On Men: Masculinity in Crisis* (2000); F. De Zulueata, *From Pain to Violence: The Traumatic Roots of Destructiveness* (1993); T. Newburn and E. Stanko, *Just Boys Doing Business* (1994); G. Pearson and M. Gilman, *Young People and Heroin* (1987); G. Sereny, *Cries Unheard: The Story of Mary Bell* (1998); Paul Wolfe-Light, 'Men, Violence and Love', in J. Wild (ed.), *Working with Men for Change* (1999).

8. Sometimes social workers will read the experience of young men through pathological models sustained through psychoanalytic theories of the Oedipus complex. These assumptions can also be reflected in assumptions made by social researchers about 'problem families' and 'inadequate individuals'. It can be helpful to question the familial assumptions underpinning Freud's Oedipal stories, so revealing the assumptions about men and masculinities that frame psychoanalytic theories. See, for example, challenging discussions in G. Deleuze and F. Guattari, *Anti-Oedipus* (1997).

9. Lisa Johnson, quoted in Joanna Moorhead, 'My Belly Was the Focus of His Anger', *Guardian* G2, 3 June 2004, p. 15. For discussions that reveal some of the dynamics of domestic violence and the different ways that crucial work has been done in different societies and cultures to interrupt these patterns of violence, see J. Pearce and T. Pezzot Pearce, *Psychotherapy of Abused and Neglected Children* (1997); D. Finkelhor and K. Yllo, *Licence to Rape: Sexual Abuse of Wives* (1985).

10. Moorhead, 'My Belly Was the Focus of His Anger', p. 15.

11. Ibid.

12. Ibid.

13. Ibid.

thirteen

1. Gary Barker, 'Introduction' to Françoise Girard, '"My Father Didn't Think This Way": Nigerian Boys Contemplate Gender Equality', *Quality/Calidad/ Qualité* 14, Population Council, p. 1.

2. See 'Programme of Action', www.un.org/ecosocdev/geninfo/populatin/ icpd.htm.

3. For some interesting explorations of how issues of gender equality are being framed within different global cultures, see Sandy Ruxton (ed.), *Gender Equality and Men: Learning from Practice* (2004); Seidler, *Transforming Masculinities*.

4. Girard, 'My Father Didn't Think This Way', p. 5.

5. For the history of the work on gender in Calibar, Nigeria, and some sense of how it developed and the issues it faced, see the Population Council publication *Quality/Calidad/Qualité* 14.

6. Ibid., p. 6.

7. Ibid., p. 7.

8. For background on diverse masculinities in Thailand and how they have developed over time, see Peter Jackson and Nerida Cook (eds), *Gender and Sexualities in Modern Thailand* (2000); Peter Jackson et al., *Lady Boys, Tom Boys, Rent Boys: Male and Female Homosexualities in Contemporary Thailand* (1999); Peter Jackson, *Male Homosexuality in Thailand* (1989).

9. Barker, 'Introduction', p. 3, referring to G. Barker, 'What About Boys? A Review and Analysis of International Literature on the Health and Developmental Needs of Adolescent Boys' (World Health Organisation, 2000, www.who.org). For a sense of the work that Gary Barker has been doing in Brazil with the Instituto Profundo, working with ECOS, Programa PAPAI in Recife Brazil and Salud y Genero in Mexico, see the Working with Young Men workbooks produced in different languages on *Sexuality and Reproductive Health, Fathering and Care Giving, From Violence to Peaceful Coexistence, Reasons and Emotions* and *Preventing and Living with HIV/AIDS.* (2002). Gary Barker has also published *Dying to Be a Man: Youth and Masculinity and Social Exclusion* (2005). For some important work around young people and sexualities in South Asia, see Jeremy Seabrook, *Consuming Cultures: Globalisation and Local Lives* (2004), his *Children of Other Worlds: Exploitation in the Global Market* (2001), and *Victims of Development: Resistance and Alternatives* (1993).

10. Girard, 'My Father Didn't Think This Way', p. 9.

11. It is a strength of Connell's work that he resists this Foucaudian move. If this has helped to introduce a concern with masculinities, it has been at the cost of being able to think about how men can change. For a sense of Connell's work in relation to young men, see Connell, *The Men and the Boys* (2000). See also interesting discussions in Bob Pease and Keith Pringle (eds), *A Man's World: Changing Men's Practices in a Globalised World* (2002). For discussions that show the importance of reflecting upon cultural masculinities in relation to Latin America, see Jose Olavarria (ed.), *Hombres: Identidad/es y Violencia* (2001); Teresa Valdes and Jose Olavarria (eds), *Masculinidades y Equidad de Genero en America Latina* (1998). For some other interesting work with young people, see *Proponer y Dialogar: Guia para el trabajo con jovenes y adolescents Irene Konterllnik* (2002).

12. Girard, 'My Father Didn't Think This Way', pp. 13, 12.

13. Ibid., p. 27.

14. Ibid., p. 26.

15. Ibid., p. 14.

16. Ibid., p. 21.

17. Ibid., p. 25.

fourteen

1. For some reflections upon the history and diversity of Thai masculinities and the shaping of different forms of gay identity and a sense of the political transformations within modern Thailand that have impacted upon

the shaping of gender and sexual relations, see Peter Jackson, *Buddhadasa: Theravada Buddhism and Modernist Reform in Thailand* (2003).

2. For some useful historical discussions about Mexico, see Donald Hodges and Ross Gandy, *Mexico under Siege: Popular Resistance to Presidential Despotism* (2002); Gerardo Otero (ed.), *Mexico in Transition: Neoliberal Globalisation, the State and Civil Society* (2004). For descriptions of the work of Salud y Genero in Mexico, see Benno di Keizer, *Masculinidad como Facto de Riesgo* (1996), and his article in Sandy Ruxton (ed.), *Gender Equality and Men* (2004).

3. For interesting work on young women's sexualities in rural Mexico, see Ana Amuchastegui, *Virginidad e Iniciacion Sexual en Mexico: Experiencias y Significados* (2001). See also Gabriela Rodriguez and Benno de Keijzer, *La Noche Se Hizo Para los Hombres* (2002).

4. For a sense of the history and development of CORIAC, a project in Mexico City that has done pioneering work with men around issues of violence and sexual health, see Juan Guillermo Figueroa and Regina Nava (eds), 'Memorias del seminario-taller "Identidad masculina, sexualidad y salud reproductiva"' (2001). For discussions of some other projects that work around issues of sexual and reproductive well-being, see A. Cornwall and A. Welbourn (eds), *Realising Rights: Transforming Approaches to Sexual and Reproductive Well-being* (2002).

5. For an appreciation of the breadth of work that the MacArthur Foundation has done in taking vital initiatives in relation to the work with young men and masculinities in Latin America, particularly Mexico and Brazil, see its publication *Population*, where much of this work is written up.

6. For background to the work that Richard Parker has done around issues of sexualities in Brazil, see R. Parker, *Bodies, Pleasures and Passions: Sexual Culture in Contemporary Brazil* (1991). See also S.B. Ortner and H. Whitehead, *Sexual Meanings: The Cultural Construction of Gender and Sexuality* (1981), T.L. Whitehead and M.E. Conway, *Self, Sex and Gender in Cross-cultural Fieldwork* (1986); Caroline Sweetman (ed.), *Men and Masculinity* (1997); A.Cornwall and N. Lindisfarne (eds), *Dislocating Masculinities: Comparative Ethnographies* (1994); N. Kabeer, *Reversed Realities: Gender Hierarchies in Development Thought* (1995); C. Moraga and G. Anzaldua, *This Bridge Called My Back: Writings by Radical Women of Colour* (1981); D. Gilmore, *Manhood in the Making: Cultural Concepts of Masculinity* (1990).

7. Margaret Neusse's comments were made in the context of a discussion organized by the Population Council that was reported in *Quality/Calidad/Qualité* 14.

8. For some reflections that have emerged from fieldwork in India, see the work of Jeremy Seabrook; for instance, *In The Cities of the South: Scenes from a Developing World* (1996), and *Children of Other Worlds: Exploitation in the Global Market* (2001).

9. For some helpful reports on the evaluations of these project see *Quality/Calidad/Qualité*, the publication of the Population Council.

10. Judith Helzner, 'Men's Involvement in Family Planning', *Reproductive Health*

Matters 7, May 1996, p. 146. See also Kirsten Moore and Judith Helzner, *What's Sex Got To Do with It: Challenges for Incorporating Sexuality into Family Planning Programs* (1996).

11. For discussions of the important work in relation to young men and masculinities that has been done in Nicaragua in recent years see Patrick Welsh, *Los Hombres No Son De Marte: Desaprendiendo el Machismo en Nicaragua* (2002). For a sense of feminist movements in Nicaragua, see M. Randall, *Sandino's Daughters Revisited: Feminism in Nicaragua* (1994). For other relevant publications from Cantera see *Identidades Masculinas* (1995, 1999) and *Sexualidad Y Masculinidad* (1996).

12. Helzner, 'Men's Involvement in Family Planning', p. 147.

fifteen

1. Chris Hedges, *War is a Force that Gives Us Meaning* (2003), p. 84. Hedges draws upon his own reflections as a veteran war correspondent. A former divinity student, he knows from his own experience that for young men who pass through it, war can be exhilarating, even addictive. 'It gives us purpose, meaning, a reason for living.'

2. The German veteran of World War I Erich Maria Remarque in *All Quiet on the Western Front* wrote of the addiction to war that quickly transforms young men. He knew the ecstatic high of violence that states readily make use of in wars and civil wars to mobilise young men, as well as the debilitating mental and physical destruction that come with prolonged exposure to war's addiction.

3. Christopher Browning, *Ordinary Men: Reserve Police Battalion 101 and the Final Solution in Poland* (1992), pp. 82–5.

4. Hedges, *War is a Force that Gives Us Meaning*, pp. 88–9.

5. Omer Bartov, in *Mirrors of Destruction* (2002), pp. 189, 193, draws attention to the disturbing effects of Ka'Tzetnik's *House of Dolls* (1986) on the education of young people in Israel and elsewhere and how it can shape young men's inner relationship with their fears and hostilities in ways that could help sustain the illegal occupation of Palestinian lands.

6. Hedges, *War is a Force that Gives Us Meaning*, pp. 98, 101. For an interesting exploration of the conflicts over the break-up of the former Yugoslavia that draws on interviews with young people as they were involved in the struggles, see Michael Ignatieff, *Blood and Belonging: Journeys into the New Nationalism* (1993). For more general background discussion, see Laura Silber and Allan Little, *The Death of Yugoslavia* (1995); Misha Glenny, *The Fall of Yugoslavia*; Michael Ignatieff, *The Warrior's Honour* (1997).

7. Hedges, *War is a Force that Gives Us Meaning*, p. 104. For an account of the horrors of those who were disappeared through the military regime in Argentina, see Margarite Feitlowitz, *A Lexicon of Terror: Argentina and the Legacies of Torture* (1998).

8. Elias Canetti, *Crowds and Power* (1962), p. 187.

9. J. Glenn Gray, *The Warriors: Reflections on Men in Battle* (1998), pp. 61–2, 90.
10. Hedges, *War is a Force that Gives Us Meaning*, pp. 100, 104, 117.
11. Hannah Arendt, in *The Origins of Totalitarianism* (1979), notes an attitude in Germany after World War II, calling it 'nihilistic relativism', which she believes was a legacy of Nazi propaganda that believed that all facts could and would be altered. As is discussed by Omer Bartov in *Murder in Our Midst* (2000), p. 72, this means reality became a conglomerate of changing circumstances and slogans that could be true one day and false the next.

bibliography

Adorno T.W., and Horkheimer, M. (1973) *Dialectic of Enlightenment*, trans. J. Cumming. London: Allen Lane.

Altman, D. (1982) *The Homosexualisation of America*. Boston MA: Beacon Press.

Anderson, B. (1991) *Imagined Communities*. London: Verso.

Arendt, H. (1958) *The Human Condition*. Chicago: University of Chicago Press.

Arendt, H. (1979) *The Origins of Totalitarianism*. New York: Harcourt Brace.

Aries, P. (1962) *Centuries of Childhood: A Social History of Family Life*. London: Jonathan Cape.

Armstrong, K. (1999) *A History of God*. New York: Vintage.

Armstrong, K. (2001) *The Battle for God: Fundamentalism in Judaism, Christianity and Islam*. New York: HarperCollins.

Armstrong, K. (2002) *Daughters of Abraham: Feminist Thought in Judaism, Christianity and Islam*. Gainesville: University Press of Florida.

Armstrong, K. (2004) *The Great Transformation: The World in the Time of Buddha, Socrates, Confucius and Jeremiah*. London: Atlantic Books.

Askew, S., and Ross, C. (1988) *Boys Don't Cry: Boys and Sexism in Education*. Milton Keynes: Open University Press.

Atkinson, P. (1995) *Medical Talk, Medical Work*. London: Sage.

Back, L. (1996) *New Ethnicities and Urban Culture*. London: UCL Press.

Barber, B. (2001) *Jihad vs McWorld*. New York: Ballentine.

Barker, G. (2005) *Dying To Be a Man: Youth and Masculinity and Social Exclusion*. London and New York: Routledge.

Bartov, O. (2000) *Murder in Our Midst*. New York: Oxford University Press.

Bartov, O. (2002) *Mirrors of Destruction*. New York: Oxford University Press.

Batra, Roger (1992) *The Cage of Melancholy: Identity and Metamorphosis in the Mexican Character*. New Brunswick NJ: Rutgers University Press.

Bauman, Z. (1990) *Modernity and the Holocaust.* Cambridge: Polity Press.

Bauman, Z. (1997) *Postmodernity and its Discontents.* Cambridge: Polity Press.

Bauman, Z. (1998) *Globalisation: The Human Consequences.* Cambridge: Polity Press.

Bauman, Z. (2000) *Liquid Modernity.* Cambridge: Polity Press.

Bauman, Z. (2001) *The Individualized Society.* Cambridge: Polity Press.

Bauman, Z. (2003) *Liquid Love.* Cambridge: Polity Press.

Battersby C. (1998) *The Phenomenal Woman: Feminist Metaphysics and the Patterns of Identity.* Cambridge: Polity Press.

Beal, T.K., and Gunn, D.M. (eds) (1997) *Reading Bibles, Writing Bodies: Identity and the Book.* London and New York: Routledge.

Beail, N., and McGuire, J. (eds) *Fathers: Psychological Perspectives.* London: Junction Books.

Beauvoir, S. de (1973) *The Second Sex.* New York, Vintage.

Benjamin, A., and Osborne, P. (eds) (1994) *Walter Benjamin's Philosophy: The Destruction of Experience.* London: Routledge.

Benjamin, J. (1990) *Bonds of Love.* London, Virago.

Benjamin, W. (1973) *Illuminations,* trans. H. Zohn. London: Collins/Fontana.

Beck, U. (1992) *The Risk Society: Towards a New Modernity.* London, Sage.

Beck, U., Giddens, A., and Lash, S. (1995) *Reflexive Modernization.* Cambridge: Polity Press.

Beck, U. (2000) *The Brave New World of Work.* Cambridge: Polity Press.

Beck, U., and Beck-Gernsheim, E. (1995) *The Normal Chaos of Love.* Cambridge: Polity Press.

Benhabib, S. (1997) *Situating the Self.* Cambridge: Polity Press.

Benjamin, W. (1973) *Illuminations,* ed. Hannah Arendt. Glasgow: Fontana.

Berlin, I. (1981) *Against The Current.* Oxford: Oxford University Press.

Berger, M., Wallis, B., and Watson, S. (eds) (1995) *Constructing Masculinity.* New York: Routledge.

Biddulph, S. (1994) *Manhood: A Book about Setting Men Free.* Sydney: Finch.

Blankenhorn, D. (1995) *Fatherless America: Confronting Our Most Urgent Social Problem.* New York: Basic Books.

Blum, L., and Seidler, V.J.J. (1991) *A Truer Liberty: Simone Weil and Marxism.* New York: Routledge.

Bly, R. (1990) *Iron John.* New York: Addison-Wesley.

Bologh, R.W. (1990) *Love or Greatness: Max Weber and Masculine Thinking.* London: Unwin Hyman.

Bordo, S. (1993) *Unbearable Weight: Feminism, Western Culture, and the Body.* Berkeley CA: University of California Press.

Bordo, S. (1999) *The Male Body: A New Look at Men in Public and in Private.* New York: Farrar, Straus & Giroux.

Borradori, G. (2003) *Philosophy in a Time of Terror: Dialogues with Jürgen Habermas and Jacques Derrida.* Chicago: University of Chicago Press.

Bourdieu, P. (2001) *Masculine Domination.* Cambridge: Polity Press.

Bowlby, J. (1980) *Loss: Sadness and Depression*, volume 3 of *Attachment and Loss*. London: Hogarth Press,

Boyarin, D. (1993) *Carnal Israel: Reading Sex in Talmudic Judaism*. Berkeley: University of California Press.

Boyarin, D. (1994) *A Radical Jew: Paul and the Politics of Identity*. Berkeley: University of California Press.

Boyarin, D. (1997) *Unheroic Conduct: The Rise of Heterosexuality and the Invention of the Jewish Man*. Berkeley: University of California Press.

Bradford, N. (1995) *Men's Health Matters*. London: Random House.

Braidotti, R. (1991) *Patterns of Dissonance*. Cambridge: Polity Press.

Brennan, T. (ed.) (1989) *Between Feminism and Psychoanalysis*. London: Routledge.

Brittan, A. (1989) *Masculinity and Power*. Oxford: Basil Blackwell.

Brod, H. (ed.) *The Making of Masculinities*. Boston: Allen & Unwin.

Brod, H., and Kaufman, M. (eds) *Theorizing Masculinities*. Thousand Oaks CA: Sage.

Brown. L.M., and Gilligan, C. (1992) *Women's Psychology and Girls' Development*. Cambridge MA: Harvard University Press.

Brown, P. (1990) *The Body and Society: Men, Women and Sexual Renunciation in Early Christianity*. London: Faber

Browning, C. (1992) *Ordinary Men: Reserve Police Battalion 101 and the Final Solution in Poland*. New York: HarperCollins.

Brugess, A. (1997) *Fatherhood Reclaimed: The Making of the Modern Father*. London: Vermillion.

Buck-Morss, S. (1978) *The Origin of Negative Dialectics*. London: Harvester.

Buford, B. (1991) *Among the Thugs*. London: Secker & Warburg.

Buhle, M.J. (1998) *Feminism and Its Discontents*. Cambridge MA: Harvard University Press.

Bull, M. (2003) *Sounds of the City*. Oxford: Berg.

Butler, J. (1990) *Gender Trouble: Feminism and the Subversion of Identity*. New York: Routledge.

Butler, J. (1993) *Bodies that Matter: The Discursive Limits of 'Sex'*. New York: Routledge.

Butler, J. (2004) *Undoing Gender*. New York and London: Routledge.

Butler, J., and Scott, J.W. (eds) (1992) *Feminists Theorize the Political*. New York: Routledge.

Canetti, E. (1962) *Crowds and Power*. New York: Viking.

Carby, H.V. (1998) *Race Men*, Cambridge MA: Harvard University Press.

Caygill, H. (1998) *Walter Benjamin: The Colour of Experience*. London: Routledge.

Chanter, T. (1995) *Ethics of Eros: Irigaray's Rewriting of the Philosophers*. London and New York: Routledge.

Chapman, R. and Rutherford, J., eds (1988) *Male Order: Unwrapping Masculinity*. London: Lawrence & Wishart.

Chodorow, N. (1978) *The Reproduction of Mothering: Psychoanalysis and the Sociology of Gender.* London: University of California Press.

Chodorow, N. (1994) *Feminities, Masculinities, Sexualities: Freud and Beyond.* London: Free Association Books.

Clare, A. (2000) *On Men: Masculinity in Crisis.* London: Chatto & Windus.

Clatterbaugh, K. (1990) *Contemporary Perspectives on Masculinity: Men, Women and Politics in Modern Society.* Boulder CO: Westview Press.

Cleaver, F. (ed.) (2003) *Masculinities Matter! Men, Gender and Development.* London: Zed Books.

Cockburn, C. (1983) *Brothers: Male Dominance and Technological Change.* London: Pluto Press.

Cockburn, C. (1991) *In the Way of Women: Men's Resistance to Sex Equality in the Organizations.* London: Macmillan.

Cohen, P. (1997) *Rethinking the Youth Question.* London: Palgrave.

Collier, R. (1998) *Masculinities, Crime and Criminology.* London: Sage.

Collins, P. Hill (1991) *Black Feminist Thought: Knowledge, Consciousness and the Politics of Empowerment.* New York: Routledge.

Connell, R.W. (1983) *Which Way is Up? Essays on Sex, Class and Culture.* London: Allen & Unwin.

Connell, R.W. (1987) *Gender and Power: Society, the Person and Sexual Politics.* Cambridge: Polity Press.

Connell, R.W. (1995) *Masculinities.* Cambridge: Polity Press.

Connell, R.W. (2000) *The Men and the Boys.* Cambridge: Polity Press.

Connolly, P. (1998) *Racism, Gender Identities and Young Children.* London: Routledge.

Cornwall, A., and Welbourn, A. (eds) (2002) *Realising Rights: Transforming Approaches to Sexual and Reproductive Well-being.* London: Zed Books.

Cornwall, A., and Lindisfarne, N. (eds) (1994) *Dislocating Masculinities: Comparative Ethnographies.* London: Routledge.

Craib. I. (1989) *Psychoanalysis and Social Theory: The Limits of Sociology.* London: Harvester Wheatsheaf.

Craig, S. (ed.) (1992) *Men, Masculinity and the Media.* Thousand Oaks CA: Sage.

Csordas, T. (1994) *Embodiment and Experience: The Existential Ground of Culture and Self.* Cambridge: Cambridge University Press.

Dawson, G. (1986) *Soldier Heroes: British Adventure, Empire and the Imagining of Masculinities.* London: Routledge.

Davidoff, L., and Hall, C. (1987) *Family Fortunes: Women and Men of the English Middle Class 1780–1850.* London: Routledge.

Davidoff, L. (1995) *Worlds Between: Historical Perspectives on Gender and Class.* Cambridge: Polity Press.

Deleuze, G. (1990) *Expressionism in Philosophy: Spinoza,* trans. M. Joughin. New York: Zone.

Deleuze, G. (1993) *Nietzsche and Philosophy,* trans. H. Tomlinson. Minneapolis: University of Minnesota Press.

Deleuze, G., and Guattari, F. (1997) *Anti-Oedipus*. Minneapolis: University of Minnesota Press.

Del Valle, T. (ed.) (1993) *Gendered Anthropology*. London: Routledge.

Dinnerstein, D. (1987) *The Mermaid and the Minotaur: The Rocking of the Cradle and the Ruling of the World*. London: Women's Press.

Dobash, R.E., Dobash, R.P., Cavanagh, K., and Lewis, R. (2000) *Changing Violent Men*. London: Sage.

Dollimore, J. (1998) *Death, Desire and Loss in Western Culture*. London: Penguin.

Donzelot, J. (1979) *The Policing of Families*. London: Hutchinson.

Dowd, N.E. (2000) *Redefining Fatherhood*. New York: New York University Press.

Dreyfus, H., and Rabinow, P. (1983) *Michel Foucault: Beyond Structuralism and Hermeneutics*. Chicago: University of Chicago Press.

Duncan, N. (1999) *Sexual Bullying*. London: Routledge.

Easlea, B. (1981) *Science and Sexual Oppression: Patriarchy's Confrontation with Women and Nature*. London: Weidenfeld & Nicolson.

Easlea, B. (1983) *Fathering the Unthinkable: Masculinity, Scientists and the Nuclear Arms Race*. London: Pluto Press.

Edley, N., and Wetherell, M. (1995) *Men in Perspective: Practice, Power and Identity*. Hemel Hempstead: Harvester Wheatsheaf.

Edwards, T. (1994) *Erotics and Politics: Gay Male Sexuality, Masculinity and Feminism*. London: Routledge.

Ehrenreich, B. (1983) *The Hearts of Men: American Dreams and the Flight from Commitment*. London: Pluto Press.

Elam, D. (1994) *Feminism and Deconstruction*. London: Routledge.

Elliot, A., and Frosh, S. (eds) *Psychoanalysis in Context: Paths between Theory and Modern Culture*. London and New York: Routledge.

Ellis, C. (1995) *Final Negotiations: A Story of Love, Loss and Chronic Illness*. Philadelphia: Temple University Press.

Elshtain, J.B. (1981) *Public Man, Private Woman*. Princeton NJ: Princeton University Press.

Eisenstein, H. (1985) *Contemporary Feminist Thought*. London: Unwin.

Epstein, D., Elwood, J., Hey, V., and Maw, J. (eds) (1998) *Failing Boys? Issues in Gender and Achievement*. Buckingham: Open University Press.

Ervø, S., and Johansson, T. (eds) (2002) *Among Men: Moulding Masculinities*, vols 1 and 2. Abingdon: Ashgate.

Faludi, S. (1999) *Stiffed: The Betrayal of the Modern Man*. London: Chatto & Windus.

Fanon, F. (1986) *Black Skin, White Masks*. London: Pluto Press.

Fasteau, M.F. (1974) *The Male Machine*. New York: McGraw-Hill.

Featherstone, M., Hepworth, M., and Turner, B.S. (eds) *The Body: Social Process and Cultural Theory*. London: Sage.

Feitlowitz, M. (1998) *A Lexicon of Terror: Argentina and the Legacies of Torture*. New York: Oxford University Press.

Figlio, K. (2000) *Psychoanalysis, Science and Masculinity*. London: Whurr.

Finkelhor, D., and Yllo, K. (1985) *Licence to Rape: Sexual Abuse of Wives*. New York: Free Press.

Flax, J. (1990) *Thinking Fragments: Psychoanalysis, Feminism and Postmodern in the Contemporary West*. Berkeley: University of California Press.

Flax. J. (1993) *Disputed Subjects: Essays on Psychoanalysis, Politics and Philosophy*. New York and London: Routledge.

Foucault, M. (1975) *Discipline and Punish: The Birth of the Prison*. Harmondsworth: Penguin.

Foucault, M. (1976) *The History of Sexuality*, Volume 1. London: Penguin.

Foucault, M. (1980) *Power/Knowledge: Selected Interviews and Other Writings, 1972–1977*. New York: Pantheon.

Foucault, M. (1994) *Care of the Self: The History of Sexuality*, Volume 3. Harmondsworth: Penguin.

Fox Keller, E. (1992) *Secrets of Life, Secrets of Death: Essays on Language, Gender and Science*. New York: Routledge.

Fraser, N., et al. (1995) *Feminist Contentions: A Philosophical Exchange*. New York: Routledge.

Freud, S. (1994 [1930]) *Civilisation and Its Discontents*. New York: Dover.

Freud, S. (1977) *On Sexuality*, Pelican Freud Library, vol. 7. Harmondsworth: Penguin.

Fromm, Erich (1963) *The Fear of Freedom*. London: Routledge.

Frosh, S. (1994) *Sexual Difference: Masculinity and Psychoanalysis*. London and New York: Routledge.

Frosh, S., Phoenix, A., and Pattman, R. (2002) *Young Masculinities*. London: Palgrave.

Fuentes, C. (2000) *Los Cinco Soles de Mexico*. Editorial Seix Barral.

Fuller, N. (2001) *Masculinidades: Cambios y permanencies*. Pontificia Universidad Catolica del Peru Fondo Editorial.

Gallagher, C., and Laqueur, T. (eds) *The Making of the Modern Body: Sexuality and Society in the Nineteenth Century*. Berkeley: University of California Press.

Game, A., and Pringle, R. (1984) *Gender at Work*. London: Pluto Press.

Gallop, J. (1982) *Feminism and Psychoanalysis: The Daughter's Seduction*. London: Macmillan.

Gallop, J. (1988) *Thinking through the Body*. New York: Columbia University Press.

Gay, P. (1988) *Freud: A Life of Our Time*. London: Macmillan.

Gay, P (1996) *Consumption and Identity at Work*. London: Sage.

Giddens, A. (1991) *Modernity and Self-identity: Self and Society in the Late Modern Age*. Cambridge: Polity Press.

Giddens, A. (1993) *The Transformation of Intimacy: Sexuality, Love and Eroticism in Modern Societies*. Cambridge: Polity Press.

Gilligan, C (1982) *In a Different Voice: Psychological Theory and Women's Development*. Cambridge MA: Harvard University Press.

Gilligan, C. (ed.) (1992) *Women, Girls and Psychotherapy: Reframing Resistance*. Binghamton NY: Harrington Park Press.

Gilligan, C., et al. (1990) *Making Connections: Relational Worlds of Adolescent Girls at Emma Willard School.* Cambridge MA: Harvard University Press.

Gilligan, C., Ward, J.V., and Taylor, J.M. (eds) (1988) *Mapping the Moral Domain.* Cambridge MA: Harvard University Press.

Gilligan, C., Lyons, P., and Hanmer, T. (1990) *Making Connections.* Cambridge MA: Harvard University Press.

Gilligan, J. (2000) *Violence: Reflections on our Deadliest Epidemic.* London: JKP.

Gillis, J. (1996) *A World of Their Own Making: Myth, Ritual and the Quest for Family Values.* New York: Basic Books.

Gilmore, D.G. (1990) *Manhood in the Making: Cultural Concepts of Masculinity.* New Haven: Yale University Press.

Gilroy, P. (1987) *There Ain't No Black in the Union Jack.* London: Unwin Hyman.

Gilroy, P. (1993) *The Black Atlantic: Modernity and Double Consciousness.* Cambridge MA: Harvard University Press.

Gilroy, P. (2004) *After Empire: Melancholia or Convivial Culture?* London and New York.

Glenn Gray, J. (1998) *The Warriors: Reflections on Men in Battle.* Lincoln: University of Nebraska Press.

Gorz, A. (1985) *Paths to Paradise.* London, Pluto.

Gramsci, A. (1971) *Selections from the Prison Notebooks.* London: Lawrence & Wishart.

Gramsci, A. (1975) *Letters from Prison.* London: Lawrence & Wishart.

Gray, J. (1999) *Men Are from Mars, Women Are from Venus.* London: Vintage/Ebury.

Green, D. (1999) *Gender Violence in Africa.* London: Macmillan.

Griffin, S. (1980) *Pornography and Silence.* London: Womens' Press.

Griffin, S. (1982) *Women and Nature.* London: Women's Press.

Grosz, E. (1994) *Volatile Bodies: Towards a Corporeal Feminism.* Bloomington: Indiana University Press.

Gutman, M.C. (1996) *The Meanings of Macho: Being a Man in Mexico City.* Berkeley and London: University of California Press.

Hall, C. (2002) *Civilising Subjects: Metropole and Colony in the English Imagination 1830–1867.* Cambridge: Polity Press.

Hall, L.A. (1991) *Hidden Anxieties: Male Sexuality 1900–1950.* Cambridge: Polity Press.

Hall, S. (ed.) *Representation: Cultural Representation and Signifying Practices.* London: Sage.

Hall, S., and Jefferson, T. (eds) *Resistance through Rituals.* London: Hutchinson.

Hearn, J. (1987) *The Gender of Oppression: Men, Masculinity and the Critique of Marxism.* Brighton: Harvester.

Hearn, J., and Morgan, D. (eds) (1990) *Men, Masculinities and Social Theory.* London: Unwin Hyman.

Hearn, J. (1992) *Men in the Public Eye.* London: Routledge.

Hearn, J. (1998) *The Violences of Men.* London: Sage.

Heckman, S.J. (1990) *Gender and Knowledge: Elements of a Postmodern Feminism*. New York and London: Routledge.

Hedges, C. (2003) *War is a Force that Gives Us Meaning*. New York: Anchor Books.

Held, D. (1986) *Models of Democracy*. Cambridge: Polity Press.

Held, V. (1993) *Feminist Morality: Transforming Culture, Society and Politics*. Chicago: University of Chicago Press.

Hewitt, R. (1986) *White Talk Black Talk: Inter-Racial Friendships and Communication amongst Adolescents*. Cambridge: Cambridge University Press.

Hochschild, A.R. (1989) *The Second Shift*. New York: Avon Books

Hochschild, A.R. (1997) *The Time Bind*. New York: Metropolitan Books.

Hochschild, A., and Machung, A. (1989) *The Second Shift: Working Parents and the Revolution at Home*. New York: Viking Penguin.

Hodges, D., and Gandy, R. (2002) *Mexico under Siege: Popular Resistance to Presidential Despotism*. London: Zed Books.

Hodson, P. (1984) *Men: An Investigation into the Emotional Male*. London: BBC Books.

Holland, J., and Ramazanoglu, C. (2004) *Feminist Methodologies*. London: Sage.

Holland, J., Ramazanoglu, C., and Sharpe, S. (1993) *Wimp or Gladiator: Contradictions in Acquiring Male Sexuality*. London: Tufnell Press.

Holland, J., Ramazanoglu, C., Sharpe, S., and Thomson, R. (1998) *The Male in the Head: Young People, Heterosexuality and Power*. London: Tufnell Press.

hooks, b. (1991) *Yearning: Race, Gender and Cultural Politics*. London: Turnabout.

hooks, b. (2000) *All About Love*. New York: HarperCollins.

hooks, b. (2001) *Salvation: Black People and Love*. New York: HarperCollins.

Hughes, T. (1999) *Tom Brown's School Days*. Oxford: Oxford University Press.

Ignatieff, M. (1993) *Blood and Belonging: Journeys into the New Nationalism*. London: BBC Books.

Ignatieff, M. (1997) *The Warrior's Honour*. New York: Henry Holt.

Irigaray. L. (1985) *Speculum of the Other Woman*. Ithaca NY: Cornell University Press.

Irigaray, L. (1985) *This Sex Which Is Not One*. Ithaca NY: Cornell University Press.

Jackson D. (1990) *Unmasking Masculinity: A Critical Autobiography*. London: Unwin Hyman.

Jackson, P. (1989) *Male Homosexuality in Thailand*. Elmhurst NY: Global Academic Publishers.

Jackson P. (2003) *Buddhadasa: Theravada Buddhism and Modernist Reform in Thailand*. Seattle WA: University of Washington Press.

Jackson, P., et al. (1999) *Lady Boys, Tom Boys, Rent Boys: Male and Female Homosexualities in Contemporary Thailand*. Binghamton NY: Harrington Park Press.

Jackson, P., and Cook, N. (eds) (1999) *Gender and Sexualities in Modern Thailand*. Seattle WA: University of Washington Press.

Jackson, S. (1999) *Heterosexuality in Question*. London: Sage.

Jardine, A., and Smith, P. (eds) (1987) *Men in Feminism*. London: Methuen.

Jagger, G., and Wright, C. (eds) (1999) *Changing Family Values*. London: Routledge.

Jameson, F. (1972) *The Prison-house of Language: A Critical Account of Structuralism and Russian Formalism*. Princeton: Princeton University Press.

Jamieson, L. (1998) *Intimacy: Personal Relationships in Modern Societies*. Cambridge: Polity Press.

Jay, M. (1973) *The Dialectical Imagination*. London: Heinemann.

Jukes, A. (1993) *Why Men Hate Women*. London: Free Association Books.

Johnson, S., and Meinhof, U.H. (eds) (1997) *Language and Masculinity*. Oxford: Blackwell.

Kabeer, N. (1995) *Reversed Realities: Gender Hierarchies in Development Thought*. London: Verso.

Ka'Tzetnik (1986) *House of Dolls*. London: Mullert, Blond & White.

Kaufman M. (1987) *Beyond Patriarchy*. Toronto: Oxford University Press.

Keijzer, B. di (1998) *Masculinidad como Facto de Riesgo*. Mexico: Salud y Genero.

Keith, M. (2005) *After the Cosmopolitan? Mulicultural Cities and the Future of Racism*. London and New York: Routledge.

Kimmel, M.S. (ed.) (1987) *Changing Men: New Directions in Research on Men and Masculinity*. Newbury Park CA: Sage.

Kimmel, M.S., and Messner, M.A. (eds) (1989) *Men's Lives*. Boston MA: Allyn & Bacon.

Kimmel, M.S. (ed.) (1995) *The Politics of Manhood*. Philadelphia: Temple University Press.

Kimmel, M.S. (1996) *Manhood in America: A Cultural History*. New York: Free Press.

Klein, M. (1957) *Envy and Gratitude and Other Works*. London: Hogarth Press

Kohut, H. (1971) *The Analysis of the Self*. New York: International University Library.

Kohut, H. (1977) *The Restoration of Self*. New York: International University Library.

Korda, M. (1996) *Man to Man: Surviving Prostate Cancer*. London: Little, Brown.

Kozol, J. (1985) *Illiterate America*. New York: Anchor.

Kristeva, J. (1982) *Powers of Horror: An Essay on Abjection*. New York: Columbia University Press.

Kristeva, J. (1998) *New Maladies of the Soul*. New York: Columbia University Press.

Laqueur, T. (1990) *Making Sex: Body and Gender from the Greeks to Freud*. Cambridge MA: Harvard University Press.

Lasch, C. (1977) *Haven in a Heartless World: The Family Besieged*. New York: Basic Books.

Lasch, C. (1991) *The Culture of Narcissism: American Life in an Age of Diminishing Expectations*. New York: W.W. Norton.

Lash, S., and Urry, J. (1987) *The End of Organised Capitalism*. Cambridge: Polity Press.

Lennon, K., and Whitford, M. (eds) *Knowing the Difference: Feminist Perspectives on Epistemology.* London: Routledge.

Lees, S. (1986) *Losing Out: Sexuality and Adolescent Girls.* London: Hutchinson.

Levinas, E. (1999) *Alterity and Transcendence.* London: Athlone.

Lewis, C., and O'Brien, M. (eds) (1987) *Reassessing Fatherhood: New Observations on Fathers and the Modern Family.* Newbury Park CA: Sage.

Lewis-Stempel, J. (eds) (2003) *Fatherhood: An Anthology.* New York: Overlook Press.

Lingard, B., and Douglas, P. (1999) *Men Engaging Feminisms: Pro-feminism, Backlashes and Schooling.* Buckingham: Open University Press.

Lloyd, G. (1984) *Man of Reason: 'Male' and 'Female' in Western Philosophy.* London: Methuen.

Lomnitz-Adler, C. (1992) *Exits from the Labyrinth: Culture and Ideology in the Mexican National Space.* Berkeley: University of California Press.

Lyotard, J.-F. (1994) *The Postmodern Condition: A Report on Knowledge.* Manchester: Manchester University Press.

Lloyd, T. (1990) *Work with Boys.* Leicester: National Youth Bureau.

MacInnes, J. (1998) *The End of Masculinity.* Buckingham: Open University Press.

Mac An Ghail, M. (1994) *The Making of Men: Masculinities, Sexualities and Schooling.* Buckingham: Open University Press.

Mac an Ghail, M. (ed.) (1996) *Understanding Masculinities.* Buckingham: Open University Press.

McNay, L. (1992) *Foucault and Feminism.* Cambridge: Polity Press.

Mahony, P. (1985) *Schools for Boys? Co-Education Reassessed.* London: Hutchinson.

Maguire, M. (1995) *Men, Women, Passion and Power.* London, Routledge.

Majors, R., and Billson, J. (1992) *Cool Pose: The Dilemmas of Black Manhood in America.* New York: Lexington.

Mangan, J.A., and Walvin, J. (1987) *Manliness and Morality: Middle Class Masculinity in Britain and America.* Manchester: Manchester University Press.

Martin E. (1991) *The Woman in the Body: A Cultural Analysis of Reproduction.* Milton Keynes: Open University Press.

Martin, L., et al. (eds) (1996) *Technologies of the Self: A Seminar with Michel Foucault.* London: Tavistock.

May, L. (1998) *Masculinity and Morality.* New York: Cornell University Press.

Mbembe, A. (2001) *On the Postcolony.* Los Angeles and London: University of California Press.

McLean Taylor, J., et al. (1997) *Between Voice and Silence: Women and Girls, Race and Relationship.* Cambridge MA: Harvard University Press.

McRobbie, A., and Nava, M. (eds) *Gender and Generation.* London: Palgrave.

Mercer, K. (ed.) (1994) *Welcome to the Jungle: New Positions in Black Cultural Studies.* London: Routledge.

Merchant, C. (1982) *The Death of Nature: Women, Ecology and the Scientific Revolution.* London: Wildwood House.

Messner, M.A. (1992) *Power at Play: Sports and the Problem of Masculinity.* Boston MA: Beacon Press.

Messner, M.A. (1997) *Politics of Masculinities: Men in Movements*. Thousand Oaks CA: Sage.

Middleton, P. (1992) *The Inward Gaze: Masculinity and Subjectivity in Modern Culture*. London: Routledge.

Miller, A. (1983) *For Your Own Good: Hidden Cruelty in Child-Rearing and the Roots of Violence*. New York: Farrar, Straus & Giroux.

Miller, A. (1984) *Thou Shalt Not Be Aware: Society's Betrayal of the Child*. New York: Farrar, Straus & Giroux.

Miller, N. (1992) *Out in the World: Gay and Lesbian Life from Buenos Aires to Bangkok*. New York: Random House.

Miller, S. (1983) *Men and Friendship*. London: Gateway Books.

Minsky, R. (1998) *Psychoanalysis and Culture: Contemporary States of Mind*. Cambridge: Polity Press.

Mirande, A. (1997) *Hombres Machos: Masculinity and Latino Culture*. Boulder CO: Westview Press.

Mitscherlich, A. (1993) *Society without a Father*. New York: HarperCollins.

Modood, T. (1992) *Not Easy Being British: Colour, Culture and Citizenship*. Stoke-on-Trent: Trentham Books.

Modood, T., and Werbner, P. (eds) (1997) *The Politics of Multiculturalism in the New Europe: Racism, Indentity and Community*. London: Zed Books.

Moore, K., and Helzner, J. (1996) *What's Sex Got To Do With It? Challenges for Incorporating Sexuality into Family Planning Programs*. New York: Population Council.

Morgan, D. (1992) *Discovering Men*. London: Routledge.

Morley, D., and Chen, K. (1996) *Stuart Hall: Critical Dialogues in Cultural Studies*. London: Routledge.

Moraga, C., and Anzaldua G. (1981) *This Bridge Called My Back: Writings by Radical Women of Colour*. Watertown MA: Persephone.

Morrison, K.F. (1992) *Understanding Conversion*. Charlottesville: University Press of Virginia.

Morner, M. (ed.) (1997) *Race and Class in Latin America*. New York and London: Columbia University Press.

Newburn, T., and Stanko, E. (eds) (1994) *Just Boys Doing Business? Men, Masculinities and Crime*. London: Routledge.

Nardi, P.M. (ed.) (1992) *Men's Friendships*. Thousand Oaks CA: Sage.

Nardi, P.M. (ed.) (1999) *Gay Men's Friendship: Invincible Communities*. Chicago: University of Chicago Press.

Nardi, P.M. (ed.) (2000) *Gay Masculinities*. Thousand Oaks CA: Sage.

Newburn, T., and Stanko, E. (1994) *Just Boys Doing Business*. London: Routledge.

Nixon, S. (1996) *Hard Looks: Masculinities, Spectatorship and Contemporary Consumption*. London: UCL Press.

Nicholson, L.J. (ed.) (1990) *Feminism/Postmodernism*. New York: Routledge.

Nicholson, L., and Seidman, S. (eds) (1996) *Social Postmodernism: Beyond Identity Politics*. Cambridge: Cambridge University Press.

Olavarria, J. (ed.) (2001) *Hombres: Identidad/es y Violencia*. Santiago de Chile: Flacso-Chile.

Olavarria, Jose (2003) *Varones Adolescentes: Genero, identidades y sexualidades en America Latina*. Santiago de Chile: Flacso-Chile.

Oliver, K. (1993) *Reading Kristeva: Unravelling the Double-Bind*. Bloomington: Indiana University Press.

Ortner, S.B., and Whitehead, H. (1981) *Sexual Meanings: The Cultural Construction of Gender and Sexuality*. Cambridge: Cambridge University Press.

Otero, G. (ed.) (2004) *Mexico in Transition: Neoliberal Globalisation, the State and Civil Society*. London: Zed Books.

Pagels, E. (1988) *Adam, Eve and the Serpent*. New York: Random House.

Pagels, E. (1995) *The Origin of Satan*. New York: Random House.

Parker, R. (1991) *Bodies, Pleasures and Passions: Sexual Culture in Contemporary Brazil*. Boston: Beacon Press.

Pateman, C. (1988) *The Sexual Contract*. Stanford CA: Stanford University Press.

Paz, Octavio (1961) *The Labyrinth of Solitude*. New York: Grove Press.

Pearce, J., and Pezzot Pearce, T. (1997) *Psychotherapy of Abused and Neglected Children*. New York: Guilford Press.

Pearson, G., and Gilman, M. (1987) *Young People and Heroin*. London: Gower Publications.

Pease, B., and Pringle, K. (eds) (2002) *A Man's World: Changing Men's Practices in a Globalised World*. London: Zed Books.

Phillips, A. (1995) *The Politics of Presence: Issues in Democracy and Group Representation*. Oxford: Clarendon Press.

Plummer, K. (1995) *Telling Sexual Stories: Power, Change and Social Worlds*. London: Routledge.

Plumwood, V. (1993) *Feminism and the Mastery of Nature*. London: Routledge.

Poliakov, L. (1974) *The Aryan Myth*. London, Sussex University Press.

Poliakov, L. (1990) *The History of Anti-Semitism*. Oxford: Oxford University Press.

Poster, M. (1998) *Critical Theory of the Family*. London: Pluto Press.

Quetel, C. (1992) *The History of Syphilis*. Baltimore: Johns Hopkins University Press.

Ramazanoglu, C. (1989) *Feminism and the Contradictions of Oppression*. London: Routledge.

Randall, M. (1994) *Sandino's Daughters Revisited: Feminism in Nicaragua*. New Brunswick NJ: Rutgers University Press.

Real, T. (1997) *I Don't Want to Talk About It: Overcoming The Secret Legacy of Male Depression*. New York: Scribner.

Rex, J. (1996) *Ethnic Minorities in the Modern Nation-State*. London: Macmillan.

Richard, G. (ed.) (1990) *The Idea of Race in Latin America 1870–1940*. Austin: University of Texas Press.

Rifkin, J. (2000) *The Age of Access*. London: Penguin.

Rifkin, J. (1996) *The End of Work: The Decline of the Global Work-Force and the Dawn of the Post-Market Era*. New York: Putnam.

Ritchie, D. (2001) *Oldham Independent Review Panel Report*. Oldham.

Robinson, S. (2000) *Marked Men: White Masculinity in Crisis*. New York: Columbia University Press.

Rodriguez, G., and de Keijzer, B. (2002) *La Noche Se Hizo Para los Hombres*. Mexico City: Population Council.

Roper, M., and Tosh, J. (1991) *Manful Assertions: Masculinities in Britain since 1800*. London: Routledge.

Rowbotham, S. (1972) *Woman's Consciousness, Man's World*. Harmondsworth: Penguin.

Rowbotham, S. (1973) *Hidden from History*. London: Pluto Press.

Rowbotham, S. (1983) *Dreams and Dilemmas*. London: Virago.

Rubin, L. (1994) *Families on the Faultline: America's Working Class Speaks about the Family, the Economy, Race and Ethnicity*. New York: HarperCollins.

Rutherford, J. (1992) *Men's Silences: Predicaments in Masculinity*. London: Routledge.

Ruxton, S. (ed.) (2004) *Gender Equality and Men: Learning from Practice*. Oxford: Oxfam.

Sabo, D., and Gordon, D.F. (eds) (1995) *Mens' Health and Illness*. Thousand Oaks CA: Sage.

Samuels, A. (1993) *The Political Psyche*. London: Routledge.

Sawicki, J. (1991) *Disciplining Foucault: Feminism, Power and the Body*. New York: Routledge.

Scott, S., and Morgan, D. (eds) (1993) *Body Matters: Essays on the Sociology of the Body*. London: Falmer Press.

Seabrook, J. (1993) *Victims of Development: Resistance and Alternatives*. London: Verso.

Seabrook, J. (1996) *In The Cities of the South: Scenes from a Developing World*. London: Verso.

Seabrook, J. (2001) *Children of Other Worlds: Exploitation in the Global Market*. London: Pluto Press.

Seabrook, J. (2004) *Consuming Cultures: Globalisation and Local Lives*. Oxford: New Internationalist Publications.

Segal, L. (1990) *Slow Motion: Changing Masculinities, Changing Men*. London: Virago.

Segal, L. (1999) *Why Feminism? Gender, Psychology, Politics*. Cambridge: Polity.

Seidler, V.J.J. (1986) *Kant, Respect and Injustice: The Limits of Liberal Moral Theory*. London: Routledge.

Seidler, V.J.J. (1987) *Rediscovering Masculinity: Reason, Language and Sexuality*. London and New York: Routledge.

Seidler, V.J.J. (1991) *Recreating Sexual Politics: Men, Feminism and Politics*. London and New York: Routledge.

Seidler, V.J.J. (1991) *The Moral Limits of Modernity: Love, Inequality and Oppression*. London: Macmillan.

Seidler, V.J.J. (1993) *Unreasonable Men: Masculinity and Social Theory*. London and New York: Routledge.

Seidler, V.J.J. (1994) *Recovering the Self: Morality and Social Theory*. London and New York: Routledge.

Seidler, V.J.J. (2000) *Man Enough: Embodying Masculinities*. London: Sage.

Seidler, V.J.J. (2001) *Shadows of the Shoah: Jewish Identity and Belonging*. Oxford: Berg.

Seidler, V.J.J. (2005) *Transforming Masculinities: Men, Cultures, Bodies, Power, Sex and Love*. London: Routledge.

Seidler, V.J.J. (ed.) (1991) *The Achilles Heel Reader: Men, Sexual Politics and Socialism*. London: Routledge.

Seidler, V.J.J. (ed.) (1992) *Men, Sex and Relationships: Writings from Achilles Heel*. London: Routledge.

Seidman, S. (1996) *Contested Knowledge: Social Theory in the Postmodern Era*. Cambridge MA: Blackwell.

Sennett, R. (1973) *The Uses of Disorder: Personal Identity and City Life*. Harmondsworth: Penguin.

Sennett, R. (1998) *The Corrosion of Character: The Personal Consequences of Work in the New Capitalism*. New York: W.W. Norton.

Sennett, R., and Cobb, J. (1972) *The Hidden Injuries of Class*. New York: Vintage.

Sereny, G. (1998) *Cries Unheard: The Story of Mary Bell*. London: Macmillan.

Shepard, S. (1977) *Rolling Thunder Logbook*. London: Penguin.

Seybold, D. (ed.) (1995) *Fathers and Sons: An Anthology*, New York: Atlantic Monthly Press.

Sherman, S. (ed.) (1992) *Lesbian and Gay Marriage: Private Commitments, Public Ceremonies*. Philadelphia: Temple University Press.

Shilling, C. (1983) *The Body and Social Theory*. London: Sage.

Snodgrass, J. (ed.) (1977) *A Book of Readings for Men against Sexism*. Albion CA: Times Change Press.

Stacey, J. (1996) *In the Name of the Family: Rethinking Family Values in the Postmodern Age*. Boston MA: Beacon Press.

Stacey, J. (1997) *Teratologies: A Cultural Study of Cancer*. London: Routledge.

Stacey, J. (1990) *Brave New Families: Stories of Domestic Upheaval in Late Twentieth-Century America*. New York: Basic Books.

Stacey, J. (1996) *In the Name of the Family: Rethinking Family Values in the Postmodern Age*. Boston MA: Beacon Press.

Staples, R. (1982) *Black Masculinity: The Black Man's Role in American Society*. San Franscisco CA: Black Scholar Press.

Stecopoulos, H., and Uebel, M. (eds) *Race and the Subject of Masculinities*. Durham NC: Duke University Press.

Steinberg, L., Epstein, D., and Johnson, R. (eds) (1997) *Border Patrols: Policing the Boundaries of Heterosexuality*. London: Cassell.

Stoltenberg, J. (2000) *The End of Manhood: Parables on Sex and Selfhood*. London: UCL Press.

Subirats, E. (1996) *El Continente Vacio*. Madrid: Anaya and Mario Muchnik.

Sweetman, C. (ed.) *Men and Masculinity*. Oxford: Oxfam.

Sydie, R.A. (1987) *Natural Woman, Cultured Men: A Feminist Perspective on Socio-logical Theory*. Milton Keynes: Open University Press.

Thomas, L.M. (1993) *Vessels of Evil: American Slavery and the Holocaust*. Philadel-phia: Temple University Press.

Thorne, B. (1993) *Gender Play: Girls and Boys in School*. Buckingham: Open University Press.

Tosh, J. (1999) *A Man's Place: Masculinity and the Middle-Class Home in Victorian England*. New Haven and London: Yale University Press.

Trachtenberg, J. (1995) *The Devil and the Jews*. Philadelphia: Jewish Publication Society of America.

Turner, B. (1984) *The Body and Society: Explorations in Social Theory*. Oxford: Basil Blackwell.

Valdes, T., and Olavarria, J. (eds) (1998) *Masculinidades y Equidad de Genero en America Latina*. Santiago de Chile: Flacso-Chile.

Viveros, M., Olavarria, J., and Fuller, N. (eds) (2001) *Hombres e Idendides de Genero: Investigaciones desde American Latina*. Santiago de Chile: Flacso-Chile.

Wade, P. (1997) *Race and Ethnicity in Latin America*. London: Pluto.

Walby, S. (1990) *Theorizing Patriarchy*. Oxford: Blackwell.

Walkerdine, V. (1990) *Schoolgirl Fictions*. London: Verso.

Walkerdine, V. (1997) *Daddy's Girl: Young Girls and Popular Culture*. London: Palgrave Macmillan.

Wallace, M. (1979) *Black Macho*. London: Calder.

Warner, M. (ed.) (1993) *Fear of a Queer Planet: Queer Politics and Social Theory*. Minneapolis: University of Minnesota Press.

Weber, M. (1970) *The Protestant Ethic and the Spirit of Capitalism*. London: Allen & Unwin.

Weeks, J. (1977) *Coming Out: Homosexual Politics in Britain*. London: Quartet.

Weeks, J. (1989) *Sex, Politics and Society*. Harlow: Longman.

Weeks, J. (1991) *Sexuality and its Discontents: Meanings, Myths and Modern Sexualities*. London: Routledge.

Weeks, J. (1995) *Inventing Moralities: Sexual Values in an Age of Uncertainty*. Cambridge: Polity Press.

Weeks, J., and Porter, K. (eds) (1998) *Between the Acts: Lives of Homosexual Men 1885–1967*. London: Rivers Oram Press.

Weeks, J. (2000) *Making Sexual History*. Cambridge: Polity Press.

Weil, S. (1962) *Selected Essays 1934–43*, ed. Richard Rees. Oxford: Oxford University Press.

Weil, S. (1972) *The Need for Roots*. London: Routledge.

Welsh, P. (2002) *Los Hombres No Son De Marte: Desaprendiendo el Machismo en Nicaragua*. London: Catholic Institute for International Relations.

West, C. (1993) *Race Matters*. Boston MA: Beacon Press.

Whitehead, S.M. (2004) *Men and Masculinities*. Cambridge: Polity Press.

Whitehead, T.L., and Conway, M.E. (1986) *Self, Sex and Gender in Cross-cultural Fieldwork*. Urbana: University of Illinois Press.

Whitford, M (1991) *Luce Irigaray: Philosophy in the Feminine*. London: Routledge.

Whyte, W.F. (1993) *Street Corner Society: Social Structure of an Italian Slum*. Chicago: University of Chicago Press.

Wild, J. (ed.), (1999) *Working with Men for Change*. London: UCL Press.

Williams, B. (1985) *Ethics and the Limits of Philosophy*. London: Fontana.

Willis, P. (1977) *Learning to Labour*. Aldershot: Gower.

Winch, P. (1989) *A Just Balance: Reflections on the Philosophy of Simone Weil*. Cambridge: Cambridge University Press.

Winnicott, D.W. (1974) *Playing and Reality*. Harmondsworth: Penguin

Wittgenstein, L. (1958) *Philosophical Investigations*. Oxford: Blackwell.

Wittgenstein, L. (1967) *On Certainty*. Oxford: Blackwell.

Wittgenstein, L. (1980) *Culture and Value*. Oxford: Blackwell.

Wolin, R. (1994) *Walter Benjamin: An Aesthetic of Redemption*. Berkeley: University of California Press.

Young, I.M. (1990) *Justice and the Politics of Difference*. Princeton: Princeton University Press.

Young, R. (1990) *White Mythologies*. London: Routledge.

Zornberg, A.G. (1995) *The Beginnings of Desire: Reflections on Genesis*. New York: Random House.

index

Elena Poniatowska